MS

Evolutionary Economics and Chaos Theory

Evolutionary Economics and Chaos Theory

New Directions in Technology Studies

Edited by
Loet Leydesdorff and Peter Van den Besselaar

With the assistance of
Peter M. Allen, Dorien DeTombe, Richard R. Nelson and Arie Rip

St. Martin's Press
New York

330.1
E93

First published in the United States of America in 1994

Printed and bound in Great Britain

ISBN 0-312-12217-9 (cloth)
ISBN 0-312-12218-7 (paper)

Library of Congress Cataloging-in-Publication Data

Evolutionary economics and chaos theory : new directions in technology
   studies / edited by Loet Leydesdorff and Peter Van den Besselaar:
   with the assistance of Peter M. Allen . . . [et al.].
      p.   cm.
   Includes bibliographical references and index.
   ISBN 0-312-12217-9 − ISBN 0-312-12218-7 (pbk)
   1. Evolutionary economics.   2. Technological innovations − Economic
aspects.   I. Leydesdorff, L.A.   II. Besselaar, Peter Van den.
III. Allen, Peter M. (Peter Murray), 1944−   .
HB97.3.E953   1994
330.1−dc20   94−1945
                                                                  CIP

Contents

List of Contributors

Peter M. Allen is the director of the International Ecotechnology Research Centre (IERC), a multi-disciplinary research centre at Cranfield University. He took a Ph.D. in theoretical physics at Hull University in 1969 and from there went to the University of Brussels. Between 1969 and 1987, he worked with Ilya Prigogine on self-organizing systems. He has published extensively in the field of urban and regional modelling as well as ecological and evolutionary theories.

Subhash C. Bhargava is a Senior Reader in Physics at St Stephen's College, University of Delhi. In addition to cellular automata, his current interests include the mathematical modelling of physical, biological and social systems.

Gertrud Blauwhof has a background in sociology and computer science. She is currently completing a Ph.D. thesis at the Department of Science and Technology Dynamics, University of Amsterdam (provisional title 'Technology as Communication').

Eberhard Bruckner Dr. Phil., studied physics at the University of Leipzig, and philosophy, economy, and sociology at the Humboldt University Berlin. He is currently head of the 'Self-Organization of Social Systems' project group at the Wissenschaftszentrum Berlin (WZB). His research interests include determinants of the description of social systems from an evolutionary point of view, processes of structure formation and evolution in social systems, and self-organization phenomena in social ensembles.

Hans-Peter Brunner took an MBA at the Free University Berlin (1980), an MA at Johns Hopkins University in Baltimore (1984) and a Ph.D. in Economics at the University of Maryland (1990). He has acted as a consultant for the World Bank, and, since 1991, has been a Research Fellow at the Wissenschaftszentrum Berlin (WZB).

Paul A. David is Professor of Economics and W. R. Coe Professor of American Economic History at Stanford University. His research interests include path dependence in technological, institutional and demographic phenomena; the interdependence of learning processes and the diffusion of innovations; standards and standardization in the past and present; coevolution of information network technologies and organizations; and the economics of open science proprietary R&D.

Dorien J. DeTombe is Assistant Professor at the Department of Systems Engineering of the Delft University of Technology. She has degrees in social science and in information science. Her research interests focus on analysing complex interdisciplinary problems, and she developed a special method, called COMPRAM, for analysing this type of problems.

Werner Ebeling, Dr rer. nat., Dr. habil., studied physics at the Universities of Rostock and Moscow. He is currently Professor of Theoretical Physics at the Humboldt University Berlin. His research topics are: statistical physics, nonlinear dynamics, and theory of self-organization and evolution.

Henry Etzkowitz is Professor of Sociology at the State University of New York at Purchase. He is the founding chair of the Section on Science, Knowledge and Technology in the American Sociological Association and co-director of the International Study Group on Academic–Industry Relations of the Science Policy Group, London. He is currently co-principle investigator (with Kevin Dougherty) of an NSF-sponsored study of 'State Science and Industry Policy'.

Dominique Foray is Professor of Economics at the Ecole Centrale de Paris and a member of the Centre National de Recherche Scientifique. He recently collaborated with Chris Freeman in editing *Technology and the Wealth of Nations* (London: Pinter, 1992).

Alfred Greiner is Assistant Professor of Economics at the University of Augsburg. His research interests focus on dynamic models of firm behaviour and their economic interpretation.

Christian Haxholdt is a Ph.D. student at the Institute of Statistics, Copenhagen Business School. He has been trained as an economist, and his research interests include nonlinear dynamics and chaos in economic systems, and statistical methods for nonlinear dynamic systems.

Miguel A. Jiménez Montaño, M.Sc., Sc.D., studies physics at the National University of Mexico. He pursued post-doctoral research at the Copernicus University, Torun, and at the University of California at San Francisco. His position is titular professor at the Department of Physics and Mathematics, Universidad de las Américas-Puebla. His research interests include computational methods in molecular biology, biolinguistics, and the evolution of natural and economic systems.

Christian Kampmann is a Post-doctoral Fellow of the Systems Dynamics Group of the Department of Physics, Technical University of Denmark. He received his Ph.D. from the Sloan School of Management, MIT, in 1992. Research interests include: dynamic, disequilibrium economic models; human decision-making and learning in complex systems; and nonlinear dynamics. The focus of his current research is on learning and adaptation in economic systems, particularly in assets markets.

Friedrich Kugler is Assistant Professor of Economics at the University of Augsburg. His research interests focus on the application of dynamic modelling to speculative markets.

Mary E. Lee recently (1993) received her Ph.D. in Sociology from Texas A&M University. The sociology of science and technology and organizational analysis are areas of interest. She previously held positions as Associate Research Sociologist with the Texas A&M University System's Texas Engineering Experiment Station and as Advanced Technology Program Specialist with the Texas Economic Development Commission.

Loet Leydesdorff is Senior Lecturer at the Department of Science and Technology Dynamics, University of Amsterdam. He has published extensively in 'scientometrics', the study of the quantitative aspects of communication in science. Current research interests include the static and dynamic analysis of network data, the evolution and self-organization of (for example, social) communication networks, and information and communication theory.

Erik Mosekilde is Professor in the Systems Dynamics Group of the Department of Physics, Technical University of Denmark. He received a Ph.D. in solid state physics in 1968. His research interests include dynamic modelling and nonlinear dynamics, and chaos theory with applications to biology, physics, medicine and economics.

Amitabha Mukherjee is a Reader in the Department of Physics and Astrophysics, University of Delhi. In addition to cellular automata, his current interests include high-energy physics, gravitation and cosmology.

Richard R. Nelson is George Blumenthal Professor in International and Public Affairs, Business, and Law at Columbia University. Before coming to Columbia, he served as Professor of Economics and Director of the Institute for Social and Policy Studies, Yale University. He has served as senior economist in the President's Council of Economic Advisors, and at the Rand Corporation. His fields of research have been technical change, economic organization, and long-term economic growth. He is probably best known for his work with Sidney Winter on evolutionary theory in economics.

Peter Nijkamp is Professor in Spatial Economics at the Free University of Amsterdam. His main research interests cover plan evaluation, regional and urban planning, transport systems analysis, mathematical modelling, technological innovation, and resource management. In recent years he has focused his research on quantitative methods for policy analysis, as well as on behavioural analysis of economic subjects.

Hoon K. Phang is a Ph.D. student of Professor Peter Allen at the International Ecotechnology Research Centre (IERC), a multi-disciplinary centre at Cranfield University. She graduated from the University of Singapore in 1988, majoring in Computer Science Information Systems. Her studies at IERC are sponsored by Toppan Moore Systems Limited, a Japanese software house. Since 1989 her major research interest has been the application of complex systems concepts to financial markets.

Aura Reggiani is Professor in Economic Programming at the University of Bologna. Her research contributions are mainly devoted to nonlinear dynamic systems (in particular, chaos, network and complexity theory) in the field of transportation science and spatial economics. She has authored and edited five books and published over 80 papers in journals, books and research memoranda.

Arie Rip studied chemistry and philosophy at the University of Leiden, and now works in the areas of science and technology dynamics, science and technology policy, and technology assessment. He is professor and head of the Department of Philosophy of Science and Technology at the University of Twente, and consults nationally and internationally.

Andrea Scharnhorst, Dr. Phil., studied physics at the Humboldt University, Berlin. Currently, she has a position at the Wissenschaftszentrum Berlin (WZB). Her research topics include application of models from the theory of self-organization and evolution to social systems, indicator research and cluster methods.

John D. Sterman is Associate Professor at the Sloan School of Management, Massachusetts Institute of Technology. His research interests include behavioural decision-making in dynamic systems; dynamic modelling, nonlinear dynamics, and chaos theory, with applications to economics, business strategy, and public policy; and organizational and individual learning.

Peter Van den Besselaar is Assistant Professor at the Department of Social Science Informatics, University of Amsterdam. His research interests include the dynamics of technological change and the implications of technological change for the workplace and employment.

Preface

Why is it timely to raise the question of the relationship between evolutionary economics and chaos theory within the perspective of new developments in technology studies? In his introduction to this volume, entitled 'Evolutionary Complex Systems: Models of Technology Change', Peter M. Allen addresses this issue.

The volume then turns to the elaboration of evolutionary economics in the light of developments in nonlinear dynamics. Richard R. Nelson – whose studies with Sidney G. Winter provided evolutionary economics with a conceptual apparatus in the early 1980s – extends the programme of evolutionary economics in a chapter entitled 'Economic Growth via the Coevolution of Technology and Institutions'. In his contribution, 'Technological Diversity, Random Selection in a Population of Firms, and Technological Institutions of Government', Hans-Peter Brunner develops a model in this theoretical tradition with a focus on policy parameters. Alfred Greiner and Friedrich Kugler show, in 'A Note on Competition among Techniques in the Presence of Increasing Returns to Scale', how assumptions about complexity in the time dimension of the economic problem may lead to chaotic effects in the results of the simulation (see, for example, Semmler 1986; Gabisch and Lorenz 1987).

The evolutionary metaphor refers to competing units. The study of competition between technologies (instead of economic units of analysis) has been the other major source of nonlinear models for technological developments. The second part of the volume contains a series of chapters at this level. First, Subhash C. Bhargava and Amitabha Mukherjee, in their chapter entitled 'Evolution of Technological Growth in a Model Based on Stochastic Cellular Automata' explain a nonlinear model for diffusion under competition. In a second chapter, entitled 'Dynamics of Competitive Technology Diffusion Through Local Network Structures: The Case of EDI Document Standards', Paul A. David and Dominique Foray take the issue a step further by using Markov random field models and perculation theory. In the chapter entitled 'Hyperselection and Innovation Described by a Stochastic Model of Technological Evolution', Eberhard Bruckner, Werner Ebeling, Miguel A. Jiménez Montaño and Andrea Scharnhorst explore the intrinsic relations between these types of model and chaos theory.

A series of chapters gathered in the third part of the volume addresses the dynamics of economic-technological systems. First, Aura Reggiani and Peter Nijkamp, in 'Evolutionary Dynamics in Technological Systems: A Multi-layer

Niche Approach' introduce an evolutionary model for these systems, and show the potential emergence of chaotic instabilities. Christian Kampmann, Christian Haxholdt, Erik Mosekilde and John D. Sterman argue in their chapter, 'Entrainment in a Disaggregated Economic Long-wave Model' that synchronization mechanisms may lead to the emergence of order in otherwise uncoordinated systems. The chapter by Peter M. Allen and Hoon K. Phang, 'Managing Uncertainty in Complex Systems: Financial Markets', develops a model that uses feedback terms for the reduction of the uncertainty in the prediction.

In Part IV, the focus is on the contribution of sociology to the development of the new paradigm. In his chapter, 'Academic–Industry Relations: A Sociological Paradigm for Economic Development', Henry Etzkowitz reports on empirical studies of the potential coevolution between knowledge production and industrial development. The sociological perspective provides us with another elaboration of evolutionary economics. In her contribution, 'Non-equilibria Dynamics and the Sociology of Technology', Gertrud Blauwhof analyses the differences and correspondences between the paradigm of evolutionary economics and recent approaches in the constructivist sociology of technology. In 'The Evolution of Technology: A Model of Socio-ecological Self-organization', Mary E. Lee discusses the modelling of technological systems on the basis of recent advances in human ecology.

What do these various types of theorizing and modelling contribute to the understanding of technological developments? This issue is addressed by one of the editors in an epilogue.

We are grateful to the members of the Programme Committee who also assisted us in selecting the contributions to this volume, namely Peter M. Allen, Richard R. Nelson, Arie Rip, and Gerald Silverberg. Dorien DeTombe took the initiative for the collection of conference proceedings, and we gratefully acknowledge her help in organizing this volume.

The Dutch Ministry of Economic Affairs, the Department of Science and Technology Dynamics, the Department of Social Science Informatics of the University of Amsterdam, and the International Science Foundation enabled us to organize the workshop under the title of 'New Developments in Technology Studies: Evolutionary Economics and Chaos Theory' and this volume financially. Thirty-one papers were presented by scholars from fourteen countries. This volume draws from this material. We also wish to thank the secretaries of the Department of Science and Technology Dynamics for their help and support.

Loet Leydesdorff and Peter Van den Besselaar
Amsterdam, September 1993

1 Evolutionary Complex Systems: Models of Technology Change

Peter M. Allen

Evolution and mechanics

In the real world we know from experience that things change: cities grow and decline, perhaps to recover, nations rise and fall as the patterns of trade and commerce evolve and as innovation and investment patterns shift and change. But can we understand these processes of change? Are they predictable? Knowing which innovations are required and will succeed would be an exceedingly valuable capacity. Or, knowing how to 'produce' innovations might be enough, as the system would then select the 'good' ones, and economic development would result. But producing innovations that fail can be extremely costly, and so what we need to know is how to find the right balance between producing innovations and concentrating on what we already know will work. This is very much the core problem that emerged in a study of fisheries (Allen and McGlade 1987a; Allen 1991). Of course, if the future could be predicted, then the answer to this question would be obvious. But the probability of being able to predict evolution and change in complex systems falls off the further ahead one looks. To base decisions purely according to the short-term advantages that can be calculated from the present situation, runs the risk that they could be completely wrong over a longer term. Short-term success may be bought perhaps at the cost of long-term failure, and therefore successful players over the longer term may have strategies that allow adaptation and adjustment in the light of events. Let us consider the basic framework of understanding and modelling for human systems.

If we examine a region, and consider the remains of populations and artefacts that litter the landscape, then after dating and classifying them, an evolutionary tree of some kind emerges, possibly with discontinuities suggesting disaster and invasion, but nevertheless suggesting a changing 'cast of characters' and of behaviours, over time (Figure 1.1). This is a fascinating study, and we can certainly spend much time attempting to classify and reconstruct the origin and evolution of the system. If, however, we want to understand the system, and in particular how its future might be affected by some choice or policy that might be

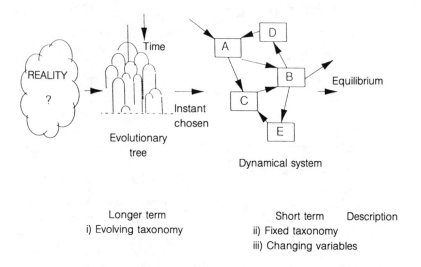

Figure 1.1 Data and classification of populations and artefacts lead to the picture of an evolutionary tree of some kind. Mathematical models have concentrated on the causal relations at a given time.

adopted, then traditionally we try to build a mathematical model of the system as it is at present and we attempt to capture the processes that are increasing or decreasing its different components. In ecology, this will consist of birth and death processes, where populations give birth at an average rate if there is enough food, and eat each other according to the average rates of encounter, capture and digestion.

In economics, the macroscopic behaviour of the economy is assumed to result from the aggregate effects of producers attempting to maximize their profits, and of customers attempting to maximize their utility. This assumes that they know the outcome of what they have not yet tried and also that transactions, production and consumption occur at average rates, changing the GNP, unemployment and other macroscopic indicators. These ideas are all based on the 'mechanical paradigm' of Newtonian physics, and assume that all individuals, producers and consumers of a given type are taken to be identical and equal to the average type.

On the left of Figure 1.1 we have 'reality'. It is drawn as a cloud, since we can say little about it other than that it includes all detail of everything, everywhere, as well as all perceptions and all points of view. However, if we simply list what we see then it includes a landscape with people of many kinds performing a variety of tasks, businesses, factories, homes, vehicles, and also fossils, disused mines and factories, closed railways, buried cities and evidence of much that has disappeared. By constructing a series of taxonomic rules concerning the differences and similarities of the objects, together with their dates, we can construct an 'evolutionary tree', showing that species, behaviours, forms, or artefacts emerged and evolved over time.

Clearly, the evolutionary tree represents the changing populations of the system over time. At any particular moment, therefore, we could identify the different objects or organisms that are present, and attempt to write down some 'population dynamics' describing the increase and decrease of each type. In other words, we can apply the traditional approach of physics, which is to identify the *components* of a system, and the *interactions* operating on these, both to and from the outside world and between the different populations of the system. From this we can capture the behaviour or functioning of the system at that time as a result of the causal relationships that are present. This gives the illusion that we have a mechanical representation of the system which can be run on a computer, to give predictions.

However, as we see clearly from our broader picture of the 'evolutionary tree', the predictions that such a model provides can only be correct for as long as the taxonomy of the system remains unchanged. The mechanical model of deterministic equations that we can construct at any given time has no way of producing 'new' types of objects, new variables, and so the 'predictions' that it generates will only be true until some moment, unpredictable within the model, when there is an adaptation or innovation, and new behaviour emerges.

In terms of Figure 1.1, the basis of scientific understanding has traditionally been the mechanical model (Prigogine and Stengers 1984; Allen 1988b) constructed from the causal relations that exist between the components of the system *at a particular time*. These are used to construct a pseudo-mechanical representation of the system which can be run forward to provide predictions, and whose component variables reflect the taxonomy of the system. In many cases a further assumption is introduced that the system is also supposed to have run itself to equilibrium, so that the correspondence between the real object and that model is made through equilibrium relations of balance between the variables. In economic geography, for example, urban form and hierarchy was supposed to express some maximized utility for the actors, where consumers had minimized distance of travel for goods and services and producers had maximized profits. This approach assumes that all the actors know what they want, know how to get it, and are doing what they would wish − given the choices open to them. Such ideas gave rise in reality to a purely descriptive approach to problems, but as computers became more powerful, the need for such strong and unrealistic assumptions gradually disappeared. System dynamics and simulation were thought to offer a path to the prediction of system behaviour, and because of this to offer a basis for rational policy and decision-making in complex systems.

Obviously, however, if we look at Figure 1.1, we see that however interesting a system dynamics model might be, it cannot anticipate the changes that may still occur in the evolutionary tree from which the 'moment' studied is taken. The taxonomy of the system will change over time, and therefore the mathematical model of causal relations will be incorrect. It might be good for some time, while the taxonomy is stable and no new classes or types have appeared. But this will only be revealed when the model is shown to be incorrect, and in need of reformulation.

Despite this, however, system dynamic models of problems have been developed, and much attention has rightly been given to the interesting behaviours of nonlinear dynamical systems. Such systems are characterized by dynamical equations of the form:

$$\frac{dx}{dt} = G(x, y, z, \ldots)$$

$$\frac{dy}{dt} = H(x, y, z, \ldots)$$

$$\frac{dz}{dt} = J(x, y, z, \ldots)$$

where G, H and J are functions which have nonlinear terms in them, leading to changes in x, y and z which are not simply proportional to their size. Also, these functions are made up of terms which involve variables x, y and z and also parameters expressing the functional dependence on these. These parameters reflect two fundamentally different factors in the working of the system:

• the values of *external* factors, which are not modelled as variables in the system. These reflect the 'environment' of the system, and of course may be dependent on spatial coordinates. Temperature, climate, soils, world prices, interest rates are possible examples of such factors.
• the values corresponding to the 'performance' of the entities underlying x, y or z, due to their *internal* characteristics such as technology, level of knowledge or strategies.

These two entirely different aspects have not been separated out in much of the previous work concerning nonlinear systems, and so the whole issue of the evolution of the populations involved in the system has not been addressed clearly. Equations of the type shown above display a rich spectrum of possible behaviours in different regions of both parameter space and initial conditions. They range from a simple approach to a homogeneous steady state, characterized by a *point* attractor, through that of sustained oscillation of a *cyclic* attractor, to the well-known *chaotic* behaviour characteristic of a strange attractor. These can either be homogeneous or involve spatial structure as well. This possibility of rich behaviours has proved to be of great significance for many fields of science.

However, in this paper, we are concerned with evolution, and that concerns modelling systems in which *adaptive* and *structural* change can occur. The internal characteristics of the participating actors change *endogenously* and new variables and new mechanisms of interaction can appear spontaneously from within the system itself, leading to a changing taxonomy. The model that we shall describe will discuss not only the evolution of improved techniques for producing a given good, but also the diversification and growth of markets into new areas.

Let us first consider the assumptions that are made in deriving system dynamics equations as in Figure 1.1. In the complex systems that underlie something like the 'economy', there is a fundamental level which involves individuals and discrete events, such as making a widget, buying a washing machine and driving to work. However, instead of attempting to 'model' all this detail, these are treated in an average way, and, as has been shown elsewhere (Allen 1990), in order to derive deterministic, mechanical equations to describe the dynamics of a system, two assumptions are required:

1. Events occur at their average rate.
2. All individuals of a given type, x say, are identical and of average type.

The errors introduced by the assumption 1 can be addressed by using a deeper, probabilistic dynamics, called the *master equation*, which essentially assumes that all individuals are identical and equal to an average type, but that events of different probabilities can and do occur. So, sequences of events which correspond to successive runs of good or bad 'luck' are included, with their relevant probabilities. As has been shown elsewhere (Allen 1988b) for systems with nonlinear interactions between individuals, what this does is to destroy the idea of a *trajectory*. The evolution is described by a probability distribution for an ensemble of systems that gradually changes its shape from being sharply peaked and centred on the initial value to spreading and splitting into a multi-modal distribution with peaks that correspond to the different 'attractors' of the dynamics. These may be point, cyclic or chaotic attractors, but clearly, if there are different possibilities then the idea of a trajectory for any single system breaks down. The fact is that unpredictable runs of good and bad luck can occur, and this means that the precise trajectory of the system does not exist in the future. Also, the fact of these deviations from the average rate of events means that a real system can 'tunnel' through apparently impassable potential barriers, the separatrices in state space, and can switch between attractor basins and explore the global space of the dynamical system in a way that the dynamical system would not itself predict.

However, in thinking about the problem of technological change and evolution, it is more important to discuss the second assumption that leads to the mechanical equations — that is, that all individuals are identical and equal to the average type. Obviously, the first and most important fact about two individuals is that they cannot be at the same place at the same time, and so spatial structure is one of the underlying issues that has been treated inadequately by population dynamics of the usual kind. In the next section we show the result of correcting nonlinear equations in order to take the effects of *microscopic diversity* into account.

In physics and chemistry the predictive models which work so well rely on the fact that the individual elements that make up the system must obey fixed laws which govern their behaviour. When molecular collisions are the source of the interactions, the collisional invariants (conservation of energy, momentum and mass) determine the observed behaviour of the whole system. In the case of chemical reactions, prediction is based on the fact that when molecules of the right kind collide fast enough, then the reaction occurs. The mechanisms are fixed, and the molecules never learn.

But let us now consider living systems. They cannot be described by such deterministic laws. To see why, let us imagine a very simple human situation, for example, of traffic moving along a highway or of pedestrians milling around a shopping centre. Clearly, movements cannot be predicted using Newton's laws of motion because acceleration, change of direction, braking and stopping occur at the whim of each driver or pedestrian. Newton's laws, the laws of physics, are *obeyed* at all times by each part of the system, but, despite this, they are not of help in predicting what will happen because the decision to coast, turn, accelerate or brake lies with the human being. Planets, billiard balls, and point particles are helpless slaves to the force fields in which they move, but people are not! People can switch sources of energy on or off and can respond, react, learn and change according to their individual experience and personality. They can see the potential usefulness for some modification in their timing, technique or tools, and they can tinker and experiment perhaps to find ways to overcome a problem, or a new way to achieve some desired result. This is where innovation comes from, and so the diversity of the experiments performed or ideas tried out will reflect the diversity of the people concerned, and the ability of these experiments to be translated into improved and new production and business will reflect the encouragement or discouragement experienced by innovative individuals, and the information flows and scanning that organizations are doing to gather and evaluate such initiatives.

Human systems are, therefore, not 'mechanical' in a billiard-ball sense because, except under conditions of total regimentation and tyranny, people perceive choices and new possibilities. Of course, many of these may prove to be illusory, but a few of them will 'take off' and be amplified and multiplied in the system, leading to its restructuring, and to the opening of new potentials for change.

Because of this uncertainty in the longer term, we cannot know what actions are best now. Even if an individual knows exactly what we would like to achieve, then because he cannot know with certainty how everyone else will respond, he can never calculate exactly what the outcome will be. He must make his decision, and see what happens, being ready to take corrective actions, if necessary. Since, in business, on the road and in the shopping centre we are all making these kinds of decision, simultaneously, all the time, it is not surprising that occasionally there are accidents, or that such systems run in a 'non-mechanical' way. An important point to remember here is, of course, that human beings have evolved within such a system and therefore that the capacity to live with such permanent uncertainty is quite natural to us. It may even be what characterizes the living. However, it also implies that much of what we do may be inexplicable in rational terms.

Because of this, the machine-like image of individuals and organizations with clear and unique responses to events that are perceived with absolute clarity is, of course, not what we find in reality. People in real life seem much less clear about their choices, as well as changeable according to their mood, and even when they are clear, the outcomes that ensue are often not what they expected. This 'mechanical' approach has been softened but not fundamentally changed by statistical models of decision processes where the probability of making a particular choice is proportional to the expected utility derived. This gives rise to probabilistic behaviour for individuals and deterministic behaviour for sufficiently large populations. However, this simple approach ignores the fact that decisions made by individuals are not really *independent* of each other, and that there is an effect of the communication between individuals. Fashions, styles and risk-minimizing strategies affect collective behaviour considerably, and mean that it cannot be derived necessarily as the sum of independent, individual responses. The current fashion for actively seeking the current *best practice* and imitating it, shows us that the assumption of independence will not be valid.

Evolutionary drive

As we have seen above, in deriving kinetic equations in order to model the system that exists at a given time, it has been necessary to derive a reduced description of reality. This is made in terms of typical elements of the system, stereotypes, according to the classification scheme that we have decided to apply. Underneath the 'model' there will always be the greater particularity and diversity of reality.

In the mechanical view, predictions can be made by simply running the equations forward in time, and studying where they lead. Is there a unique 'attractor', into which all initial states eventually fall, or are there many possible final end-points? Does the system continue in a series of eternal cycles? Or does it display chaotic behaviour, as the trajectory wraps itself around a 'strange attractor'? Fascinating stuff, but of course only of any significance if the equations and the fixed mechanisms within them remain a good description of the system. Explanation of the world is obtained then in terms only of the internal functioning of the system. But, from the picture of the evolutionary tree in Figure 1.1 that we know really characterizes complex systems, the taxonomy of the system, the variables present and the mechanisms which link them actually change over time. Because of this, the dynamical system that we are running as a model of the system will only be a good description for as long as there is no evolutionary change, and no new variables or mechanisms appear. In other words, the predictions of the dynamical system model will only be correct for as long as the model itself is a correct description of the system, and this is only for some unpredictable length of time.

Figure 1.1 offers us a conceptual framework within which we can place the different pieces of research in the field of technological evolution. First, the interesting behaviour of deterministic nonlinear systems is being studied by simulations concerning, for example, the explanation of business cycles and long waves as dynamic phenomena. Similarly, cellular automata studies and percolation models can examine pattern formation and diffusion processes within a fixed and deterministic framework. However, recognizing the limitations of the deterministic equations, the master equation approach can be used to take into account the fact that events do not occur at their average rate (assumption 1 above). Thus, stochastic differential equations can be generated to look more correctly at the probabilistic dynamics. Stochastic cellular automata simulations can also explore the spatio-temporal behaviour of systems in which it is affected by randomness. Various 'urn problems' can also be used to demonstrate the effects of path-dependent dynamics, but they seem useful mainly for pedagogical demonstrations, since they are less general then master equation descriptions of non-linear systems, where, for example, the emergence and evolution of spatial structure can be taken into account.

In order to describe evolutionary change, we must try to suppress assumption 2, discussed above, and put back the effects of innovators. The first idea is to discuss what kind of actor/firm can successfully 'invade' the system, and this leads to a 'criterion' for evolutionary change to occur (Allen 1976b). Despite the interesting insights that this approach offers, it still treats the innovators as exogenous factors coming from 'outside' the system, and in addition the possible behaviours are all set up initially and deterministic equations govern their dynamics. As before, of course, the deterministic equations can be replaced by the master equation approach which leads to stochastic differential equations describing the survival of innovations (Allen and Ebeling 1984; Bruckner *et al.* 1993; Bruckner *et al.*, this volume), but the 'source' of innovations still needs to be made endogenous in some way.

Nelson and Winter (1982) have set out a seminal framework for economics in which internal variabilities and the differential survival of firms are explicitly taken into account as they compete in the production of a particular good. The evolution concerns returns on investment and techniques of production, and has been the basis for many later studies (Goodwin *et al.* 1984; Anderson *et al.* 1988; Silverberg *et al.* 1988; Lorents 1989; Saviotti and Metcalfe 1991). Clark and Juma (1988) have also set out the essential points concerning the difference between the long- and short-term view of economic systems, and how this leads to an evolutionary view.

Returning to the general conceptual framework of Figure 1.1, we see that in order for us to understand and model a system that can change its taxonomy endogenously we must 'put back' what assumptions 1 and 2 took out in order to get to the deterministic description of nonlinear dynamics. Clearly, the future of any system will be due to two kinds of term: changes brought about by the deterministic action of the typical behaviour of its average components; and structural qualitative changes brought about by the presence of non-average components and conditions within the system.

We really have a dialogue between the 'average dynamics' of the chosen description (a process that results in what we may call 'selection') and the exploratory, unpredictable 'non-average' perturbations around this that result from the inevitable occurrence of non-average events and components – a search or exploration process that generates information about the 'pay-offs' for other behaviours. This leads to the new concept of *evolutionary drive*.

In order to explore the behaviour of systems with endogenously generated innovations and selection, we define a 'possibility space', a space representing the range of different techniques and behaviours that could potentially arise for the different types of firms present (Figure 1.2). In practice, of course, this is a multi-dimensional space of which we would only be able to anticipate a few of the principle dimensions. This 'possibility space' will be explored by firms which research and try out new techniques. In biology, genetic mechanisms ensure that different possibilities are explored, and offspring, offspring of offspring and so on, spread out over time from any pure condition. In human systems the imperfections and subjectivity of existence mean that techniques and behaviours are never passed on exactly, and therefore that exploration and innovation are always present as a result of the individuality and contextual nature of

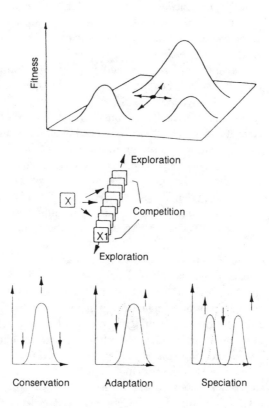

Figure 1.2 In 'possibility space', an initially pure behaviour will diffuse outwards as a result of imperfect imitation, learning and details of the local context. Differential success provides 'selection'.

experience. Local conditions, materials and needs differ and therefore any 'pure' technique or behaviour that migrates into a locality will rapidly diverge in its nature and intent. The diversity of existence itself generates complexity, and hence complexity feeds on itself.

Physical constraints mean that some behaviours do better than others, and so imitation and growth lead to the increase of some behaviours and the decline of others. If possibility space is seen as a kind of 'evolutionary landscape', with hills representing behaviours of high performance, then our simulations lead to the amplification of populations which are higher on the hill, and the suppression of those which are lower down.

By considering dynamic equations in which there is a 'diffusion' outwards in character space from any behaviour that is present, we can see how such a system would evolve. If there is a hill of advantage, of higher and lower pay-off, then the diffusion downhill is lost gradually, as it is decreased by selection, while any diffusion 'uphill' is gradually amplified, and moves the 'average' for the whole population higher up the slope. This demonstrates the vital part played by the exploratory 'diffusion' of behaviour, corresponding to imperfect copying, in driving evolution. By making populations with different intensities of 'error-making' or 'imperfect reproduction' it is found that the steeper the slope, the better it was to have behavioural exploration (Allen and McGlade 1987a).

Evolution selects, therefore, for populations with the ability to learn, rather than for populations with optimal, but fixed, behaviour. This corresponds to the selection of 'diversity-creating' mechanisms in the behaviour of populations, initially involving genetics, and later cognitive processes.

The self-organizing geographic models developed previously (Allen 1978; 1984; 1988b; Allen and Sanglier 1978; 1979; 1981) are a simple particular case of these general ideas. Instead of some 'behaviour' space, what we have is real, geographic space. Individuals of any particular type, X, all differ from one another by being located at different points in space. By using distributions of choice and behaviour around an average, the microscopic diversity of individuals is taken into account, and this allows the 'exploration' of seemingly unpopular, irrational and non-average decisions. In this way, changes in the 'pay-offs' for novel behaviour can be detected in the system, and innovations can take off. In this case, it concerns 'spatial' innovations, such as the spontaneous emergence of new centres of employment, or of peripheral shopping centres, of industrial satellites and so on. Because of the presence of positive feedback loops, there were many possible final states to which the system could tend, depending on the precise position and timing of non-average events, and therefore simply to study the final equilibrium states open to the system is rather pointless. What will matter in a real case is the 'path' that the system follows, and the stresses and strains that occur along the way. Because of these, responses and adaptations may emerge as a result of the particular strains resulting from the path of evolution followed by the system. Models such as ours are therefore more useful if they are used in a constant monitoring exercise, learning how the system is changing over time, and to what extent the average behaviour that is enshrined in the model equations is still coping with events.

An important point that arises is that the shape of the 'hills' in possibility space (potential pay-offs) not only reflects purely exogenous and objective factors related to the performance of a technology in absolute terms, but also results from the interaction between the different firms and players as they compete and cooperate in the market. Instead of thinking of firms competing to produce a common good, evolving better techniques as they go, in the model here they can also choose to move up or down market, or into other neighbouring markets. In this way, the 'landscape' reflects the details of which behaviours happen to be present, and whether they help or hinder any proposed activity. The landscape of *potential* pay-offs will be a subjective picture, depending on the beliefs and imagination of each actor, and therefore there are in principle as many 'landscapes' as there are agents in the system, and if people's actions reflect their vision of the landscape, then, of course, only some actors will succeed in 'getting it right'. Information flows will play an important role in recounting the apparent advantages and disadvantages of particular techniques, technologies, locations or behaviours, but this will be influenced by needs of an actor to present whatever happened in the most advantageous way possible. The 'true' worth of a product is probably impossible to ascertain. Advertising, slanted reporting and the selective use of statistics, together with people's need to justify themselves and their actions, mean that much of what occurs in the world reflects these needs rather than any 'real' advantages. But information can only come from the paths that were actually taken, not from those that were not. Because of this, patterns of technological change feed upon themselves, and self-reinforcement of growth and decline are the result. Instead of an objective rationality expressing genuine comparative advantages, the beliefs and the structures coevolve (Allen and Lesser 1991).

In some further theoretical models, instead of considering the evolution of techniques and behaviours in a fixed landscape expressing higher or lower pay-offs, it has been shown how 'adaptive landscapes' are really generated by the mutual interaction of behaviours. In the space of 'possibilities' closely similar behaviours are considered to be most in competition with each other, since they require similar resources, and must find a similar niche in the system. However, we assume that in this particular dimension there is some 'distance' in character space, some level of dissimilarity, at which two populations do not compete with each other so that they can grow and multiply on the basis of some other market. In its turn, this new type increases until it, too, is limited by internal competition, and once again there is a pay-off for deviants, particularly for those on the outside of the distribution, as they climb another self-made hill towards unpopulated regions of the potential market space. In this way, innovators spread out, gradually filling possibility space with an 'economy' made up of firms and sectors of activity.

Competition helps to 'drive' the exploration process, and Figure 1.3 shows an 'evolutionary tree' that results from a simulation based only on competition. If we now take into account the other dimensions of interaction that can exist between behaviours in a complex system, which can result either in positive or negative feedback, the landscape of advantage experienced by any one behaviour depends in a complex way on the presence or absence of others. What is observed is that a

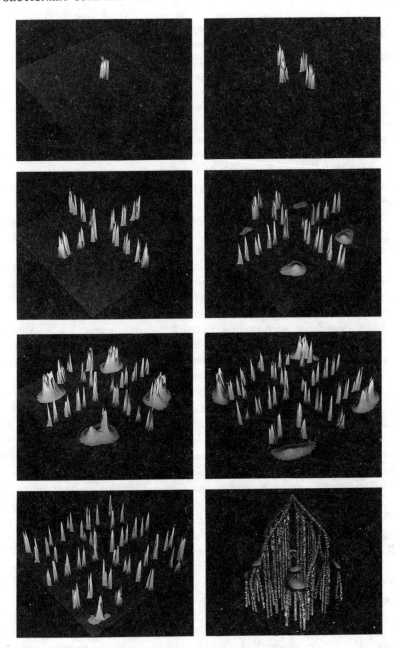

Figure 1.3 A visualization of a mathematical model simulating the coevolution and emergence of a simple ecology of behaviours.

system with 'error-making' explorations of behaviour evolves towards structures which express *synergetic complementarities*. In other words, evolution, although driven to explore by error-making and competition, evolves *cooperative structures*.

In a typical simulation we start with a single type of behaviour in a possibility space. Because of the micro-diversity, there is an exploration process with behaviours emerging and declining, until, after some time, the average level of synergy per individual rises from zero to some positive value, and the level of competition per individual declines. The synergy can be expressed either through 'self-symbiotic' terms, where the consequences of a behaviour, in addition to consuming resources, is favourable to itself, or through interactions involving pairs, triplets, and so on. This corresponds to the emergence of 'hypercycles' (Eigen and Schuster 1979).

The system evolves to a complex concatenation of behaviours which, although they compete at some level, favour each other! Free markets are not, therefore, just about competition, but also about synergy! A successful and sustainable evolutionary system will be one in which there is freedom for imagination and creativity to explore at the individual level, which seeks out complementarities and loops of positive feedback, providing the stability and structure that humans need to feel themselves part of a community.

In human systems, such positive feedback systems abound. Much of culture may well be behaviour which is fixed in this way. In most situations imitative strategies cannot be eliminated by the evolutionary process, and so fashions, styles and indeed cultures rise and decline without necessarily expressing any clear functional advantages. Indeed, 'culture' should perhaps be viewed less as being 'the best' way of doing things somewhere, than as resulting from ignorance of other ways of doing things. Particular technologies can trap or liberate their followers, without it necessarily being clear at the outset which it will be. Cities are extreme examples of 'positive feedback' traps. They can grow far beyond the point at which they function well, trapping capital investment, infrastructure and human enterprise in what may be a congested and inferior environment. People can only grow and develop within the framework which they inherit, using the paths and levers that exist, and building on what went before. They cannot start from a clear slate, and formulate their ideal choices. Indeed, their values and skills will automatically reflect the setting in which they exist, and so structure is locked into perceptions and values, as well as into the organizations and institutions through which we must work. Positive feedback traps create structure and organization, and the changing circumstances due to new technology and new desires stress these stable entities. If there are insufficient ways to modify structure, then eventually there will be a sudden collapse and reorganization. Again, diversity maintained at the level of individual experience can help constantly to question and modify existing structures and organizations so that they may adapt to changing circumstances.

Discussion

The idea that evolution leads to a community of interlocking behaviours is an important result. The history of the successful economic development of a region is largely a tale of increasing cooperation and complementarity, not competition. If competition dominated it would 'spread things out', rather than building dense concentrations of people and activities. An economy is a 'complex' of different activities that to some extent 'fit together' and need each other. Competition for customers, space, or for natural resources is only one aspect of reality. Others are of familiar suppliers and markets, local skill development and specialization, coevolution of activities to each other, networks of information flows and solidarities, that lead to a collective generation and shaping of exchanges and discourse within the system.

From a single type of firm, evolution can generate an ecology/economy, and a dynamic one since the identity/practices of each participant is maintained by the balance between a continual exploration of innovators outwards into character space, and the differential reproduction and survival that are due to the presence of the other firms in the economy. Random events which occur during the 'development' process will affect which technologies and products arise, and so it is not true that the evolution represents the discovery of pre-existing 'niches'.

Such a system operates beyond the mechanical paradigm, because its response to external interventions can involve changes in structure and in the 'identity' of the participants in the system. Penalizing particular types in such a system will provoke a complex response from the rest of the system. The identity of each type of firm depends on that of the others, and on the accidents of its particular history. Removing or severely depleting one or several types will, therefore, set in motion a series of responses, and changes in behaviour of others which may look very like (and indeed be) a form of learning. Deviant behaviour, which hitherto encountered a negative pay-off, may instead be reinforced, and in addition the responses may be essentially unpredictable.

Instead of viewing evolutionary dynamics as the inevitable progress of technologies and knowledge of a given (if complex) landscape, our models show how the landscape itself is produced by the behaviours in interaction, and how the detailed history of the exploration process itself affects the outcome. Evolution is endogenous, rather than exogenous. Innovators are present to a constant degree all the time, but sometimes the feedback loops of the system can 'control' their influence, and a period of stability results, while at other times the flow of 'innovations' cannot be controlled by the feedback loops, and structural change ensues.

Technological evolution is not about a single type of firm 'winning', through its superior behaviour, since, as we see, evolution is characterized more by increasing variety and complexity than the opposite. Instead, it is about the emergence of self-consistent 'sets' of activities, with mutually helpful effects on each other, that characterizes evolutionary dynamics. Potential 'supply' and 'demand' are not given independently of one another. People cannot consume what is not produced, but can only experience and react to what is produced. Their lifestyle, demands and preferences are shaped by the supply that really occurs, and so a 'learning' dialogue shapes the patterns of consumption that develop in the system. These patterns emerge, and the chance details of the process of emergence alter what is finally 'revealed'. Supply affects demand, and vice versa, and cultural structures are formed by the effects of positive and negative feedbacks – imitation, economies of scale, learning by doing and so on, are positive; and competition for attention, market and resources negative.

This brings us to the important question of speculation and beliefs in human systems. Clearly, the expected return on an investment is what derives investment in an innovation, but this can only be based on an imperfect grasp of the perceptions of potential customers. Their perceptions could be based either on an understanding of the 'fundamental' usefulness of the innovation, or alternatively on the basis of the observed trend in price, or imitation of other actors' decisions. What people believe affects what happens, and what happens affects what people believe! This is a positive feedback loop which can be understood on the basis of the kinds of model which we are developing. It severely affects the outcome of 'free markets', as we have seen repeatedly in commodity cycles, land speculation, the prices of almost anything of which there is a limited supply. Instead of free markets leading to a sensible and effective allocation of investment and resources, we find that prices, although they are 'numbers', are still driven by people's beliefs, and these feed on each other resulting in peaks and troughs, and often in massive misallocations of resources and waste. Clearly, the fact that 'trend creates trend' offers a considerable opportunity for instability and chaos, and this is only rendered manageable by the diversity of perceptions and motivations of human actors. Models can and are being developed to 'learn' robust, mutually consistent strategies, and also how to encourage diversity in the face of the mass media, and instantaneous shared information.

For diversity is absolutely vital to the functioning of the system. Transactions can only occur if two actors are different. If they are both identical and 'average', then there can be no useful interchange. The evolution of the urban or regional landscape therefore reflects the specificities of individuals who have different aims, different information and different resources. Imperfect knowledge and plain ignorance play a role in smoothing the responses of a population to a given situation, and as decisions are made by some individuals, so they change the conditions and constraints on others, provoking successive responses and adjustments to the evolving circumstances.

The idea that we can solve our problems by simply releasing the forces of the 'free market' is an illusion. The real complexity of the world involves the *fact* of collective structure, which is not amenable to any simplistic solution, be it central planning or free markets. The goals and strategies, the ethics and the understanding of individuals, fashion the collective structure that emerges, and give it complex properties, which act on each individual uniquely, and which cannot easily be summarized in a few criteria. Similarly, the collective structure that emerges enriches and constrains the experiences and choices that are open to individuals, and so one is dealing with the dialogue between individual freedom and beliefs, and the social, cultural, technological and physical realities in which they are embedded and which they shape. The existence of cycles of over- and undersupply, and the real effects of speculative investment have affected most of us through spiralling house prices and mortgages, or boom and recession, and so it seems clear that the idea that 'the market knows . . .' is contrary to our everyday experience. Neither is it true that 'the planner knows . . .', since whatever the generosity of spirit, the real interdependencies and potentials exceed the grasp of any single person or group.

This discussion of self-organization in complex systems hopefully teaches us humility. Science has revealed its own limitations, and this, too, is an achievement. Knowing that we cannot know is an important step on the road to wisdom. If we are to learn from the way that the natural world copes with its inability to predict the future, then we see that parallelism, micro-diversity and local freedom are key factors in its ability to deal with whatever happens. Conceiving an economic and social system which can adapt and change its technologies as well as its organizations in a similar way will presumably require the translation of these ideas into the economic, managerial and research and development practices that we should adopt, and this will be the aim of future work.

PART I: Evolutionary Economics Elaborated

2 Economic Growth via the Coevolution of Technology and Institutions

Richard R. Nelson

Introduction

This essay is a contribution to the rapidly expanding body of evolutionary economic growth theory. The purpose is to locate this theory intellectually within the broader body of evolutionary theorizing in economics and social science that is represented by the various essays in this volume.

A glance through the collection here testifies that the recent surge of writing in economics and social sciences that calls itself 'evolutionary' is very diverse in nature. Some of it is concerned with explaining the 'evolution' of a particular variable — science, say, or the organization of the modern business firm. Some is concerned with the 'evolution' of complex structures involving several different kinds of variable. Thus Sidney Winter and I (Nelson and Winter 1982), Silverberg *et al.* (1988), Soete and Turner (1987) and Metcalfe and colleagues (Metcalfe and Gibbons 1986; Metcalfe and Saviotti 1991) have developed a class of evolutionary models in which technology and the structure of industry coevolve, and this process leads to growth of productivity which is a statistical property of the system as a whole. This essay is in this latter group, concerned with the evolution of a quite complex structure.

In a number of writings the term 'evolutionary' is used to connote that the variable or structure under study changes over time in a strongly path-dependent manner, but the analysis of that process makes little use of notions analogous to 'natural selection'. Sometimes the connotation is that of a more or less natural development or 'unfolding' of traits latent in an earlier form. In other studies, particularly those influenced by chaos theory, small perturbations may set the time path off on a radically different direction than it would otherwise have taken. But in neither case does the term 'evolution' carry the connotation of variation and selection as the mechanisms driving change.

On the other hand, in the evolutionary growth models noted above, it does. And it does as well in some of the more narrowly focused evolutionary theories, like Campbell's (1974) that science evolves, or Vincenti's (1990) that technology does. This essay definitely falls into that branch of evolutionary theory in which systematic selection on somewhat random variation plays a central analytic role.

Much of the evolutionary writing is quite formal, but within this group the nature of the formal modelling varies a lot. Some of the models are completely determinate. Some contain essential probabilistic elements. Some specify full-blown selection systems operating on extant distributions of entities. On the other hand, many of the evolutionary writings invoke no formal model at all.

Regarding formalization, the present essay, or rather the objective of the work the essay attempts to motivate, stands betwixt and between. Its principal purpose is to help bridge the large gap that exists at present between formal theories of economic growth, and studies of growth that take the form of economic history. Contemporary formal growth theories concocted by economists – both evolu-tionary and neoclassical – treat growth as almost all 'quantitative'. Various magnitudes, like per-capita income, or capital intensity, rise over time, while others, like the share of labour in national income or the rate of return on capital, may stay constant, but nothing much happens qualitatively. In the historical accounts lots of qualitative things are happening, such as the emergence of distinctly new technologies, new forms of business firms, dramatic changes in industry structure, the emergence of new institutions, and so on. Put another way, development is going on and it is not simply a matter of things getting bigger or smaller.

One of the principal reasons why I am attracted to evolutionary theories of economic growth is that the language of evolutionary theory seems so natural to employ to describe and explain the detailed empirical studies. While the language certainly abstracts and simplifies the picture, it does not seem to distort it greatly, nor does it force one to ignore large parts of it. Using a term Sidney Winter and I coined some years ago, evolutionary theory is good appreciative theory about the phenomena in question.

The other principal reason why I am attracted to evolutionary theory is that it is amenable to powerful formalization, which permits the analyst to see into the logical structure of the mechanisms described verbally, to check whether the system so described hangs together, and whether or not it actually 'explains' what it purports to. However, it is my strong methodological belief that squaring the appreciative theory with the empirical evidence is an essential first step towards real understanding, and that the formal modelling needs to be disciplined by the appreciative theory.

While many historical accounts of economic growth are concerned with whole economies, I believe that, for the purpose at hand, the best way to make progress is by trying to develop industry- or sectoral-level models. There is too much diversity across economic sectors to hope that a model that aggregates them all can achieve the contact with empirical developmental history I am seeking. There is a better chance of fruitful sector-level modelling.

The model, the basis of which I lay out here, is directed towards manufacturing. The question of whether the same general model fits all or most of manufacturing will be explored along the way. My objective here is to describe the basic ingredients that will ultimately go into the model. I have not yet built that model and, as will become apparent, there are some major problems that need to be resolved before one is up and running.

I shall proceed as follows. In the next two sections, I describe and try to link two broad bodies of evolutionary theoretic writing. The first proposes that a new technology develops along a relatively standard track from the time it is born, to its maturity, and that firm and industry structure 'coevolves' with the technology. The other is concerned with the development of institutions in response to changing economic conditions, incentives, and pressures. The fourth section will then be concerned with 'punctuated equilibrium'.

Then, in the penultimate section, I will consider several economic developmental implications that flow from the model, although my argument is not yet as clean as I would like. The essay concludes with a reprise on formal modelling.

The coevolution of technology and industry structure

It is analytically convenient to begin by discussing a body of research that purports to identify a 'life cycle' through which many technologies seem to go. At the present time a number of scholars, including both economists and organization theorists, are doing work that I would put in this category. However, much of the contemporary formulation was offered over fifteen years ago by Utterback and Abernathy (1975) and Abernathy and Utterback (1978) who had been working on automobiles. The basic starting argument is that when a new technology comes into existence there is considerable uncertainty regarding which of a variety of possible variants will succeed. Different ones are tried out by different parties. However, after a period of time and competition one or more of these variants come to dominate the others, and attention and resources become concentrated on these at the expense of the others. In the parlance of several of the workers in this field, a **dominant design** emerges.

There are several different stories about how a dominant design comes into existence. In the most straightforward of these, one variant simply is better than the others and, with time and experimentation, the best basic design comes to be identified and widely recognized. However, there are other more complex stories.

If the competing technologies are cumulative, an early advantage, which could have been simply a matter of chance, of one over the others may lead to the race ending very shortly. If one technology gains an advantage over its competitors, there are strong incentives for resources to be drawn away from trying to advance its rivals, since major advances may be needed to make them competitive. And once resources come to be largely focused on the leader, further improvements may soon make it and its further development the only economic way to proceed because competing designs are left so far behind. Winter and I suggested this as a possibility some time ago, and some of Arthur's (1988a) recent modelling can be interpreted this way. In such a context there is no reason to believe that the dominant design society fixes upon is the best one. It could well be that other broad configurations would have turned out better had resources been allocated to advancing these in the technological race.

Still a third story, or rather a family of stories, has some commonalities with the second, but stresses systems aspects. In particular, the focus is on interaction economies that may occur when the number who own and use a particular variant grows, as skills develop that are particular to a certain variant, or through investments in complementary products designed to fit with a particular variant (see, for example, David 1992a; Arthur 1989; and Katz and Shapiro 1985). While sometimes used more generally, the special term 'standard' tends to be used to denote the key mechanism or configuration that defines and delineates the dominant 'system' when it emerges. As the authors writing in this field argue convincingly, there is no reason why the standard that emerges and, in effect, 'locks' in the system, need be optimal.

In the original Abernathy and Utterback story, once a dominant design comes into existence, radical product innovation slows, and product design improvements become incremental. There may, however, be a considerable period of time where there is substantial improvement of process technology. If the advancing process technology is specific to a particular product design, cumulative process innovation further locks in that design and makes it even more difficult for different designs to compete. This storyline is quite consistent with that being spun by economists interested in systems technologies and standards.

When Abernathy and Utterback first spun out the dominant design story, they based it on detailed observation of only one industry – automobile manufacturing. Since that time the basic storyline has been tried, and found fitting, in a wide range of industries (see, in particular, Tushman and Romanelli 1985; Tushman and Anderson 1986; Tushman and Rosenkopf 1992; and Utterback and Suarez 1993). Some writers clearly believe it is a universal. I confess some scepticism about that. The story seems to fit best industries where the product is a 'system', and where customers have similar demands. It is not at all clear if the notion of a dominant design fits the experience of the chemical products industry, where often a variety of quite different products are produced for similar uses, or pharmaceuticals, where customer needs are divergent and specialized. Nevertheless, dominant design theory certainly has proved illuminating in a wide range of industries.

And where it does seem applicable, that theory raises very interesting and troubling questions about the nature of economic explanation, about whether one can presume that market forces generate efficient outcomes, and even about what one means by market forces. In the first 'story', economic logic prevails. But in both the second and third stories of how a dominant design emerges, there are stochastic forces at work that can be decisive. Particularly in the third, there also may be processes of coalition-building that can nudge the outcome one way or another, which may have little to do with projections of long-run economic efficiency (see, for example, David 1985; 1992a; and Tushman and Rosenkopf 1992). Some writers have gone so far as to argue that it is power, or social consensus, rather than economic efficiency, which determines which broad path ultimately is followed. This raises the question of how far economic selection arguments can take one in an evolutionary analysis of economic change, and the extent to which political and social forces need to be taken explicitly into account not simply in influencing transient or short-term developments but in determining the broad paths along which technology proceeds. More on this later.

There is another body of research which uses concepts similar to those employed in the technology life cycle literature, but with a different focus – in particular, what happens to firm and industry structure as a technology matures. Abernathy and Utterback (1978) were interested in this question, but it was not the central focus of their earlier articles. Indeed, until recently, the bulk of the research in this area has been done by economists, who made little reference to the above technology cycle literature. A number of economists have contributed to this line of research and 'story-telling'. Mueller and Tilton (1969) wrote a pioneer piece along these lines. Recently, Gort and Klepper (1982) and Klepper and Graddy (1990) have developed the empirical and theoretical argument further. Over the past few years there has been convergence. Utterback and Suarez (1992), coming from the technology life cycle tradition, has gone into the industrial organization literature. Klepper (1992), coming from the latter, has found the former.

In any case, the basic propositions tend to be these. During the early period of experimentation and flux, before a dominant design emerges, there are no particular advantages to incumbency. Market demand is fragmented across a number of variants. Firms producing particular designs tend to be small. Model change may be frequent. There is a considerable amount of exit from and entry into the industry.

However, after a dominant design becomes established, firms that do not produce a variant of it tend to drop out of the industry, or into small niche markets. With product design more stabilized, learning by incumbent firms becomes more cumulative, and potential entrants are increasingly at a disadvantage. With the market less fragmented and more predictable, firms try to exploit latent economies of scale, and advances in process technology both reflect and enforce this. Generally scale-intensive technology is capital-intensive as well, and so the cost of entry rises for this reason, too. There is 'shake-out' in the industry and structure becomes more concentrated, with the surviving firms tending to be relatively large.

As with the theory about dominant designs, there is a question about how universal is the proposed pattern of industry evolution. The empirical work by Gort and Klepper (1982) and Klepper (1992) shows that the basic story does seem to fit a wide range of industries in the United States. Utterback and Suarez (1993) similarly claim widespread applicability. However, there certainly are exceptions. The companies that got into the (then) new pharmaceuticals business in the 1930s and after the Second World War were, by and large, the old strong chemical products companies, rather than new entrants.

It should also be noted that almost all the empirical research on the topic has been on patterns in the United States. At least since the Second World War, there is reason to believe that new products that were pioneered by new firms in the United States, were pioneered (somewhat later) by established firms in Europe and Japan. If so, these international differences seem interesting to explain.

The evolution of supporting institutions

By and large, the evolutionary processes discussed above proceed in a market setting, and involve competition among firms, with selection determined to a good extent by market forces. One can see a route towards formal modelling drawing ideas from various industry models Winter and I have developed, from Arthur and colleagues, and from Klepper. A society's institutions – both general and specific to the broad sector that contains the developing industry – will influence the parameters of the model, and perhaps even its broad shape. Thus the ability of a firm with a better product to eliminate its competition may depend on its ability to attract funds to exploit its advantage.

However, a number of detailed historical accounts document that various features of the institutional environment themselves tend to adapt and change in response to pushes and pulls exerted by the development of a new industry. The processes involved here are not market processes, at least not of the standard variety, but involve the forming of collective bodies, decisions of voluntary organizations, government agencies and political action.

One important development that almost invariably occurs as a new industry develops is that the people in it become conscious that there is a new industry, and that it has collective interests and needs (see Granovetter 1985). Industry or trade associations form. These may be active in the standard setting discussed earlier. More generally, they give the industry a recognized organization that can lobby on its behalf for regulation to its liking, for protection from competition from outside the group, for public programmes to support it, and so on. This is another feature of an industry's evolution that can lock in the status quo.

If the technology on which the industry is based has novel characteristics, new technical societies and new technical journals tend to spring up. In some cases whole new fields of 'science' may come into being.

Research by Nathan Rosenberg and myself (Nelson and Rosenberg 1993) has called into question certain popular notions about the relationships between science and technology. Conventional wisdom has it that the sciences, in general, do not aim to solve practical problems but rather to advance basic understanding of nature, but that enhanced basic understanding makes technological advances possible even if the work is not aimed to do that. Thus the work of Maxwell on electromagnetism, which was an exercise in pure science, ultimately led to radio. The case of Sadi Carnot, who launched the field of thermodynamics largely because he wanted to understand what was going on in steam engines, is recognized but generally considered something of an exception.

Our research suggests that these kinds of 'exception' may well be the rule. Quite often when a new technology comes into existence, there is very little scientific understanding relevant to it. However, the appearance of that new technology then induces scientific research to understand it, and lay the basis for its subsequent development. The result may be the creation of a new scientific field related to that technology. Thus the field of metallurgy came into existence because of a demand for better understanding of the factors that determined the properties of steel. Computer science is the field that was bought into existence by the advent of the modern computer. Chemical engineering and electrical engineering arose as fields of teaching and research because of industry demand for them that occurred after the key technological advances that launched the industries.

The appearance and development of these technology orientated sciences tend to tie industries to universities, which provide both people trained in the relevant fields, and research findings which enable the technology to advance further. The development of these sciences naturally tends to lend extra strength to prevailing technologies. On the other hand, the presence of university research tends to dilute the extent to which firms in being have knowledge advantages over potential entrants. Also, research at universities just may become the source of radically different technological alternatives.

Recognition of the role of technical societies and universities in the development of modern technologies opens the door to seeing the wide range of institutions that may coevolve with technology. Often legal structures need to change. Thus there may be intellectual property rights issues that need to be sorted out — biotechnology is a striking contemporary case in point. There almost always are issues of regulation, as was prominently the case in radio and, in a different manner, biotechnology again. Hughes (1987) has described in great detail the wide range of legal and regulatory matters that had to be decided before electric power could go forward strongly, and how the particular ways they were decided affected the evolution of the technology and the industry.

In many cases new public sector activities and programmes are required. Thus mass use of automobiles required that societies organize themselves to build and maintain a system of public roads. Aeroplanes required airports. The development of radio required mechanisms to allocate the radio spectrum. Development of commercial television required that as well, and also depended on governmental decisions about standards.

These examples indicate that the evolution of institutions relevant to a technology or industry may be a very complex process, involving not only the actions of private firms, but also organizations such as industry associations, technical societies, universities, courts, government agencies, legislatures, and so on. The 'new institutional economics' started with a broad theoretical stance that, somehow, institutions changed optimally (if perhaps with a lag) in response to changes in economic circumstances that called for those changes. Recently, however, scholars in that field are beginning to highlight the interest-group conflict often involved in public responses, and the strong sensitivity of outcomes to political structures and processes (see, for example, Shepsle and Weingast 1981; North 1990; and Cohen and Noll 1991). Not only is there an abandonment of the assumption of 'optimality' of institutional response. There now is strong recognition that one needs a process model to predict and understand what the institutional accommodations will be.

Punctuated equilibrium

This leads me to another set of strands I want to gather here: those concerned with what happens in a mature industry when radical new developments come about that call for significant change. An example would be the effect of the advent of transistor and later integrated circuit technology on the mature electronics industry which had been dedicated to vacuum tubes. Another would be the effect of the advent of biotechnology on the mature pharmaceuticals industry.

Perhaps the largest body of writing addressing this issue has been concerned with who adopts and brings to practice such a new technology. In particular, do incumbent firms adopt it, or does its adoption depend on new entrants? The proposition advanced by this literature is that the answer depends on whether the new technology employs roughly the same kinds of understanding and skills as does the old. If so, firms in the industry tend to be able to switch over to it. If not, new firms will tend to enter the industry, and the failure rate among incumbents may be very high. Work along these lines has been done by Tushman and Romanelli (1985), Tushman and Anderson (1986), Hannan and Freeman (1989) and Henderson and Clark (1990), among others. However, as with the empirical literature on the evolution of firm and industry structure described above, virtually all of this work has been on the United States. As I noted earlier, there is reason to believe that in Europe and Japan new firms do not seem to enter the picture so readily, and incumbent firms thus have more time to adjust.

A broader question, of course, is whether the larger set of institutions supporting the established technology and industry are able to adapt, or whether their conservatism makes it difficult for established firms to shift away from old practices, or for new firms to enter and to take over. Lazonick (1990), among others, has elaborated the theme that the broad organization of work and institutions for training labour that worked so well for British industry in the late nineteenth century became a handicap in the twentieth. Veblen's (1915) famous essay on the rise of Germany as an economic power stressed more generally that British industry was in effect sorely handicapped in adopting the new technologies that were coming into place around the turn of the century by an interlocking set of constraints associated with her institutions and past investments, whereas Germany could work with a relatively clean slate.

The most sweeping of the propositions along these lines has been made by Perez (1985) and Freeman (1991), who have developed the concept of a 'techno-economic paradigm'. Their argument starts along lines developed by Schumpeter many years ago: different eras are dominated by different fundamental technologies. They then propose that to be effective with those technologies a nation requires a set of institutions compatible with and supportive of them. The ones suitable for an earlier set of fundamental technologies may be quite inappropriate for the new. Their arguments clearly are similar to those of Veblen, in the particular case he addressed. Thus while Britain lagged, Germany and the United States had or quickly adopted institutions that could support the rising chemical and electrical industries that were the basic ones in the era from 1910 to 1960 or so. Perez and Freeman propose that the period since around 1970 has seen the rise of 'information technologies' as the new basis of economic effectiveness, and argue that effective accommodation requires a very different set of institutions than those required in the earlier era. They see Japan as coming closest to having them.

One can be sceptical about these propositions simply because they are so grandly stated. However, I think that the basic point, that new technologies often are not well accommodated by prevailing institutional structures and require institutional reform if they are to develop effectively, squares with the historical record.

Economic growth and the formation of comparative advantage at a sectoral level

In the introduction, I stressed that virtually all formal growth theory focuses on the quantitative aspects of growth and captures little either of the developmental or the qualitative features of the detailed historical accounts.

Regarding the quantitative aspects, the appreciative theory sketched above certainly does suggest a 'developmental' flavour to the time paths of measured worker productivity, capital intensity, and total factor productivity as an industry matures, and also some interesting connections between these variables and firm size and industry structure. In particular, the argument leads one to expect that rising capital intensity and the development of large-scale units are phenomena that go together and occur after a dominant design or mode of production has been established. One might suspect that these developments would also be associated with an acceleration of growth both of labour productivity and of total factor productivity. However, particularly if effective use of the potential latent in a new technology requires significant institutional accommodations, it might take a long time before there is much effect on productivity. David's (1991) study of electric power is consistent with this story.

For me, perhaps the most intriguing implications of the life cycle appreciative theory concern the factors it suggests may lie behind the establishment of comparative advantage in a new industry. The 'new trade theory' recognizes, in stylized form, that comparative advantage in certain fields is created rather than being innate in broad country-level variables, and that both private and public actions may be needed for comparative advantage to be built. However, the stories sketched above provide a much richer and variegated account of how comparative advantage is built.

Among other things, they suggest that different factors may be operative early in an industry's history than later. Regarding the determinants of comparative advantage when an industry is new, the technology cycle story calls attention to the fact that countries clearly differ in the ease with which new firms can form and get funding and in the degree to which markets are open to new sources of supply. They also differ in the speed with which universities are able to adopt new sciences, in how adaptable legal structures are to changing demands put on them by new technologies, in how supportive public sector programmes are of the new as contrasted with protective of the old, and so on. On the other hand, once a dominant design is established, different features of a nation's institutional environment become important – ability to finance large-scale investment, for example; ability to train labour for the specifics of the jobs, for another.

A reprise on formal theorizing

This essay has been on appreciative theorizing. In the introduction I stated my conviction that it is important to get appreciative theory reasonably well worked out before one embarks on the business of building formal theory. Otherwise there are few restraints preventing formal modelling from going amuck, and little that pulls the enterprise towards being about real phenomena. On the other hand, given the existence of a reasonably well-worked-out appreciative theory, formal theorizing can be a very helpful part of the intellectual enterprise.

There is, centrally, the problem that the informality of appreciative theorizing makes if difficult to check out the logical completeness and correctness of the 'causal' arguments in that theory. The exercise and discipline of formalizing the argument can reveal a lot about what is incomplete or problematic in the appreciative causal story. As someone who has played this game a number of times, I can attest that much is learned even before a formal model is fully developed and capable of serving as an analytic engine – for example, through the process of discovering that various appreciative theoretic causal propositions or 'predictions' will not go through formally unless one makes certain ancillary assumptions. In turn, one might be quite willing to make these, or one might go back and reconsider the appreciative theoretic logic. Once a formal model is up and running, the same dialectic between appreciative and formal theorizing continues, as one discovers that the hypothesized conclusions hold only for certain sets of parameter values, or that the model is generating certain kinds of outcome regarding which the appreciative theory was mute. Again, one is forced to revise or qualify or extend the appreciative theory, or at least learn to interpret it differently in terms of how it can be appropriately formalized.

In that spirit, what are the key issues that I, right now, would like to explore with a carefully constructed formal model? (I indicated above that I am sure that once one is up and running I will discover a lot of matters that I have not thought about.) First of all, I think the logic of the various processes that have been argued to lead to the emergence of a dominant design ought to be worked through in the context of a complete evolutionary model, with diverse firms, whose growth or decline is tied to their profitability, and who are locked in in varying degrees to particular technologies. The model certainly should contain diverse customers, who have various degrees of rigidity in their preferences, and who may or may not want to buy what others have bought. The model should build in various mechanisms that generate different forms and degrees of dynamic increasing returns. The Pólya urn scheme that, up until now, has been virtually the only way the dominant design question has been formally analysed, strikes me as possibly missing a number of interesting complications.

Second, the relationships between the evolution of a technology and the evolution of firm and industry structure surely can be illuminated by formal modelling. How much difference does it make, for example, if the broad technology is available to new entrants, because, say, much of it is codified in a scientific discipline? How does the diversity of customers affect how industry structure evolves? And so on.

As I indicated earlier, I think I see a reasonably clear road towards modelling these kinds of things, drawing from early Nelson–Winter and related models, from Arthur, and from Klepper. I think it will be far more difficult to model the coevolution of institutions.

There are two reasons. One is that it is not clear exactly how various institutions ought to be represented. Thus how should one model an 'industry association' or a 'technical society'? How should one treat MIT and Stanford as parts of the institutional structure supporting the US semiconductor industry? What activities do they perform? How do they affect the behaviour and performance of firms in the industry? We have 'appreciative theory' about this. It will not be easy to translate that theory into formal theory, however. That is exactly the reason why it is important to try to do so.

The second reason is that the 'evolutionary processes' through which new academic disciplines are formed, or blocked, or the ways in which new law comes to be created, or old law modified, are very different from the processes built into extant formal evolutionary models. We have 'appreciative theories' about these matters, but virtually no work trying to formalize those theories. It should be fun, but not easy, to try to do so.

3 Technological Diversity, Random Selection in a Population of Firms, and Technological Institutions of Government

Hans-Peter Brunner

D33

B25

Introduction

The notion of technological change as determining an economy's competitive advantage in the late twentieth and early twenty-first centuries enjoys increasing attention in both the popular press and economic circles. The fear of being overtaken by technological changes induces governments to facilitate techno-logical change in their countries' productive sectors with industrial policies. Policy-makers proceed with their programmes without being familiar with the mechanism that links policy inducement to technological change and competitive advantage. Indeed, only very recently have economists attempted to examine such linkage mechanisms of feedback loops. Schumpeter was first in thinking that technological change generates competition and that this competition works to the benefit of technologically advancing firms. His work greatly influenced recent research on the technological development of industries. Now it is widely held that new, radically superior technologies displace old, inferior ones and create relative competitive advantage. Exactly how this process works still remains nebulous, despite the need for providing guidance to industrial policy pro-grammes.

One reason for the inexact formulation of the technological renewal process in industries is that most economists' models do not reproduce differences in firm characteristics, especially those indicative for technological know-how, which ultimately drive upwards an industry's average productivity. In this paper I venture an evolutionary way of thinking about the processes interacting for technological diversity. I also formalize the mechanisms underlying the creation of diversity leading to change. I show ways in which various types of industrial policy affect both industry structure and technological diversity, and thus induce technological change.

In an evolutionary mode of thinking productivity change is driven by fluctuating population size which is subjected to variations in frequencies of

events and performance characteristics. So I will have to examine frequencies and
their probability distributions for a model of the sort I am proposing. As Metcalfe
(1989: 56) states:

whereas in typological [neoclassical] thinking variation is a nuisance, in population
thinking it is of all-consuming interest because it is the variety in the system which
drives the evolutionary process. Moreover the changes over time in statistical moments
derived from the characteristics distribution are an index of the rate and direction of
evolutionary change . . .

The frequency of firm attributes is the result of a stochastic process of
innovation and imitation. Technological change can be detected and felt only at
the higher, macro level, but the change is the outcome of individual (firm)
behaviour that fluctuates and that is susceptible to three distinct forces:
competition (turbulence), technological diversity, and appropriability conditions.

As empirical evidence suggests, the industrial policies of deconcentrating
economic sectors and of accelerating diffusion of know-how can make the
whole economy and particular industries in it internationally more competitive.
From empirical work of both myself and others, I have come up with a flow
diagram (Figure 3.1) which depicts how important processes interact in
producing turbulent technological change in a population of firms. I proceed in
five steps with formalizing and analysing the interaction of the processes as
sketched in Figure 3.1. First, I tell the story how the processes interact for
technological diversity. The story helps me to specify mechanisms of technological change. Second, based on that story I interpret the model, which is
presented formally in the Appendix to this paper and which specifies the
relationships producing technological change. Third, I highlight the instrumen-
tal role of the institutions of government for creating technological diversity.
Fourth, I subject the model to simulation experiments. Fifth, I compare the
results with my empirical stories.

Description of the processes interacting for technological diversity

A review of the articles by Winter (1984), Metcalfe (1989), Radzicki (1990) and
Dopfer (1991: 54) leads me to conclude that three interacting essential processes
of change are necessary as well as sufficient to produce the kind of variety in firm
size (industry structure) and technological advance observed in different empirical
studies of industrial sectors (Acs and Audretsch 1990; Brunner 1991a). The three
evolutionary processes are: economic selection via entry and exit; new technology
absorption; and diffusion of such new technological information among firm
populations.

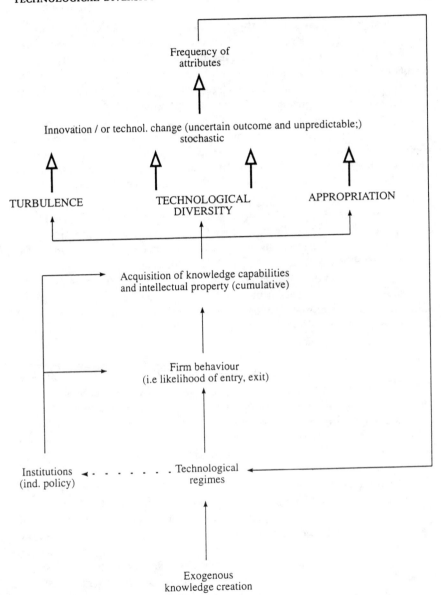

Figure 3.1 A map of the model.

The first pillar of the process tripod has to be the mechanism of population change. Firms are the individual members that make up the population of firms in an industry. The industry becomes the unit of analysis in my model. Populations are subject to immigration and deaths, as firms enter or leave an industry. Economic selection produces fluctuations in population size, and entry and exit rates are an expression of that selective pressure itself.

Even the simplest evolutionary process of change contains one mechanism that generates random variety in at least one characteristic of a given population, and one mechanism that dampens variety. Variety is the response of a population (of firms) to incoming flows of inputs from their environment. The input foremost of interest to me is technological information. Firms then absorb such information to a different degree by producing innovative products. Technological variety is the result. Firms then hold on to competing varieties of products long enough for selection to operate in the form of market or sales success, for example. As a consequence, accumulated inputs available to firms will vary — stocks of skilled human capital, for example, resulting in varying types of output.

An evolutionary model must also include a mechanism that disperses the effects of environmental inputs: such a mechanism can be a diffusion process. Techno-logical knowledge is diffused through both innovation (adaptation of technology) and imitation by rival firms. The diffusion process of technology then becomes the third pillar in my model.

Stochastic processes incorporate uncertainty — or, as Nelson (1981) suggests they allow for 'vagueness' — in the groping process of research and imitation. Nelson mentions that we deal with a search process of sequential nature, where one success builds on the previous one, or possibly on a previous failure. Poisson processes, a special type of stochastic process, are ideally suited for representing these vague, groping processes mathematically. We will deal not only with a process sequential in nature but also one where events, such as innovations, can and do occur at any time.

The frequency of firm attributes itself feeds back on the emergence of technological regimes. (This latter loop, however, which facilitates punctuated equilibria, is not included in this small version of my model.) An entrepreneurial regime endogenously selects producers who are specialists in a niche of the product market. Appropriability of returns from innovation is low. That is, innovation can be imitated at low cost. Information density is increasingly high. Technology variation is low. The strong diffusion process overpowers the creation of technological diversity. Short-lived differentiation of products is required, in order quickly to appropriate the benefits from minor innovations, before erosion of benefits occurs from close competitors. Firms that do not withstand the competitive pressure are forced to exit the industry. Fewer firms appropriate larger slices of the market. Industry concentration gradually increases. Large generalist firms emerge in a routinized regime. Firms can now justify large investment in R&D by high appropriability – that is, benefits are not easily eroded from competitors or potential entrants. Technological distance between firms is relatively large. However, that increase of distance leaves room for smaller, entrepreneurial firms to enter the product market with radically new technologies.

Model mechanism

In general, evolutionary models consist of positive and negative feedback relationships. The loops give structure to an evolutionary model. Their identification helps formalizing the process story given. In my model two countervailing loop structures, subordinate to the grand overall loop, influence the firms' innovation activities in an industry.

The first loop structure relates accumulated technological knowledge to technological change via innovative and imitative behaviour under the influence of turbulence (entry and exit of firms) and technological diversity. An increase in competition (competition can be expressed in turbulence) will enhance technological progress, however at the expense of technological diversity (see the first subsection of the Appendix). Yet a wider variety of technologies used in one industry leads to high selective fitness of the industry. It avoids premature technological lock-in.

The second loop structure relates accumulated technological knowledge to technological change via innovative and imitative behaviour under the influence of appropriability conditions and technological diversity. Klepper (1992) argues that large firms, because by definition they have a larger share of the market, can appropriate a larger share of the benefits from innovation than smaller firms can (see the second subsection of the Appendix). However, smaller firms are more flexible and faster in introducing new technologies in the market, thus they introduce more technological diversity. As I have mentioned, higher technological diversity increases the overall selective fitness of an industry, but it slows down the pace of technological change.

The degree of competition is expressed not only in the level of diversity, but also in the degree of turbulence to which an industry is subjected. Turbulence, in my model entry and exit, is higher in industries with a large number of small and medium-sized firms. Both entry and death rates for particular industries relate directly to the degree of concentration in an industry: the relationship is to be non-monotonic though (see the third subsection of the Appendix). It also varies over time. Entry increases with the population, but at a decreasing rate as the level of competition increases.

The expected change in firm population is then determined by the entry rate, and the rate of exits or death rate. But those rates change over time, according to the maturity of an industry. In a new industry a large number of firms will enter, attracted by high expected appropriation of benefits from new technology (assuming that relative low deterrence to entry exists). Firms expect that increasing competition in the industry leads to a decline of appropriation rates. This will lead to a lower rate of entry and a higher rate of exit. There may be a period where the exit rate exceeds the entry rate. This means that the absolute number of firms in the industry will then decrease until the industry will approach a steady-state number of firms.

My model predicts that differences in levels of both technological density parameters and of turbulence parameters, due to, let us say, different policy environments, lead to different outcomes in industry structure, technology variation and technological change.

The role of institutions of government

The strength of the interacting forces is not considered to be solely exogenously determined. The identification of the ways in which government influences the model mechanism will help formulate effective industry policy programmes. Governmental institutions can set parameters that influence the strength of particular forces in particular industries at a certain time. From empirical studies (Hannan and Freeman 1989: 121; Brunner 1991b) it is again clear that two dimensions of institutional control and regulation seem relevant to the ease of starting and exiting: regulatory control of economic concentration, and degree of 'licensing' of entry and exit.

Government policies can restrict competition between technologies of different firms – for example, Grabowski and Vernon (1987) make a good story of patent regulation and institutions in the US pharmaceutical industry. Policies that help or hinder technological imitation, such as copyright laws and enforcement procedures, are important to an examination of government impact. Finally, government research and development support, particularly in technologies which need massive financial and human resources beyond the capabilities of a single firm, could help the spread of a new technology.

The simulation experiments

With two simulation experiments I test the model's sensitivity to changes in policy parameters. Every industrial sector can draw on a fund of relevant technology, called from now on the 'level of latent productivity' (LP). That fund increases exogenously and continuously.[1] It paints thus a type of moving technology frontier, which serves as an orientation and a barrier for firms of an industry in their technological efforts.[2] Firms can draw on that fund of latent knowhow through either innovation or imitation of rival firms' innovations.

In the following simulation experiments, one with $\pi = 0.05$ (standing for the low technological opportunity regime), and the other one with π set to 0.15 (standing for an entrepreneurial technological regime), four policy parameters (β, γ, $\bar{H}$ and X) take on a high (+) and low value (−). The simulation is run over 100 time periods 15 times for each of the 16 combinations of high and low values of the four policy parameters for each experiment. β and γ are government entry and exit policy parameters, respectively (for example, foreign investment, bankruptcy laws), $\bar{H}$ stands for the level of desired competition (for example, antitrust laws), and X represents a host of technology policy conditions. Tables 3.1–3.3 present the results of the 15-run samples for all policy parameter combinations.

Simulation results

The interaction coefficients of the model show the elasticity or sensitivity of the five key independent variables to changes in policy parameters. The model turns out to be very responsive to changes in entry, exit and government restrictions on concentration. For example, a one-point increase in the exit policy parameter γ decreases firm population by approximately 75 ($\pi = 0.05$) and by 56 ($\pi = 0.15$). A one-point increase in the technology policy parameter X decreases the technology level (the lower the technology level the faster technological advance) by 13 ($\pi = 0.05$) and by 14 ($\pi = 0.15$). The tendency towards lower firm population is stronger in the first than in the second experiment. Entry is less sensitive to an increase in the entry policy parameter, but exit is more sensitive to an increase in the exit policy parameter than in the higher exogenous technological change case. An increase in the policy target Herfindahl leads to a more rapid decline in population size in the first experiment than in the second, confirming the first result. But surprisingly a change in $\bar{H}$ has a stronger concentrative effect in the second experiment. The reason may be that the second experimental set-up reacts to $\bar{H}$ changes with higher variance in market shares of firms. Indeed, as Clarke and Davies (1982) demonstrated theoretically, H is influenced largely by the variation in market shares.

An increase in entry and exit rates decreases technological variance distinctively more in the experiment with the lower exogenous technological opportunity than in the one with higher technological opportunity. An increase in the concentration policy target is more effective in terms of reducing technological variance in the low technological opportunity scenario. Or, to state it differently, an antitrust policy is more effective in an environment of high technological competition (yet of lesser urgency). A policy which strengthens technological acquisition and capacities of firms is also more effective in the latter scenario than in the former.

Table 3.1 Interaction coefficients of the model ($\pi = 0.05$)

Policy parameters	Independent variables				
	Firm population	Herfindahl concentration	Variance market shares	Technology variance	Technology level
β	19.38	−0.0514	−0.000 955	−17.159	8.0375
γ	−75.4	0.0206	−0.000 315	−149.782	−74.39
$\bar{H}$	−55.9	0.0334	0.000 575	−70.129	24.0375
X	12.13	−0.0091	−0.000 378	13.191	−12.9625

Table 3.2 Interaction coefficients of the model ($\pi = 0.15$)

Policy parameters	Independent variables				
	Firm population	Herfindahl concentration	Variance market shares	Technology variance	Technology level
β	39.25	−0.0453	−0.001 195	94.314	6.7113
γ	−56	−0.0055	−0.001 005	−147.051	−74.2143
$\bar{H}$	−29	0.0755	0.001 982 5	−24.049	32.8418
X	5.5	−0.0263	−0.001 035	32.269	−14.2608

Table 3.3 Initial values of policy parameters

	β	γ	$\bar{H}$	X
high (+)	2	0.1	0.8	5
low (−)	0.5	0.01	0.2	1

As far as the technology level is concerned, both regimes, the high and the low opportunity one, lead to approximately the same outcome after 100 periods of simulation. The way I have designed the model, the effects of turbulence and of technological diversity on the technology level approximately cancel each other out.

Conclusion

Technological variety drives the evolutionary process modelled here. Variety is the result of the interplay of three forces only: economic selection; creation of technological diversity; and competitive diffusion of technological knowhow. The model allows me to explain inter-industry variations in market structure and technological competitiveness simply by differences in four key industrial policy parameters such as regulatory control of economic concentration, degree of 'licensing' of entry and exit, and research and development subsidization rates. The model may thus serve as a manageable framework for empirical studies on effects of industrial policies. Econometric estimates of the model parameters are routinely given in industrial organization studies.

The simulation illustrates that government intervention or the absence of intervention has a significant influence on the level of technological competence of an industry. Moreover, the simulation validates the consistency of the model with stylized facts from different empirical studies of industrial sectors. In a technological environment where lots of variety is exogenously introduced, the results show a lesser concentrative tendency of the model, but also a tendency towards more extensive coverage of the technological space, or high information density.

Appendix

Productivity and technology variance (diversity)

The technology diffusion process can be represented mathematically as a discrete state space, continuous-time Markov process, or Poisson process, with variable rate λ and varying changes in the level of productivity $p_i(t)$:

$$P\{\bar{X}(t) - \bar{X}(t - \Delta t) = 1\} = \lambda\,(t)\epsilon + o(\epsilon),$$

where the last term denotes a general unspecified remainder term, and $\bar{X}$ is the incidence of technological change (of varying degree) in a short time period.

Expected accumulated productivity is:

$$E\,[p_i(t)] = p_0 \exp\left(-at/v\,(t - \Delta t)\right)$$

where p_i is the price–performance ratio of firm i; p_0 is the starting value; and

$$a = f(X)$$

X being a vector of technology policy variables. The variance or diversity $v\,(t - \Delta t)$ is:

$$v\,(t - \Delta t) = \int_{-\infty}^{+\infty} \left(p\,(t - \Delta t) - \mu\right)^2\ f\!\left(p\,(t - \Delta t)\right)\,dp\,(t - \Delta t)$$

where $f\!\left(p\,(t - \Delta t)\right)$ is the density of an exponentially distributed random variable $p\,(t - \Delta t)$ and $\mu\,(t - \Delta t)$ its mean.

Productivity and appropriability

The increase in a firm's market share MS_i is positively, linearly related (Meyer 1990: 277) with parameter a^* to its periodical technological advance $dp_i(t)$, as well as to its market share. Hence

$$\frac{dMS_i\,(t)}{dt} = a^*\,\frac{dp_i(t)}{dt}\,MS_i\,(t - \Delta t)$$

Turbulence in a firm population

Entry is represented by the following equation:

$$y\,(t) = q(t)^{1+H} \exp\left(-Aq(t)\,(1 - H)\right) \qquad A > 0; 0 < H \le 1$$

where A represents an intrinsic entry rate, and H stands for Herfindahl, or the industry concentration index. $q\,(t)$ is the number of firms in the industry (population). The first exponentiated factor on the right-hand side of the equation stands for a networking effect of firm foundations. The more firms there are in an industry the higher the potential information sources, or resource pools for entry. The second exponentiated factor, however, deals with the intensification of competition for new firms with increasing competition.

Exit is given by the following relationship:

$$x(t) = q(t) \exp\left(-Bq(t)H\right)$$

where B represents an intrinsic death rate. Exit rates are low for a small industry population, but are rising rapidly, once competition erodes any appropriability benefits from technological advance. Yet the networking effect somewhat counterbalances increases in the exit rate which are due to increasing competition.

In the above equations

$$A(t) = \left(|H(t) - \bar{H}|\right)/\beta \Delta p(t) > 0$$

$$B(t) = \left(|\bar{H} - H(t)|\right)/\gamma \Delta p(t) > 0$$

where $\bar{H}$ is an imaginary or stationary degree of concentration, used as policy goal; β is a policy parameter for 'licensing of entry', γ is the equivalent policy parameter for 'licensing of exit'.

Notes

1. A technology defines in advance limits to performance: a position of technological maturity ($t \to \infty$) implicit in the particular set of design principles. That is to say, chemical and physical properties of materials and the laws of thermodynamics put limits to performance of microprocessors (see also Metcalfe 1986: 39 on this subject).
2. Following Meyer (1990: 279–80), exogenous increases of the technology fund LP, and thus induced declines in the price–performance ratios of products, occur at a constant rate π. Thus $LP(t) = LP_0 \, e^{-\pi t}$.

Acknowledgement

I would like to thank Michael Scheutzow and Manfred Fleischer for helping with the simulation.

4 A Note on Competition among Techniques in the Presence of Increasing Returns to Scale

Alfred Greiner and Friedrich Kugler

D24

Recently Amable (1992) presented an evolutionary model in which he investigates the diffusion process of two competing technologies producing the same good for a certain market. As a result he finds out that the dynamic system describing the evolution of the produced goods always converges to a rest point where the market shares of product 1 and 2 stay constant over time. The respective amounts of the goods produced depend on the rate of returns to scale prevailing in the production process. In this paper we show that this result changes drastically if we use a discrete time framework instead of a continuous one as does Amable. Then convergence to a rest point need no longer necessarily hold and regular or even erratic fluctuations of the amounts produced may occur.

The outcome of completely different results is due to the fact that we create a completely different economic model by employing a discrete-time formulation. Therefore, it is clear that the substitution of a first-order difference equation by a first-order differential equation does not yield the same dynamic outcome − Sparrow (1980) and Medio and Gallo (1989) have shown how to transform a system with a fixed delay into a continuous one such that the dynamic behaviour is preserved. It is a questionable assumption that economic agents would not take their decisions continuously. But on the other hand, there are many models in the economic literature which use a discrete-time formulation (see, for example, volume 40 of the *Journal of Economic Theory* of 1986). There are even economists asserting that a discrete-time framework is preferable since decisions of economic agents only occur at certain points in time − cf. the book review by Eckalbar (1992) who mentions six arguments in favour of discrete-time modelling. For these reasons we assert that the model presented by Amable does also make sense in discrete time and therefore investigate the dynamic properties of this new model. For a further discussion of the nature of time see, for example, Gandolfo (1981).

Let us now come to the economic model. Amable considers a market for two goods (y_t^1, y_t^2), which are perfect substitutes for each other. The evolution of the demand for these goods in discrete time is given by the logistic pattern

$$y_{t+1}^1 = y_t^1 + \beta y_t^1(D - y_t^1 - y_t^2) \tag{4.1}$$

$$y_{t+1}^2 = y_t^2 + \beta y_t^2(D - y_t^2 - y_t^1) \tag{4.2}$$

where β is a positive imitation coefficient and D is the maximum attainable level of demand for the goods. The level of saturation D is determined endogenously:

$$D = a_0 - a_1 p \qquad a_0 > 0; a_1 > 0 \tag{4.3}$$

where p is the price which is the same for the two goods.

The growth rate of production capacity for the technique used to produce good i, x_t^i, is assumed to be a positive function of unit profit Π_t^i:

$$\frac{x_{t+1}^i - x_t^i}{x_t^i} = \sigma \Pi_t^i \qquad \sigma > 0 \tag{4.4}$$

Π_t^i is defined as

$$\Pi_t^i = p - c^i = p - c_0^i - c_1^i x_t^i \qquad c_0^i > 0, c_1^i \neq 0. \tag{4.5}$$

Assuming that demand equals supply, the equilibrium condition is $x_t^i = y_t^i$ for all t.

By combining equations (4.4) and (4.5), solving for p and substituting the result in equation (4.3) and the D in equation (4.1) and (4.2), the evolution of x_t^1 and x_t^2 is given by

$$x_{t+1}^1 = x_t^1 + A_1 x_t^1(B_1 - x_t^1 - C_1 x_t^2) \tag{4.6}$$

$$x_{t+1}^2 = x_t^2 + A_2 x_t^2(B_2 - x_t^2 - C_2 x_t^1) \tag{4.7}$$

with

$$A_i = \frac{\sigma\beta(1 + a_1 c_1^i)}{\sigma + a_1\beta}, \ B_i = \frac{a_0 - a_1 c_0^i}{1 + a_1 c_1^i}, \ C_i = \frac{1}{1 + a_1 c_1^i} \qquad i = 1,2$$

In what follows we will confine out investigations to the case where the saturation levels for the two techniques, B_1, B_2, are positive, an assumption which makes sense economically. Moreover, we will allow for increasing returns to scale, that is, $c_1^i < 0$, but assume that they are not too strong such that $C_i > 0$ holds.

As in the continuous-time case we can state that there are four equilibrium points in this model, that is, situations for which $x_{t+1}^i = x_t^i$ holds for all t (i = 1,2), namely (0,0), (0,B_2), (B_1,0) and $\big((B_1 - C_1B_2)/(1 - C_1C_2), (B_2 - C_2B_1)/(1-C_1C_2)\big)$. Computing the eigenvalues of the Jacobian of the linearized system shows that the trivial solution (0,0) is always unstable. Stability conditions for all other points may be determined technically but cannot be interpreted economically. Therefore, we will instantaneously resort to numerical simulation in order to demonstrate that any sort of dynamic behaviour will be possible in that model.

Using the equality $A_1C_1 = A_2C_2$, we can rewrite equations (4.6) and (4.7) as follows:

$$x_{t+1}^1 = x_t^1 + A_1x_t^1(B_1 - x_t^1 - C_1x_t^2) \tag{4.8}$$

$$x_{t+1}^2 = x_t^2 + A_1(C_1/C_2)\, x_t^2(B_2 - x_t^2 - C_2x_t^1) \tag{4.9}$$

For the numerical example we make use of the following parameter values: C_1 = 0.06; C_2 = 0.052; B_1 = 0.6; B_2 = 0.4. A_1 serves as bifurcation parameter. The initial conditions are set to x_0^1 = 0.01, x_0^2 = 0.02. Note that in this case both technique 1 and technique 2 show decreasing returns to scale. Computing the eigenvalues of the Jacobian of the linearized system then gives $\lambda_1 = 1 + 0.567A_1$, $\lambda_2 = 1 - 0.461\,538A_1$ for the steady state values (x^1, x^2) = (0,0.4) and $\lambda_1 = 1 + 0.425\,538A_1$, $\lambda_2 = 1 - 0.6A_1$ for (x^1, x^2) = (0.6,0), showing that both equilibrium points are unstable (recall that $A_1 > 0$). For the fourth equilibrium which is given by (x^1, x^2) = (0577 802 7, 0.369 954 2) with the parameter values of our example we get $\lambda_1 = 1 - 0.421\,933A_1$, $\lambda_2 = 1 - 0.582\,74A_1$; that is, this point is stable if $A_1 < 3.432\,062\,3$.

Figures 4.1 and 4.2 show the bifurcation diagrams for x_t^1 and x_t^2. It can be seen how the solution bifurcates for the value $A_1 \approx 3.43$.

Increasing the value of A_1 further, we finally observe completely erratic fluctuations of the variables x_t^1 and x_t^2 for values of A_1 greater than about 4.35. Now we have chaos, or more strictly speaking 'topological' chaos in the sense of Li and Yorke (1975).

In Figures 4.3—4.5 the time paths for x_t^1, x_t^2 are presented for different values of A_1 (the dotted line denotes x_t^2). In Figure 4.3 A_1 = 2.5, showing that the variables converge to their stationary values. In Figures 4.4 and 4.5 A_1 = 4.25 and A_1 = 5, revealing periodic oscillations of period 4 and completely aperiodic oscillations, respectively.

Figures 4.6—4.8 finally show strange attractors for different values of A_1 (100 000 iterations). The values for A_1 are A_1 = 4.53, A_1 = 4.6, A_1 = 5 for Figures 4.6—4.8, respectively. The Lyapunov exponents corresponding to the

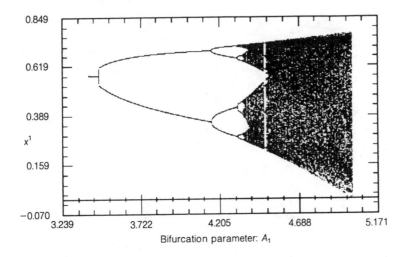

Figure 4.1 Bifurcation diagram for x_t^1

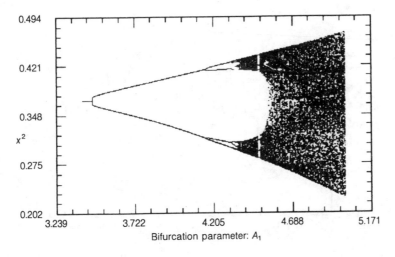

Figure 4.2 Bifurcation diagram for x_t^2

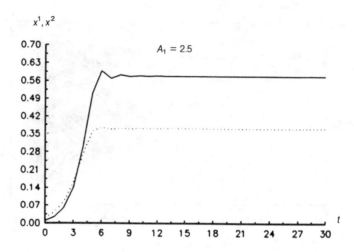

Figure 4.3 Constant time path for x_t^1, x_t^2

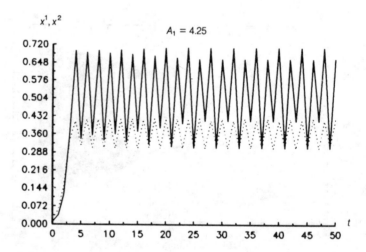

Figure 4.4 Cyclical oscillations of x_t^1, x_t^2

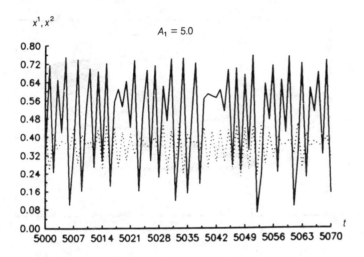

Figure 4.5   Erratic oscillations of x_t^1, x_t^2

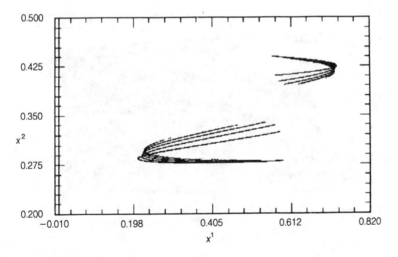

Figure 4.6   Strange attractor for $A_1 = 4.53$

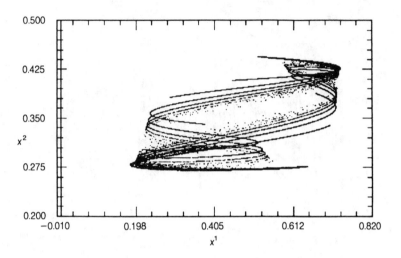

Figure 4.7   Strange attractor for $A_1 = 4.6$

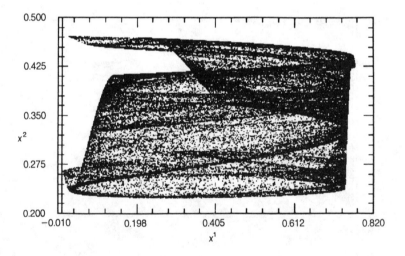

Figure 4.8   Strange attractor for $A_1 = 5.0$

values of A_1 are $0.306\,763$, -1.0456 for $A_1 = 4.53$; $0.335\,924$, $-0.695\,448$ for $A_1 = 4.6$; and $0.473\,521$, $-0.188\,07$ for $A_1 = 5$, confirming our results.

The economic interpretation of that result seems to be straightforward. Besides the possibility of an equilibrium solution with constant production and unchanging market shares, as in the original model, we observe that persistent fluctuations may be the outcome of that model where competition among the two techniques prevents the system from converging to a rest point. So, on the one hand, there may be regular, periodic cycles stating that production in that market occurs cyclically with the distribution of the market shares between technique 1 and technique 2 showing periodic fluctuations. In that case the period during which technique 1 will gain a larger share of the market than technique 2 can completely be predicted. On the other hand, there may be erratic fluctuations stating that production and the distribution of the market shares are subject to continuous and unpredictable change. In that case we may reason that none of the techniques is capable of achieving a position in which it will gain a higher share of the market than its competitor for a predetermined period of time.

We have seen that, all other parameters constant, A_1 determines the stability properties of that model, with a more complex dynamic behaviour being obtained for larger values of that parameter. It can easily be shown that for a given cost structure (C_1 constant) A_1 positively depends on both the imitation coefficient β and on σ, the coefficient giving the dependence of the growth rate of the two production techniques on profit. Therefore we can state the following. The larger the influence of profit on the growth rate of production of technique 1 and technique 2 and the larger the imitation coefficient β, the more likely is the emergence of complex dynamics. The imitation coefficient β may also be termed a reaction coefficient, giving the speed of adjustment of demand for goods 1 and 2 to their saturation levels.

Our results were derived under the assumption of decreasing returns to scale in the two production technologies. Allowing for increasing returns, no concrete outcome could be observed. Simulation runs, however, suggest that instability of this model is more likely if technologies with increasing returns are introduced. As to that point, see also Brock (1988).

A final remark seems to be necessary concerning the formulation of the model in discrete time. As shown, we were able to demonstrate that erratic time paths of economic variables, frequently observed in reality, may result endogenously. But given the Li–Yorke theorem stating that period 3 implies chaos, and with due regard to the technical details, any *ad-hoc* postulated 'tent shape' difference equation may reveal erratic fluctuations for a certain parameter constellation. Although that theorem was proved only for one-dimensional systems, there is strong evidence that the coupled combination of two equations of that form may also lead to chaotic behaviour of the variables. For that reason empirical research seems to be indispensable to gain insight into real-world economic phenomena showing aperiodic fluctuations in order to clarify whether they are merely the result of stochastic shocks or the outcome of nonlinear dynamics.

Acknowledgement

This chapter has benefited from valuable comments from participants of the workshop.

PART II: Technology Dynamics: Competing Technologies

5 Evolution of Technological Growth in a Model Based on Stochastic Cellular Automata

Subhash C. Bhargava and Amitabha Mukherjee

D33

Introduction

Whenever a new technology is introduced it invariably competes with the existing technology. In situations where the new technology 'satisfies the need better', as suggested by Fisher and Pry (1971), a competitive substitution of one technology by the other takes place. However, in many situations, though competitive substitution occurs at the beginning, it never reaches completion. For example, in many developing countries both colour and black and white television coexist. In fact both technologies evolve by forming separate market *niches*. This *niche* formation could be due to economic considerations (a section of the population cannot afford the cost of colour TV in spite of its attractiveness) or due to other reasons.

The substitution of an 'old' technology by a 'new' one, in general, is not a simple process: the replacement of the old by the new could be complete, or both may coexist, or the trend might even reverse after some time. Since the theory of competition and formation of *niches* is better understood in the context of ecological growth, we begin by recalling that two competing biological species feeding on a common resource (Volterra 1931; 1982) will result in extinction for one of them; the species which can exploit the resources better has an advantage and it invariably displaces the other. If the resources are not identical both the species can coexist. The equations which describe these processes are the well-known Lotka–Volterra competition equations:

$$\frac{dX}{dt} = a_1 X (M_1 - X - b_1 Y)$$

$$\frac{dY}{dt} = a_2 Y (M_1 - Y - b_2 X)$$

where X and Y are the two species, the a_i are related to the intrinsic rate of growth of these species, the b_i define the coefficients of interaction between the species, and the M_i the level to which the species can grow in the absence of interaction. If Y is initially zero, its subsequent behaviour corresponds to that of a fluctuation. Using the idea of self-organization in non-equilibrium systems (Nicolis and Prigogine 1977), Allen (1976a) derived conditions for growth of such a quantity, and used it to explain the evolution of ecological systems.

It was Lenz (1962) who first said that technological growth follows a dynamics which is quite similar to that of biological growth. For example, the logistic equation, which is extensively used in the modeling of economic growth, can be obtained from the Lotka–Volterra (LV) equations (Lotka 1925; Volterra 1931), as was indicated by Volterra himself. In addition, Goodwin (1967), Samuelson (1971), Montroll (1972) and Marchetti (1983) have pointed out that biological growth equations such as the LV equations are useful in describing social and economic behaviour. In particular, these ideas were used by Batten (1981) to explain the path of industrial evolution, by Silverberg (1984) to explain the dynamics of technical change, by Karmeshu et al. (1985) for providing a rationale for the empirical law of technological substitution, and by Bhargava (1989) to show that LV equations are general enough to describe various known models of technological substitution.

All the models mentioned above are formulated in the form of a single ordinary differential equation (ODE) or a set of ODEs which give no information about the spatial distribution of adopters of a given technology. Another problem is that the actual data are not continuous and are available at discrete time steps. Since differential equation models deal with continuous time, one will have either to make sure that use of discrete data in the description of continuous functions is reasonable, or to look for models which are essentially discrete. The present paper exploits one such class of models, namely cellular automata (CA). Since technology substitution is usually governed by parameters which vary in a random manner, we modify the commonly used CA, which are essentially deterministic, in such a way that the state of a system at step $t+1$ is determined not only by the state at step t, but also by parameters which are essentially random in nature. CA with this property are called stochastic cellular automata. They have been used recently by Bhargava et al. (1993) to model diffusion of an innovation.

In this paper, an attempt is made to understand the evolution of technological growth in a model based on stochastic cellular automata. The purpose of the paper is threefold: to examine the growth of two competing technologies using stochastic CA models; to simulate situations where one of the technologies substitutes the other; and, finally, to see if a possible mechanism of technology substitution emerges from the simulations. Our main finding is that when competing technologies evolve they carve out their own market niches and that the technology which exploits the resources better ultimately captures the whole market. We describe our model in the next section, while a final section contains results and discussions.

Our model

In our model, the market is represented by a square array of identical cells. With a cell, which is identified by its row and column indices i,j, we associate a number $n(i,j,t)$, the occupation number at time t. Since we are interested in studying how two technologies (or products) compete when placed in a given marketplace, an occupied cell in our model is defined to contain either an adopter of the first technology, which we represent by -1, or an adopter of the second technology, denoted by $+1$. An empty cell represents a potential adopter, indicated by 0. Thus in our model $n(i,j,t)$ takes one of three possible values, ± 1 and 0.

Here we shall assume that in a real market situation, adoption of a product or a technology by an individual depends on the influence exerted on him by the neighbours (adopters) with whom he interacts. Thus in the model the fate of a cell, that is, adoption of a technology by a potential adopter, depends on the number of its neighbours. We denote by $\nu_-(i,j,t)$ and $\nu_+(i,j,t)$, respectively, the number of neighbours of the cell i,j adopting the two technologies.

It is not only the number, but also how successfully the neighbours of each type influence the individual through interaction, that determine the spread of a technology. Therefore, in calculating $\nu_\pm(i,j,t)$, each neighbouring cell is counted with a *probabilistic weight factor*, to take into account the random nature of successful interaction. This is done by introducing a parameter χ lying between 0 and 1. To compute the contribution of each neighbour, we generate a random number η, which lies between 0 and 1. If $\eta > \chi$, we count the neighbour, otherwise we ignore it. Thus $1-\chi$ represents the *average effectiveness of interaction*. In addition, we also allow for interaction between a cell and its 16 next-to-nearest neighbours, by including them in the counting for $\nu_\pm$, though with a smaller weight factor. This is achieved by comparing η with $\sqrt{\chi}$. Thus we define $\nu_\pm(i,j,t)$ by

$$\nu_\pm(i,j,t) = \sum_{\substack{|i'-i|=1,\ |j'-j|\le 1 \\ \text{or } |i'-i|<1,\ |j'-j|=1}} \pm\theta(\eta-\chi)\theta(\pm n(i',j',t))\, n(i',j',t)$$

$$+ \sum_{\substack{|i'-i|=2,\ |j'-j|\le 2 \\ \text{or } |i'-i|<2,\ |j'-j|=2}} \pm\theta(\eta-\sqrt{\chi})\theta(\pm n(i',j',t))\, n(i',j',t) \tag{5.1}$$

where either all the upper signs or all the lower signs are to be taken. Here θ is the Heaviside step function which has the property that when its argument is positive its value is 1 while, otherwise its value is 0. The first term in the equation (5.1) represents the effect of nearest neighbours, while the second term represents that of next-to-nearest neighbours. Since η is different each time it is used, the θs in equation (5.1) ensure that each neighbour is counted with a probabilistic weight, which is higher for nearest neighbours than for next-to-nearest neighbours.

Having counted the 'number of neighbours' of the (i, j)th cell at time step t as above, the fate of the cell at time step $t+1$ is determined by the following rules:

1. *The habit rule.* If a cell has one or no neighbour of each type its state remains unchanged. The interpretation is that an adopter left to himself does not adopt a new technology. Old habits die hard.

2. *Majority or conformity rule.* A cell which has unequal numbers of neighbours of each type is taken over by the type which has a majority, provided that there is more than one neighbour of that type. (In the case of a $1-0$ majority, the habit rule prevails.) This rule does two things: it leads to growth for a single technology; and in competitive situations it opposes the existence of pockets of dissimilar technologies.

3. *The competitive advantage rule.* This rule comes into operation when rule 2 cannot determine the outcome, that is, when a cell has equal numbers of neighbours (exceeding one) of both types of adopters. A fixed parameter ρ, lying between 0 and 1, determines the competitive advantage of technologies. To implement this rule a new random number η' is generated and compared with ρ. Depending on which of η' and ρ is greater, the occupancy of the cell becomes $+1$ or -1. If $\rho = 0.5$ neither technology has an advantage: since η' lies between 0 and 1, it is greater than ρ as often as it is less than ρ. A bias in growth can be introduced by taking any other value of ρ. That is, if $\rho < 0.5$, $+1$s will tend to grow at the expense of -1s, while if $\rho > 0.5$ it will be the other way around.

Mathematically the above stated rules can be expressed in the following form:

$$
n(i, j, t+1) = \begin{cases} n(i, j, t) & \text{if } \nu_+(i, j, t) \le 1,\ \nu_-(i, j, t) \le 1 \\ \pm 1 & \text{if } \nu_\pm(i, j, t) > \nu_\mp(i, j, t) \\ & \text{and } \nu_\pm(i, j, t) > 1 \\ 2\,\theta(\eta' - \rho) - 1 & \text{if } \nu_+(i, j, t) = \nu_-(i, j, t) > 1 \end{cases}
$$

Note that randomness, which is characteristic of growth in real social environments, enters both in the definition of $\nu_\pm$ and in the computation of $n(i, j, t+1)$ with given $\nu_\pm(i, j, t)$.

The growth is measured by $N_\pm$, the number of cells containing ±1, at time t. Our 'market' is a 100×100 array of cells. Initially both technologies are assumed to be confined within a 'seed region' in the form of a square grid (typically 12×12), which is filled with an equal number of $+1$s and -1s, randomly distributed. This is allowed to evolve with the rules stated above, for two values of χ (0.82 and 0.92) and three values of ρ (0.2, 0.5 and 0.8 for $\chi = 0.82$; 0.0, 0.5 and 1.0 for $\chi = 0.92$). A number of computer runs are taken for each set of parameter values.

Results and discussion

Our main findings can be summarized as follows. First, for all values of χ and ρ and for all grid sizes, we observe the phenomenon of market segregation. That is, each technology carves out its own *niche*. Even though in the initial configurations the adopters of the two technologies are randomly intermixed, after a certain number of time steps they are found to occupy distinct spatial regions with a sharply defined boundary. This phenomenon is illustrated in Figures 5.1(a)–(d) and 5.2(a)–(d) for $\rho = 0.5$.

Second, both the growth and the formation of *niches* is considerably slowed down at the higher value of χ, corresponding to a very low probability of acceptance (of either technology) by an individual potential adopter, that is, a situation of fierce competition. This is clearly seen by comparing Figure 5.1 ($\chi = 0.82$) and Figure 5.2 ($\chi = 0.92$). The level of segregation reached in Figure 5.1(b), that is, after five steps, is reached only in Figure 5.2(d), which shows the position after 30 steps.

Third, a bias in growth, introduced through the value of ρ, clearly favours one of the two technologies. Figures 5.1(e)–(f) show the outcomes of biased growth under favourable conditions ($\chi = 0.82$), starting from the same initial configurations and after the same number of steps as Figure 5.1(d). Figures 5.2(e)–(f) show the same phenomenon for $\chi = 0.92$, that is, under relatively unfavourable conditions. This shows that the technology which can exploit the market better eventually displaces the other.

If we assume that our CA model provides a reasonable description of actual technological growth and that the rules which we have defined broadly represent the real system, we are led to the conclusion that the immediate outcome of competitive evolution of technologies is market segregation. The formation of market *niches* is quite a common experience. One can find examples of this phenomenon in almost every country and over a wide range of technologies.

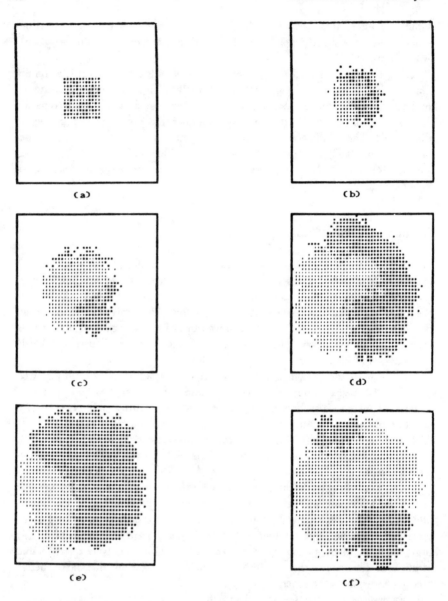

Figure 5.1   Growth with randomly placed +1s and −1s in a 12×12 seed grid with χ = 0.82 and formation of market *niches*: (a) initial configuration, $t = 0$; (b) $t = 5$, $\rho = 0.5$; (c) $t = 15$, $\rho = 0.5$; (d) $t = 30$, $\rho = 0.5$; (e) $t = 30$, $\rho = 0.2$; (f) $t = 30$, $\rho = 0.8$.

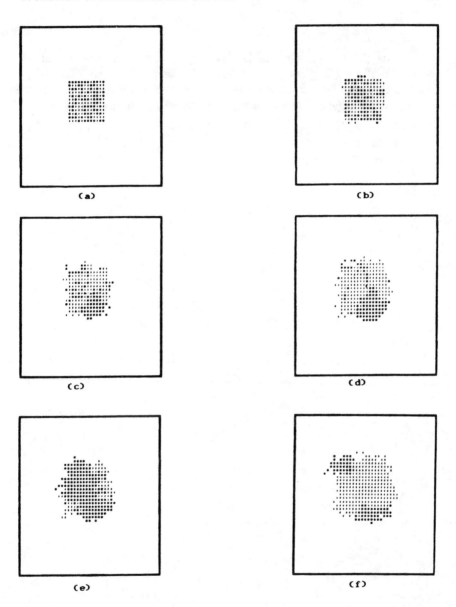

Figure 5.2   Growth with randomly placed +1s and −1s in a 12×12 seed grid with χ = 0.92 and formation of market *niches*: (a) initial configuration, $t = 0$; (b) t = 5, $\rho = 0.5$; (c) $t = 15$, $\rho = 0.5$; (d) $t = 30$, $\rho = 0.5$; (e) $t = 30$, $\rho = 0$; (f) $t = 30$, $\rho = 1.0$.

Acknowledgements

One of us (SCB) is grateful to Dr Ashok Jain and other members of the mathematical modelling group at the National Institute of Science, Technology and Development Studies, New Delhi, for many useful discussions, and to the Council of Scientific and Industrial Research, New Delhi, for financial support.

6 Dynamics of Competitive Technology Diffusion Through Local Network Structures: The Case of EDI Document Standards

Paul A. David and Dominique Foray

Dp3   D 33

Introduction and motivation

Convergence between telecommunications and computing technologies requires a viable means of automating the transfer of information between organizations. The immediate aim of the collection of hardware and software technologies and the implementation techniques associated with electronic data interchange (EDI) is to enable the electronic transmission of intelligible business documents – such as electronic funds transfers (EFT) – among trading partners in the 'seamless', user-initiated way that telephoning is done today. More profoundly, EDI is viewed by many information industry observers and business management experts as the most promising method for catalysing the fundamental changes in business practices which will be necessary to realize the full benefits of inter-organizational information transfer.

Although the widespread adoption of new technologies supporting inter-organizational networks for EDI would seem to offer great opportunities for economic benefit, this is by no means an assured outcome of decentralized decision-making on the part of the organization involved.

Inter-organizational networks, like other 'network technologies', require standards that assure the compatibility and interoperability of the network's components (David and Greenstein 1990). Special problems arise in assuring interoperability when the autonomy and scope for extra-network operations on the part of components or 'nodes' has to be preserved. A still further level of complications present themselves in the case of EDI document standards, which are supposed to govern the terms, forms and procedures used in both inter-firm and intra-firm transactions, thereby permitting the data-processing apparatuses of distinct business entities to interact with one another directly. Standards for EDI documents are simply a means of reducing ambiguities and diminishing translation costs entailed in such transactions. Although an enormous array of diverse and incompatible proprietary and industry-specific EDI document standards currently are in use, a much smaller number of major alternatives appear to be evolving within the main markets and organizational contexts. In North America most companies have directly or indirectly adopted standards conforming to the ANSI X.12 format. By contrast, the majority of European users are considering adopting the United Nations document standards known as EDIFACT (David and Foray 1992).

In this paper we argue that decisions to implement EDI with one or another available specific document standard are likely to spread in a population of firms through positive feedback effects from an initial core of users; direct transactions cost savings and indirect benefits are realized by marginal (potential) adopters as positive externalities generated by the intra-marginal group of users. The problem we address is that of developing a suitable analytical framework for studying the dynamics of such processes. 'Pólya urn models' recently have been introduced to economists as a vehicle for studying competitive technology diffusion under conditions of positive feedbacks (David 1985; 1988; Arthur 1989). Analysis of this class of models which we discuss in the next section, reveals that the mere presence of potential positive network externalities is not sufficient to induce the emergence of a unique, global standard from a competitive technology diffusion process involving a large population of potential adopters. But the practical policy insights gained from those probabilistic models go little beyond suggesting that the source of the problem of incomplete standardization lies in the positive feedbacks not being 'strong enough'. Furthermore, it will be observed that the specifications of the Pólya urn model do not adequately correspond to certain key structural features of the EDI document standards situation.

For those reasons, in the third section of this paper, we take up consideration of another class of stochastic models which appear more suitable for the analysis of the behaviour of economic agents embedded in local networks of transactions. Positive network externalities can be limited, in such models, to subsets of the entire potential user community, a situation that is readily described using the terminology of Markov random field theory. Drawing specifically upon insights from the related and comparatively new field in stochastic process analysis referred to as 'percolation theory', we are led to account for the observed coexistence of multiple EDI document standards as a manifestation of the 'sub-criticality' of the inter-organizational transactions system. A particular standard fails to 'percolate' throughout when the connection probabilities between typical nodes in the system remain below a critical level.

We maintain that the pre-existence of various finite 'clusters', or sub-groups of firms among whom there is a history of close commercial relations, will greatly influence the design and diffusion patterns of documents standards by multiplying the occurences of idiosyncratic forms (like natural languages and local dialects thereof), and leading, at least at the outset, to even further fragmentation or 'balkanization' of the transactions system. EDI networks, as a practical matter, must be implemented so as to conform with local coordination structures that have arisen historically from firm and sectoral specificities, geographical neighbourhood, and industry conventions in describing the highest-frequency forms of transactions. The sub-criticality of the system as a whole is, thus, likely to be the result of the historical process that created an antecedent routine of coordination.

In the concluding section of the paper some basic analytical results in percolation theory are drawn upon for insights as to the nature of policies that would be most efficacious in removing the condition of sub-criticality and fostering a decentralized process leading to more universal standardization.

Properties of the diffusion of EDI document standards: analytical preliminaries

From the foregoing discussion it should be evident that the proximate subject of the proposed analysis is not the operation of any particular EDI network through which messages and data can pass among the participating business entities. Rather, we seek to characterize the dynamic process whereby such a network can be implemented; and, in particular, the process through which firms acting independently would adopt a common set of EDI document standards, as a consequence of decisions shaped by the particular configuration of their respective prior transactions patterns. Those transactional relationships may be conceptualized as connecting groups of firms in 'network-like' sub-systems. But, at the same time, it is important to keep clear the distinction between the metaphoric 'network' of business relationships among firms, and the physical, electronically implemented networks supporting EDI. Adoption of document standards (and the physical telecommunications infrastructure and protocols) permitting electronic implementation can lead to enhancements of the degree of *intelligibility of the relational network*, or transactions system − by enabling the firms involved to send and receive messages and data among themselves in a consistent, more efficient form.

Since the primary interest here lies with the way in which an economic transactions system attains the minimum level of intelligibility represented by the establishment of an EDI network, our attention has been directed to the configuration of the transactional connections established among firms, viewing such 'relational networks' as structures within which acceptance of a standard will spread. The initial configuration, and the particular dynamics of these structures will determine whether spontaneous diffusion of a single, universal standard is possible and likely; or, in the case of breaks in the structure of connectivities, a multiplicity of local standards may coexist in the absence of more concerted, hierarchically directed policies of standardization.

Pólya urn process: basics

The problem in hand lends itself to the application of a particular class of dynamic resource allocation theories, that is, models of stochastic systems that are characterized by positive feedbacks and possess a multiplicity of locally stable equilibria, or 'absorbing states'. Among these, one well-known model is the generalized Pólya urn scheme, which has been introduced to economists recently by W.B. Arthur.[1] Formal analysis of this model derives theorems about the existence and properties of the limiting distribution of the contents of an urn initially containing balls of different colours, when the urn is randomly sampled repeatedly with 'over-replacement' (of balls of the same colour as the one drawn) in each round. The principal property of this model is that when the degree of over-replacement is sufficiently strong, the contents of the urn will converge in the limit to a population of balls that is uniform in colour, with one of the colours initially present having been 'selected', by the accidents of the sequence of random draws, to emerge as the universal standard for the urn. The latter implication, and collateral propositions regarding the possibility of sub-optimal outcomes, has been quite illuminating in suggesting how *de facto* standardization occurs in some contexts. Some cases in point are the emergence of QWERTY as the standard for typewriter keyboards, the victory of the VHS format over the Sony Betamax format in the market for video–cassette recorders, and the dominance of the light water reactor technology in the population of nuclear power plants of the world's electric utilities. But, as will be seen shortly, the generalized Pólya urn scheme is not so suitable for the case of EDI document standardization, or other *de facto* standardization processes that share its principal structural features.

EDI features and the Pólya urn process

The essential dynamics described in the Pólya urn scheme is driven by the continuous growth of a population, the members of which have to make their choices sequentially in an order that is random with respect to their *inherent* preferences among the set of available alternatives. By contrast, our present purpose is to understand the properties of a sequence of choices within a *finite* population, that is, a configuration of (actual and potential) adopters among whom the initial distribution of technology choices can be observed. Indeed, the technico-organizational decision of a firm in this area can be viewed as a sequential process consisting of the decision to implement an EDI system, and the selection of a standard. Thus, we will posit a population of firms already committed in terms of EDI infrastructures but having to make (or reassess) a choice between two alternative document standards.

As we wish to characterize the evolution of the share held by each variant standard within a finite adopter population, we must focus on the revision and reassessment policies of the adopters. A second property of the Pólya urn scheme makes it poorly suited for this analytical task: it supposes that each agent decides only once, and irreversibly, at the time of entering the population. Hence, the share of each variant in the total installed base can only change if there are additions made to the stock. Although this assumption (tantamount to infinite durability of commitments) might be suitable in case studies dealing with technologies embodied in long-lived physical infrastructures, it is out of place where the firms can alter their choice of a document standard with the passage of time (at some cost, of course). The present phase of EDI standardization belongs exactly to that class of situations: despite the existence of switching costs, revisions of choice are very popular in the EDI world.[2]

From both EDI features described above, we infer that the essential dynamics of the EDI standard competition is driven by *the process of revision of choices within a finite population*. Clearly, the properties of the Pólya urn scheme do not accommodate these features. A third feature further impairs the Pólya urn scheme's ability to capture the essential dynamics of the EDI document standards competition: in applying the Pólya process to represent the outcome of a sequence of decentralized decisions involved under conditions of positive externalities, it is assumed that micro-decisions are directly influenced by positive feedbacks from the *macro-state* of the system. Thus, the probability of adding a ball of one colour rather than another to an urn at each moment is assumed to improve as a function of the *global* proportion of the balls in the urn that currently are of that colour. There most certainly are real-world situations that fit reasonably easily into this framework. For example, Cowan (1990) has made a persuasive case for the view that, among the agencies responsible for the selection of the designs for nuclear reactors to be installed in electric power plants in the industrial nations of the West, from the late 1960s onwards, considerations of the distribution of global experience with the construction and operation of various reactor types proved to be paramount over local conditions; what reactor technology might have been adopted in the neighbouring province or country carried comparatively little weight.[3]

Toward local network modelling

Local versus global feedbacks in technology adoption

There are many other technological circumstances involving networks, however —
and the case of EDI standard is one such — where specifying the dominance of
feedbacks from the macro–state in micro–decisions-making is not appropriate. A
railway engineer selecting the gauge of the track gauge would give prime
consideration to the opportunities of making easy connections with railway lines
in the immediate surrounding territory, and would be likely to care little if at all
about the gauge choices made for railways on different continents. Likewise, the
communications manager for a firm choosing an EDI document standard will be
most concerned about the choices made by business entities located in the present
and immediately foreseeable 'transactional territory'. The firm is likely to care
only about the ease of direct electronic data exchanges with its major suppliers,
sub-contractors, important customers, collaborators in R&D projects — and not
with parties drawn at random who are representative of the entire population of
EDI users. In other words, individual decision agents each are limited to
considering only the actions of the members of a particular reference group, or
subset of 'significant others' within the collectivity (David 1992b). This property,
namely, *the locally bounded nature of the positive feedbacks that stem from network
integration benefits*, should be assumed to characterize the individual decision
agent in many cases of technology adoption. This consideration would seem to
call for application of a set of analytical tools different from the ones we
introduced in the previous section.[4]

Markov random field structures

Concepts, terminology and a simple example: the voter model
Simply put, the structure of the 'competitive diffusion' process we would like to
study now is the following: members of a finite population of agents each make
(recurrent) standard selections at random intervals in time (corresponding to a
stochastic replacement process), subject to the positive influence of the currently
prevailing standard usage among a subset of neighbouring agents; the neighbourhoods are not completely segregated. This structure is that of a heuristic model,
initially known under the form of the 'voter model' elaborated by T.E. Harris
(1978) and presented in Kinderman and Snell (1980). This heuristic model is
based on a particular branch of probability, called Markov random field theory,
the extension of which to the economics of competition between technological
alternatives is introduced in David (1988; 1992b). It displays several important
features.

First, this model is concerned with the features of an adoption process made up essentially of interlinked local structures. The crucial limitation of this model, which must be borne in mind when interpreting the results, is that interconnectivities within a structure and between structures are assumed always to be equivalent.

Second, in this model, the share of each standard will vary on account of choice revisions made by agents and not because of the arrival of new agents. Despite the recurrent reassessment of choices, the global process of sequential decisions will be seen to display the property of non-reversibility.

Third, unlike the Pólya urn scheme, it is possible *ex ante* to assign probabilities of eventual 'victory' to each of the competing standards, simply on the basis of information concerning the initial distribution of the agents' choices.

Leaving aside technicalities, it is possible briefly to describe this framework in order to consider the competition as a stochastic path-dependent process in which knowledge of the initial conditions enables one to make predictions on the limiting macro-states of the system. Following the notation by Kinderman and Snell (1980), we may begin with the basic definitions relating to Markov random fields.

Let $G = (O,T)$ be a graph with $O = (o_1 \, o_2 \ldots o_n)$ the vertices (i.e. the set of organizations) and $T = (t_1 \, t_2 \ldots t_m)$ the edges (that is, the set of transactional lines). Assume a simple connected graph with five vertices and five edges. A *configuration* x is an assignment of an element of the finite set S to each point of O. We denote this configuration by $x = (x_o)$ where x_o is the element of S assigned to vertex o. If we let $S = [u,a]$ represent assignments of two possible standards, then a configuration would be an assignment of either o_u or o_a to each of the points in O. A *random field p* is a probability measure $p(x)$ assigned to the set X of all configurations, such that $p(x) > 0$ for all x. By the *neighbours* N (o) of the point o we shall mean the set of all points o' in O such that $(o'o)$ is an edge. A random field p is called a *Markov random field* if

$$p\{x_o = s \, x_{O-o}\} = p\{x_o = s \, x_{N(o)}\}$$

That is, in trying to predict the value at o (either u or a in the example), given the values at all other points of O, we need know only the values assigned to the neighbours of o.

Assume now, that associated with each point of a graph we have a firm and with each firm we have a reference set of other firms (possibly including the firm itself). Then the model may be described informally as follows: each firm selects a standard u or a. At random points in time it will reassess its choice. At these times it will commit to the choice u with a probability equal to the proportion of u-assigned firms in its reference set. Consider the graph consisting of the points $[-N, -N_{+1} \ldots, 0,1, \ldots, N]$. The reference set of i consists of the points i_{-1}

and i_{+1} for $-N < i < N$. The reference set for N consists of the points N_{-1} and $-N$, and for $-N$ it consists of $-N_{+1}$ and N. This particular neighbourhood arrangement could represent a transaction matrix that has a 'ring' structure: a firm receives impulses from a preceding one and sends impulses to a succeeding one, the last firm being connected with the first in the array.[5] One important feature of the local structures described in the inter-firm 'ring' model is that the reference sets or relational 'neighbourhoods' are not disjoint. Because one of the neighbours of an agent is also a neighbour of another agent, individual units' decisions become linked indirectly by the interlocking networks of local relationships, which serve to transmit their effects.

The dynamics of this model are quite simple, as it is assumed that the times between successive reassessments made by any given organization follow an exponential distribution with mean duration 1. Thus, the occurence of micro-level re-evaluations at each node is independent of the timing of reorientations that might take place among the other firms that share the same neighbourhood. Where a significant number of symmetrically influential organizations constitute the subsets of neighbours, this simplifying assumption does not seem unreasonable.[6]

The global process of migration between competing standards now can be described by a finite-state continuous-time Markov chain, with states being configurations of the form $x = (u, a, u, u, a, \ldots, u, a, u)$ where $x(i)$ is the choice of firm i. Several properties follow from this:

1. It is evident on even the briefest consideration that the extremal states $x^u = (u, u, u, \ldots, u, u, u)$ and $x^a = (a, a, a, \ldots, a, a)$, in which there is a perfect correlation of standards choices throughout the population, constitute *absorbing states* for this system. Once such a state is entered, there can be no further change.
2. A somewhat less obvious proposition, also true, is that for any starting state x the chain eventually will end up in either x^u or x^a. Thus, *in the limit*, the process must become *locked-in* into one of its extremal solutions.
3. There exists a limiting probability distribution over the macro-states of the system, which is non-continuous, such that starting in x, the probability that the chain will end in x^u is equal to the proportion of u in the initial configuration x (without regard to their position in the array), and the probability that it will end up in x^a is equal to the proportion of a in the initial configuration x. Therefore, although subject to random influences, *the asymptotic macro-state of the system can be readily predicted from information on the initial conditions.*

What do these results mean in the context of technology studies? This model foresees the emergence of a single standard (in certain conditions which will be examined more closely below) in the space defined by the entire body of users. The certainty that the outcome will be one of those extreme solutions means that the network integration benefits will be fully exploited in the future – which should increase the expected value for an individual firm of belonging to it. Further, an outside observer who knew the actual distribution of the agents' initial choices among the available standards would be able to calculate the odds of each standard emerging as the eventual victor in the competition, so long as such information remained irrelevant to the individual agents' actions.

Generalizations in dimension and size: qualitative properties of the voter model
The foregoing asymptotic properties will hold for Markov random fields defined in two-dimensional graphs.[7] For example, the decision units located in geographical and 'industrial complementary' space could be represented as the nodes of a square lattice, such that each has 'four nearest neighbours' (east and west, and north and south). Sequential binary neighbours made under the influence of additive local interactions with these near neighbours would, in the limit, converge to one or the other uniform configuration; and the outcome will be predictable, as has been seen, simply from the proportions in which the alternative policy assignments were made in the initial configuration.

Intuitively, one would not expect these results to be robust to further generalizations of the model in the direction of higher dimensionality.[8] Thus, when agents' decisions are subject to 'network externality effects' of such complexity that they cannot be reduced to a two–dimensional representation, there is no guarantee of their policies becoming *perfectly* correlated in the long run; all possible assignments of policies for any particular finite set of agents will have positive probability in the limit. But, at the level of three dimensions, some strong correlation still can be expected to emerge.

There is another direction in which the foregoing model cannot be generalized without losing the qualitative properties of eventually locking in to an extremal solution, and of having that outcome be predictable on the basis of some 'initial' or 'intermediate' configuration. Those properties will hold strictly only for finite populations of agents. The behaviour of very large finite systems, however, may well be better indicated by that of an infinite population – a continuum of agents. For the case of a continuum, a random walk being performed on all the real integers, it is found that there will not be a time after which the system remains in an absorbing state; the process oscillates between the extrema of perfectly correlated policies – with all firms adopting one standard at one moment, and all firms adopting the other policy at some other.

What may we surmise, if the evolution of collective behaviour in extremely large networks with positive local externalities is likely to resemble that of the infinite population case? Even under stationary structural conditions, such populations should not be expected to become inextricably 'locked in' to one of a number of locally stable equilibria. But, as noted below, they may linger for many periods of time in those neighbourhoods.

What can then be said with regard to the qualitative macro-behaviour of smaller ensembles of interacting decision agents, when these remain isolated from external interference and their internal structural relations remain undisturbed? If there is no inherent tendency for the behavioural orientation of the individual agents to undergo 'spontaneous' changes, that is, changes not prompted by interactions or signals received from the macro-state of the system, these systems will be most prone to exhibiting the working of history in its strongest form: convergence to an indefinitely persisting equilibrium (that is, 'lock in') characterized by perfectly correlated individual policy choices. Moreover, the prevailing collective policy or behavioural norm arrived at will have been 'selected' adventitiously, as a result of some particular concatenation of small events on the historical path. Inasmuch as the policy thus settled upon may well be one that is globally inefficient, indeed, collectively disastrous, this may be a reason why small systems of social and economic interaction appear historically to have a greater tendency to become extinct or absorbed into larger systems.

In dynamic models where the orientation (say, a or u) of the individual particles are subject to continuous *spontaneous* random perturbations, as well as to the influence of positive feedback from the macro-state of the system (say, the difference between the global proportions of positive and negative particles), the expected time interval separating the transitions the system makes between the neighbourhoods of its local equilibria will lengthen rapidly if the number of particles in the (finite) system is increased. An intuitive explanation can be given for this size effect: it is the spontaneous random perturbations of the system's micro-units that serve to push it out of the neighbourhood of one potential minimum and beyond the point of instability, whence it can move towards the other point of locally minimum potential. In a larger population it is a lower-probability event that enough independently distributed random perturbations will be positively correlated to produce such a 'shock'. This is the same principle that prevents a large herd of horses that are tethered together from moving any great distance in finite time, whereas, as any cowboy knew, a small band of horses tied together for the night could easily be out of sight by the sunrise.

Percolation and criticality of positive feedback systems

There is, however, one important qualification that renders application of the 'voter model' to competitive technology diffusion studies less than completely straightforward. This qualification arises from the assumptions of the model with respect to the 'mixed percolation probabilities' of the global system.

Percolation concepts and theory

The stochastic feature of the 'voter model' described in the preceding sub-section is confined to the reorientation of the standard selected by the node organizations, and is made conditional on the orientations of the set of their neighbours. The population of firms portrayed in this set-up is homogeneous in a twofold sense: first, all of the firms are taken to be equally ready to implement a particular standard in response to the external influence exerted upon it by the currently reigning choices of their trade partners; and second, the structure of inter-organizational connections is symmetrical, in that a similar pattern of transactional relations characterizes all of the reference sets. These homogeneities are, further, assumed to take a rather special form which renders the transmission of influence among the organizations completely deterministic. It is for this reason that we noted, above, that the source of randomness in the model had to do not with whether or not particular firms might be open to the influence of particular neighbours, but rather with the direction of the reorientation that such influences would bring about. The concepts and terminology of *percolation theory* provide a precise way of describing these specifications, and showing their relationship to a more general specification of the model.

By the term *percolation process* we refer to the dual of a diffusion process. 'Diffusion', to speak strictly, refers to the random movements of particles through an ordered, non-random medium, as in the case of the diffusion of molecules of salt in water; whereas the term 'percolation' conjures up the image of droplets of water moving under the deterministic pull of gravity through a disordered random medium such as a filtration tank filled with sand, and pebbles of different sizes. When the water, entering at some source sites, eventually finds its way into enough open channels to pass throughout, wetting the entirety of the interior surfaces, *complete percolation* has occured − whence the statistical models of analogous processes take their name.

Adapting the notation of Hammersley and Welsh (1980) to the Markov random field framework, let G be a graph in which some, none, or all of the edges may be directed. Thus G consists of a set of vertices or *nodes*, O, connected by a set of (possibly directed) edges or *connections*, T. Thus, we begin again with a set of *node organizations*, $O = (o_1 \ o_2 \ \ldots \ o_n)$, and a set of transactional lines connecting them, $T = (t_1 \ t_2 \ \ldots \ t_m)$. An *operative path* in G from an organizational o_1 to an organization o_n in a finite sequence of the form $\{t_{12} \ o_2 \ t_{23} \ o_3 \ldots t_{n-1,n} \ o_n\}$, where t_{ij} denotes a relational line connecting o_i to o_j. The graph G is *connected* if for each pair of organizations o_i and o_j there is a path in G from o_i to o_j. We now construct a *random maze* on G, as follows. Let each organization o of G be *open*, or responsive to the influence of any of its neighbours' standards choices, with probability p_o, or *closed* (unresponsive to local network externalities in deciding on its standards) with probability $q_o = 1 - p_o$. Similarly, each inter-organizational transactions line t_{ij} attains some minimal or *threshold density* of transactions between i and j (which is sufficient to influence decisively the ith and/or the jth firms' choices of a standard) with probability p_t, or it fails to do so with probability $q_t = 1 - p_t$. Moreover, we shall assume all these events are to occur independently of each other.

An operative path, $\mathbf{d} = \{t_{12} \ o_2 \ t_{23} \ldots t_{n-1,n} \ o_n\}$ from o_1 to o_n is said to be 'open' if all its transactional links attain the minimum sufficient density and all its organizations are influenced by network externalities in selecting their standard. Thus, the probability that the particular path $\mathbf{d}$ is 'operational' in that sense is given by $(p_o \ p_t)^{n-1}$

Let $\mathbf{R}$ be some given set of source organizations, from which a particular transactional standard emerges into $\mathbf{G}$. The decisions to adopt that standard can flow along any open path from a source organization and will then similarly reorientate the other organizations on such a path ('wetting' them, to use the natural percolation metaphor). The *percolation probability* $P(p_o, p_t \ \mathbf{R}, \mathbf{G})$ is the probability that $\mathbf{R}$ can thus reorient some infinite set of nodes in $\mathbf{G}$. We call the parameters p_o, p_t the *receptivity* and the *connectivity* of the process, respectively. In other words, in a large population, it can be expected that a proportion p_o are receptive to their neighbours' choices of a standard, while a proportion $1 - p_o$ are unreceptive. The transactional lines of $\mathbf{G}$ connect neighbouring pairs of organizations and the model supposes that an 'infected' organization (one already committed into a given standard) has a chance p_t of 'infecting' a neighbour provided that the latter is receptive. Then $P(p_o, p_t \ \mathbf{R}, \mathbf{G})$ is the probability that a standard initially established in the source organizations $\mathbf{R}$ will become adopted universally.

Suppose that $\mathbf{R}$ and $\mathbf{G}$ are fixed, that $\mathbf{G}$ is infinite and that we abbreviate

$$P(p_o, p_t \ \mathbf{R}, \mathbf{G}) = P(p_o, p_t) = P$$

then, clearly, the mixed percolation probability P is a non-decreasing function of p_o and p_t, and $P(0,0) = P(1,0) = P(0,1) = 0$, while $P(1,1) = 1$. Thus, $P_o(p) = P(p_o \ 1)$ and $P_t(p) = P(1 \ p_t)$ are, respectively, called the *node percolation* and *connection percolation* probabilities of this system.

A fundamental mathematical property of the percolation process is that there exist some critical values of $p_o > p_o^*$ and $p_t > p_t^*$ beyond which there will be a positive probability that percolation occurs, and below which the percolation probability is zero.[9] In other words, the system undergoes a 'phase transition' when these underlying critical probabilities are attained. There are corresponding critical values at which the node-percolation and edge-percolation probabilities, respectively, become positive. These define the endpoints of a region above which a 'mixed-percolation process' (one for which it is not certain that either all nodes or all edges of the graph are open) will have positive probability of achieving complete percolation.

The special percolation conditions of the voter model

If we now return to the process described by the 'voter model', the limiting outcome (lock-in to one of the extremal configurations whose identity may be predicted from initial configuration) may be seen to obtain under the special conditions: $P_o(p) = P_t(p) = 1$.

It is clear, however, that the pair of homogeneity specifications which correspond to those conditions does not correspond well with the realities characterizing populations of users. First, some firms (for example, those with a very high ratio of internal to external message transactions) are not likely to be highly responsive to the choices their trade partners have made with regard to electronic document formats. Either the internally orientated EDI users may expect to incur high fixed costs in converting all their data processing to work with some new, externally compatible format, including some disruptions of their internal control and decision-making structures in the switch-over; or they may fear some increases in their vulnerability to external disruptions created by the existence of inter-organizational networks that render their internal operations informationally transparent. These firms, therefore, pay little or no attention to the problems arising from the incompatibilities of the formats in which they exchange information with outside entities. They are ready to bear high per-transaction conversion costs in order to maintain their internal data-coding and data-processing procedures in the status quo. Under such conditions, some of the organization nodes of our graph, G, will be closed, so that for the randomly drawn (representative firm of the system) the node percolation probability will be less than 1. Indeed, it could be so degraded that the system was 'sub-critical' and there would be no possibility whatsoever of the occurence of a spontaneous percolation of a given standard throughout the population.

Secondly, some transactional lines may be closed, so that the bond percolation probability (the connectivity of the system) may be less than 1. Indeed, certain local structures (reference sets) are weakly (or not) connected to the rest of the network — in other words, some reference sets are isolated while others are fully 'embedded' in the global transactions system. Moreover, the patterns of interactions within each reference set may be very different. In other words, it appears that structural heterogeneity in subsets of adopters (in terms of internal connectivity between the agents), as well as fragmentation into essentially free-standing sectoral networks of local relationships, are two possible features of the global relational network that are very important in determining the possibility of *de facto* EDI standardization as a dynamic process. This structural heterogeneity at both the inter- and intra-neighbourhood levels can be more rigorously formulated within the framework of percolation theory.

Thus, recognition of the presence or absence of significant relational structures in the adopter system is important. If we return now to the 'voter model' and its assumption regarding the mixed percolation probabilities $\left(P_o(p) = P_t(p) = 1\right)$, it is clear that those assumptions impose considerable restrictions upon the applicability of the analysis: structural heterogeneity in the node and connection percolation probabilities certainly plays a key role in the dynamics and the eventual equilibrium outcome of the system. This conclusion gives rise to the following questions. What happens if both node and connection percolation probabilities are degraded? Are the results of the 'voter model' (lock-in to an extremal solution and predictability) altered? Are there critical probability levels for node and connection percolation, above which the system can take on the properties of a finite-state continuous-time Markov chain and reach limiting configurations characterized by perfect or very strong correlation among standards choices? We conjecture that both questions can be answered affirmatively, but, to our present knowledge, the relevant theorems have not been proved and these propositions remain to be formally demonstrated for the case of a 'voter model' with a mixed-percolation process.[10]

Asymmetry of node degradation and channel degradation: some concluding policy implications

The modern economic analysis of compatibility standards suggests clear and strong grounds for setting information technology policy the broad goal of encouraging the selection and diffusion of a single universal EDI standard.[11]

The framework developed here, based on Markov random field theory and percolation probabilities, points to specific and important policy issues in this regard, and offers some guidance in the choice among alternative strategies. One approach is the one that can be referred to as the 'bottom-up' strategy of standardization: to create the appropriate percolation conditions that would induce spontaneous emergence of a standard from a sequence of individual decisions. Simply put, such a policy should aim to increase the mixed-percolation probabilities $[P]$, so that the EDI user system approaches the results that were obtained in the case of the 'voter model'. The mixed-percolation framework provides a useful basis for discussing the rationale of such a policy. Indeed, the parameters p_o and p_t (the receptivity and the connectivity of the system, respectively) are not perfectly symmetric in their influence on the percolation probability P. In other words, the receptivity of the system is more 'brittle' than its connectivity. The following general property of P:

$$P_o(p) < P_t(p) \text{ whenever } 0 < p < 1$$

suggests that a standard percolates more easily via an imperfect set of connections between receptive nodes than through a completely connected graph whose nodes (organizations) are imperfectly receptive. A further generalization of this is provided by the theorem due to Hammersley and Welsh (1980):

$$P(p_o \beta, p_t) < P(p_o, p_t \beta) \text{ whenever } 0 < p_o < 1, 0 < p_t < 1, 0 < \beta < 1$$

This inequality can be given the following epidemiological interpretation: to prevent a pandemic (universal adoption) it is more effective to reduce the receptivity of members of a population than to reduce the probability of infectious contacts among them (the connectivity among organizations). In other words, if one degrades the node probability p_o, the percolation probability is lower than if one equiproportionally degrades the connection probability p_t.

Thus, when the costs of alternative policy actions are identical at the margin, the proper policy course for raising the percolation probability – so that a user system approaches the Markov random field model's properties – would be one that was 'receptivity-directed' rather than 'connectivity-directed'. The indicated policy would not rely on efforts to increase the density of external transactions. Rather, it would open the 'closed nodes' by subsidizing the initial commitment of the reluctant firms (those firms characterized by a high ratio of internal to external information exchanges) to implement the standard which dominates their local structures.

Notes

1. See references in Arthur (1989) to contributions in this vein earlier in the 1980s. Still earlier precursors can be found: the French mathematician Guilbaud (1955), in his comments on Schumpeter's evolutionary dynamics, explored the role of positive feedbacks in the generation of waves of innovations, stressing in particular the bounded nature of the cumulative process of innovations. He suggested a new way of modelling innovation dynamics by extending the use of Pólya urn processes to the analysis of evolution in the economic sphere.
2. However, let us be clear that while the choice of a standard may be subject to revision, the firm's commitment to EDI as a technology of inter-organizational network is treated here as completely irreversible.
3. But such is by no means universally the case. It is recognized in the industry that any particular utility has a strong motive to achieve internal standardization across the designs of the nuclear power plants it builds, especially when these are constructed on a common site. Furthermore, the self-reinforcing mechanisms that tended to promote the international dominance of light water reactor designs were considerably more intricate, and involved the complex intertwining of political, institutional and technical considerations to a degree that is difficult to represent by reference to analytically tractable stochastic processes in which there is a simple form of positive feedback.
4. Puffert (1987), in an early paper, developed a stochastic simulation model of the choice of railway gauge, in which both local and global positive feedbacks were represented. Cowan and Cowan (1993), in a more recent paper, develop a model that has both

global and local adoption externalities. The local externalities are positive (localized compatibility) while the global effects appear in the decreasing returns in the production of the capital goods in which the new technology is embodied. Thus the global externalities are always negative.

5. The closed nature of this production structure proves particularly convenient for heuristic purposes, in that it avoids the problems of having otherwise to deal with the special influence exerted by sectors that lie at the boundaries of the system – primary suppliers, and/or final demanders, so to speak.

6. The role of 'dominant users' in influencing the standardization process, however, cannot be well represented within the framework of this model – except through the device of assigning satellite organizations of the dominant firm to a 'collective territory' that is completely under the dominant firm's control as far as the choice of standards is concerned. The notion of 'collective territory' is introduced by Schelling (1971) in his dynamics models of residential segregation. In the present context collective territories are territories 'belonging' to a certain network standard, wherein population entrants will adopt the local standard with virtual certainty. Through the device of defining 'collective territories' one can allow for the entry of new users under conditions which would prevent the process from being perturbed in a way that would cause it to become unpredictable and undergo continuous random fluctuations between the extremes.

7. This follows from the fact that random walks in two dimensions, like those in one dimension, intersect with probability 1 in infinite time.

8. The mathematical reason is that there is no certainty of intersections among random walks performed in three-dimensional or still higher-dimensional spaces.

9. The more usual terminology in the mathematical literature associates the vertices and edges of G with 'atoms' and 'bonds', respectively, and so refers to the probabilities of atom percolation and bond percolation.

10. Our conjectures in this regard have received support from preliminary simulation studies, upon which we intend to report in future papers. The authors acknowledge the excellent assistance of J.M. Dalle (Ecole Polytechnique and IEPE) with these preliminary exercises.

11. See David and Greenstein (1990) and David and Foray (1992), for the conditions under which a universal standard represents a socially better outcome than the persistence of different and incompatible standards.

7 Hyperselection and Innovation Described by a Stochastic Model of Technological Evolution

Eberhard Bruckner, Werner Ebeling, Miguel A. Jiménez Montaño and Andrea Scharnhorst

Introduction

In physics, a tradition has developed (since the introduction of thermodynamic descriptions in the nineteenth century at the latest) where systems with large numbers of subsystems are considered. The many-subsystem approach has brought about a distinction between microscopic and macroscopic considerations, which emerged at about the same time as modern industrial society. This situation, where the system is very large and the elements are very small is well known in other disciplines where it has also led to the differentiation of microscopic and macroscopic processes. In physics, the relationship between micro- and macro-level descriptions became important and led to questions of fundamental relevance which still exist today. The whole history of self-organization and synergetics is focused on a surprising new understanding of the relationship between micro- and macro-level descriptions. One of the main results of these historical findings was that, more or less regardless of the nature of the subsystems, the manner of their coordination is what is important in the demonstration of the well-known macroscopic phenomena of spontaneous structure formation. The macroscopic effect results from the coherent behaviour of the subsystems, resulting in a cooperative effect. This fact generates a trend towards general models. To describe the manner of coordination, the mechanisms might be considered without providing them with a substantial physical or biological meaning. Formally, mechanisms from different disciplinary contexts might be integrated. Thus, the self-organization research tradition has led to a generalization which opens up new application areas, one of them being technological innovations.

Technological innovations have been investigated by means of substitution and diffusion as well as evolution models, each of them dealing with different aspects of the innovation problem. The evolutionary point of view has been proposed in earlier works on self-organization models of complex systems by Feistel and Ebeling (1976), Bruckner (1980), Jiménez Montaño and Ebeling (1980), Silverberg (1984) and later demonstrated by, among others, Silverberg et al. (1988), Bruckner et al. (1989), Troitzsch (1993) and Saviotti and Mani (1993).

The evolution aspect of the innovation problem mainly involves its description as an (amplified) structural fluctuation. Following earlier work (Bruckner et al. 1989) a general modelling framework is introduced in the next section, which allows a formal description of evolutionary processes for a particular application to social systems. An enumerable set of fields (such as biological species, technologies or areas of scientific behaviour) is considered, each field being characterized by the number and the properties of its representatives (occupying elements). By introducing probabilities for the elementary processes of spontaneous generation, identical self-reproduction, error reproduction, death and transitions to other fields, a Markov process in the occupation number space can be defined. At any time, only a finite set of fields is occupied, and the appearance of a representative of a field with 'better' properties is possible.

If this general modelling framework is to be applied to the problem of technological evolution, one has to respecify the system, subsystems (fields), elements and the elementary processes. As fields we consider different technologies represented by plants (as parts of firms) using them. The plants are assumed to be the smallest production units possible. A firm contains different plants using different technologies. The growth and decline of a technology, the transfer to other technologies and the introduction of new technologies in this manner are related to the creation, closure and re-construction of plants by the firm management, according to given market (or non-market) conditions.

To describe technological change as a macro-economic change process in an evolutionary conceptual framework, the micro-economic carriers of the change process have to be identified. In our view, two types of micro-economic carrier, the plants (represented by firms) and the technology elements are combined (or recombined) to bring about the micro-economic coordination process responsible for the observed macro-economic changes.

Regarding the innovation problem, the macro-economic (system) level and the micro-economic (firm) must also be distinguished. On the macro-economic (system) level, innovation is understood as the first appearance of a new technology in the system under consideration. On the micro-economic (firm) level most combination and recombination processes associated with the two different carriers include an innovative effect. Creation of the two types of carrier as well as the combination and recombination processes between them are taken as elementary processes of the evolutionary model. The model will then describe an innovation as a structural fluctuation in the dynamics of the system.

Innovation in its first stage may be understood as infection. The main question of an infection experiment is whether and how the system structure will change. The stability properties of the global state then represent the selection value of the new technology appearing either by a transition process, by diffusion or by innovation. In the stochastic picture, stability is related to a maximum of the probability function over the states. To obtain answers concerning the behaviour of the system against an infection with a new technology, in principle one should determine the time behaviour of the probability function by solving the corresponding master equation.

To concentrate on the problem of hyperselection in the third section of this paper, we consider a two-dimensional model to describe the process of substitution of an old technology by a new one. Competition is introduced by the constraint that the overall number of plants in the system must remain constant. In particular, we deal with a specific type of nonlinear growth properties, which leads to a hyperselection situation. In this way the once-and-for-all selection occuring in the deterministic description can be overcome in the stochastic picture.

Initially in the literature we obtain analytical expressions for the survival probabilities of a new technology in smaller or larger ensembles. We show how a hyperselection situation (Ayres 1991) might be removed in a stochastic picture and thresholds against the prevailing of a new technology in a step-by-step process can be overcome. In particular, we show that the survival probability of a new technology depends not only on the growth rates, but also on the size of the ensemble and the initial conditions. Particularly in small ensembles, the survival probabilities change dramatically. On this basis we show a specific niche effect which is responsible for the remarkable change of the competition conditions in local areas.

Because of the existence of a local dimension within a large system with the Markov property, a limitation of the competition area is in principle always possible. Although many systems – in particular social systems – require strong historical constraints, the Markov property is demonstrated in such systems. In particular, this property can be understood as a short-term adaptation of local decision-making agents and processes to the current state of the art in the global system. The status quo of the global system influences the microscopic behaviour to a significant extent. On the other hand, in such systems local decisions have a certain degree of independence from the larger context, although they are not uncoupled from it. This local independence of micro-decision-making could be stated as follows: a macro-economic change can be divided up into a chain of small steps, where each small step is associated with a local decision, itself to a certain extent independent of the global economy. Deviations which are not too much above the normal range of independence of local (micro-economic) decision-making are in general of insufficient interest in recognizing them, since they easily may be considered as unimportant. A technology which exists in small numbers may thus be of insufficient interest to be recognized globally, but of sufficient interest to be recognized locally, which leads almost automatically to the creation of a limited competition area.

A stochastic model of technological evolution

Technological change is usually imagined as a macro-economic change process – for example, from the radio tube to the transistor. To describe it as an evolutionary process one has to identify its micro-economic carriers, which in a coordinated activity govern and cause the macro-economic change process. In our view firms (or plants) as well as technologies are considered as micro-economic carriers of technological change. Therefore, to describe the process of technological change not only technological change has to be taken into account. The new events appear within the system

(a) by new micro-economic carriers;
(b) by combination and recombination of existing and new carriers.

Even a recombination of existing carriers (for example, existing plant recombined with existing technology) represents from the point of view of the firms an innovation process, if the technology has not been in the firm before. Thus, concerning the innovation problem the macro-economic level (system level) and the micro-economic level (firm level) have to be differentiated.

Macro-economically an innovation appears in the system if a new technology has been produced. On the micro-economic level all combination and recombination possibilities (excluding the process, which represents non-innovative firm extension) include an innovative effect.

An overview of the creation and (re)combination processes for the two types of carrier of technological change is given in the following:

(a) Creation of a small firm (firm = unit) combined with creation of a new technology.
(b) Creation of a small firm combined with choosing an existing technology.
(c) Creation of a new production unit combined with a new technology (firm extension (twice innovative)).
(d) Creation of a new production unit combined with an existing technology on the system level (firm extension (innovative)).
(e) Creation of a new production unit combined with an existing technology on the firm level (firm extension (non-innovative)).
(f) Creation of a new technology, combined with an existing production unit.
(g) Recombination of an existing production unit with an existing technology.

To describe the technological evolution process a good model should be able to fit the creation as well as the (re)combination possibilities of micro-economic carriers occurring in the system. In reality, the multitude of possible technologies forms an infinite continuous set. Here we assume that the number of potential technologies is infinite but discrete and countable.

Let us now specify our model by introducing an industrial state as a set of integers

$$(N_1, N_2, \ldots, N_i, \ldots) = \{N_i\} \qquad (7.1)$$

where N_i denotes the number of production units (plants) using the technology i. The plants using technology i might belong to different firms. Furthermore, we assume that the system is open − that production units can be created (new plants enter the system) and closed down (plants leave the system). The production units may also change (plants change to a different technology). Such decision processes in the model occur as transitions of plants between technologies (Nelson and Winter 1982). If we assume that all decisions leading to a change of the set $\{N_i\}$ depend mostly on the present state, we can apply a Markov process.

In order to have a sufficiently general basis for the description of evolutionary processes we need a stochastic birth, death and transition model involving many interacting fields (Bruckner et al. 1989). We assume that a set of fields of different type is present or potentially present in the system. The reservoir of possible fields may be very large or even infinite. A given N_i means that the field of type i is occupied by a population of N_i representatives. The occupation numbers N_i are integer functions of time. The complete set of occupation numbers $N_1, N_2, \ldots,$ N_s determines the state of the system at a given time. Due to the large number of potential fields most of the occupation numbers are zero. The probability that the system at time t is in a particular state may be described by the distribution function $P(N_1, N_2, \ldots, N_i, \ldots, N_s, t)$.

To describe the change of the probability distribution over time we assume that we can determine elementary processes, which, in one time step, change only the number of representatives of a single field: that is, $N_i \rightarrow N_i + 1$ or $N_i \rightarrow N_i - 1$ (which describes spontaneous generation, identical self-reproduction, error reproduction and death). An additional process which simultaneously changes two occupation numbers is: $N_i \rightarrow N_i + 1$ and $N_j \rightarrow N_j - 1$ (describing transitions to other fields). Introducing the corresponding transition probabilities as functions of the occupation numbers, we define a Markov process in the occupation number space. In particular, we consider the nonlinear growth properties associated with the emergence of new fields.

At any time, only a finite set of fields is occupied, and the appearance of a representative of a field (first population) with 'better' properties than the previously occupied fields produces an instability in the system.

In this way, we can formulate an equation of motion for the distribution function, taking into consideration the four fundamental processes of evolutionary behaviour: self-reproduction and error reproduction; decline; transition between fields (innovations or imitations); and input from external sources (cf. Bruckner *et al.* 1993).

Hyperselection and innovation

The (post)modern society is characterized by rapid changes. In particular, some industrial branches are characterized by very fast growth processes (up to saturation), which must be described by non-linear growth rates.

Using the framework of our evolutionary model of technological change we assume that the system is occupied by N_1 'master' producers with reproduction rate E_1 and we infect the system with a few producers using a new technology with rate E_2. Further, we assume that the total number of producers is a constant $N = N_1 + N_2$. This condition leads to competition where a new technology can only succeed if it replaces the old one.

The dynamics of such a process of rapid growth is described in a corresponding deterministic model by:

$$\frac{d}{dt} N_i = B_i N_i^2 - k_0 N_i \qquad i = 1, 2 \tag{7.2}$$

The condition of a constant overall number, N, of production units leads to

$$k_0 = \frac{B_2 N_2^2 + B_1 N_1^2}{N} \tag{7.3}$$

Introducing the condition $N_1 + N_2 = N$, for some constant N, we reduce the two-dimensional problem in a certain sense to a one-dimensional problem. First, let us consider the states in which the system is in a stationary behaviour.

The stationary points of the model given by equations (7.2) and (7.3) ($dN_1^s/dt = 0$, $dN_2^s/dt = 0$) are:

$$\text{(i) } N_1^s = N; N_2^s = 0$$

$$\text{(ii) } N_1^s = 0; N_2^s = N \tag{7.4}$$

$$\text{(iii) } N_1^s = \frac{NB_2}{B_1 + B_2} \quad N_2^s = \frac{NB_1}{B_1 + B_2}$$

The system exhibits bistability. The stationary states $(N_1^s = N; N_2^s = 0)$ and $(N_1^s = 0; N_2^s = N)$ are stable. State (iii), which lies between 0 and N, is unstable and separates the stable states. It is a separatrix. (The model in this case corresponds to the competition of hypercycles in the Eigen theory (Eigen and Schuster 1977–8).) Then the fate of the new technology depends on the initial conditions, and the chances of survival of a new variant starting with a few elements are not very large. Let us introduce the ratio between the growth rates of the technologies, $\alpha = B_2/B_1$, as an expression for the selection advantage of the new technology 2. If the initial number of the new firms is lower than the threshold

$$N_2(0) < \frac{N}{\alpha + 1} \tag{7.5}$$

the new technology has no chance of survival within the deterministic picture. The threshold value corresponds to state (iii). For example, for an initial condition below the unstable stationary point, technology 2 is located in the attractor basin of the stable state $(N_2^s = 0$ and $N_1^s = N$ correspondingly) and cannot leave it. If $N = 200$ and $\alpha = 2$, the new technology must start with 67 firms, to substitute the old one with certainty. If $N_2(0) < 67$ the new technology has no chance of substituting the old one. Such an initial condition can hardly be realized. On the other hand, if $N = 200$ and the new technology starts with around 10 firms, then α must be around 20 for the new technology to survive. We see that the hyperselection situation, which is in many cases not unrealistic, is hard to overcome and thus we have to look for possibilities of a real substitution in a stochastic world.

In a stochastic dynamics which is based on integer particle numbers $N_i = 0, 1, 2, \ldots$ the picture changes completely. Let us assume that N_1 is the number of plants using the old technology and N_2 the number of plants using the new one and furthermore that $N_1 + N_2 = N$, for some constant N. The elementary stochastic process is assumed to be a substitution, that is, one plant substitutes the new technology for the old one, or, in mathematical terms, we have the transition:

$$N_1 \to N_1 - 1, N_2 \to N_2 + 1 \tag{7.6}$$

Under the condition that N is constant in the state space only certain states or transitions are possible. Then, the transition probabilities can be written in terms of the number of firms using the new technology as probabilities of gain (W^+) and loss (W^-) processes for the new technology as follows:

$$W^+ = W(N_1-1, N_2+1|N_1, N_2) = B_2 \frac{(N - N_2)N_2^2}{NV} \tag{7.7}$$

$$W^- = W(N_1+1,\ N_2-1|N_1,\ N_2) = B_1 \frac{(N-N_2)^2 N_2}{NV} \qquad (7.8)$$

Now, the transition probabilities contain a quadratic and cubic term in N_2, e.g., we consider growth processes accelerating with N_2.

From the transition probabilities introduced above, a master equation can be derived. If an analytical solution of the master equation as a whole is not accessible, we can investigate analytically the behaviour of the system in the limit $t \to \infty$. The calculation of the stationary distribution $P(N, t \to \infty)$ corresponds to the analysis of the stationary states in the deterministic description.

For a birth and death process in the case of a two-dimensional system (with $N_1+N_2 = N$, for some constant N, and two absorber states, $N_2 = 0$ and $N_2 = N$) the final stationary distribution must have the shape (Ebeling et al. 1981; Ebeling and Feistel 1982):

$$P(N_2, t \to \infty) = \sigma\delta(N, N_2) + (1-\sigma)\ \delta\ (0, N_2) \qquad (7.9)$$

where σ is the survival probability of the new technology 2 in the stationary state and δ is the Kronecker delta function:

$$\delta(N, N_2) = \begin{cases} 1 & N_2 = N \\ 0 & \text{otherwise} \end{cases}$$

In this case the survival probability σ can be derived from just one constant of motion.

Results

With the transition probabilities introduced above we obtain the following formula for the survival probability of the new technology:

$$\sigma_{N_2(0),N} = \frac{1 + \displaystyle\sum_{j=1}^{N_2(0)-1} \left(\frac{B_1}{B_2}\right)^j \binom{N-1}{j}}{\left(1+\dfrac{B_1}{B_2}\right)^{N-1}} \qquad (7.10)$$

The survival probability now depends not only on the selection advantage but also on the degree of infection (initial conditions of the new technology) and the size of the ensemble in which the competition takes place.

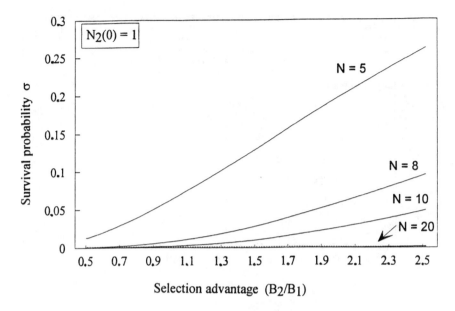

Selection advantage (B_2/B_1)

Figure 7.1 Survival probability, σ, of a new technology in the hyperselection situation as a function of the selection advantage, α, and ensemble size, N (N_2 (0) = 1).

The probability of survival is in general a smooth function which is continuously increasing with the relative advantage. There is no sharp difference between the better and the worse technologies.

In the hyperselection situation, as we have seen, the deterministic model shows that the survival of a new technology initially may require a third of the firms of the total existing population, which is in standard economic situations impossible to fulfil. In the more realistic stochastic model represented by equation (7.10) the picture is somewhat less distinct but the chances might be considered to be still worse. If $N = 200$, $\alpha = 2$ and the new technology starts with 67 firms, the probability of survival is around 50%. To have a survival probability of 90%, one must start in this case with 75 firms. On the other hand, in contrast to the deterministic model, if the new technology starts with fewer than 67 firms, it still has a certain chance of survival (with 65 firms, 40%; with 60 firms, 10%). If N is around 200, the new technology starts with 10 firms ($N_2(0) = 10$) and α is around 20, the new technology has a survival chance of around 50%. To have a survival probability of 90%, α must be around 30.

As will have been seen, the only real possibility of overcoming the hyperselection effect is to create a niche by limiting the competition area. As Figure 7.1 shows, a finite population size in any case improves the survival probability of the

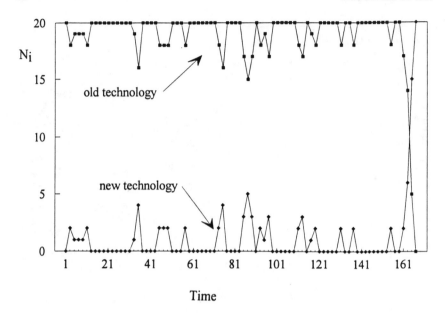

Time

Figure 7.2 Tunnelling through the separatrix after several unsuccessful trials (parameters $B_2/B_1 = 3$, $N = 20$, $N_2 (0) = 1$).

new technology. This effect is essential since it guarantees the survival of mutants in hypercyclic systems with finite population size.

Locally developed niches may play a constructive role in the technological evolution process. The new variants in the niche may first grow to considerable numbers and thus afterwards in the global system the hyperselection situation may be overcome.

Figure 7.2 shows in a simulation experiment how a new technology can 'tunnel' through the separatrix. The survival probability of the new technology increases if the degree of infection of the substitution process is increased (Figure 7.3).

Discussion

Evolution of technologies is a complex dynamical process which is connected with innovations, competition and selection. In this paper, some basic elements of a stochastic evolutionary theory of technological change were presented. It is proposed that this theory provides the framework for a deeper analysis of the processes of technological change and dynamic competition. Competition is

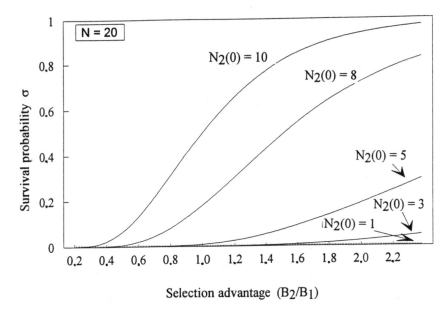

Figure 7.3 Survival probability, σ, of a new technology in the hyperselection situation as a function of the selection advantage, α, and initial conditions $N_2(0)$ ($N = 20$).

introduced by imposing constraints, which limit the number of firms sharing a market. Therefore technologies (as fields) 'are competing' for firms or plants (as elements). In other words, firms using different technologies compete for higher growth rates.

The model reflects the fact that any new achievement in technology is due to research and development, in the same way as the origin of any progress in biology is due to mutations. A new element in the evolution of technologies as compared with molecular evolution seems to be imitation of successful technologies. The importance of this process has been underlined by Nelson and Winter.

A fundamental role for the evolution of technologies is played by the behaviour of new participants in the game. This leads to the basic importance of random effects for technological evolutionary processes.

We consider an important result the fact that limited competition areas act as niches for the survival of variants which are present in the system in small numbers. In such niches the global selection rules are neutralized to some extent. In the hyperselection situation the niche is the only possibility for a 'good' technology to overcome the one-and-for-all selection predicted by the deterministic theory. Better new technologies can win the competition if the competition area is sufficiently small, say $N \ll 100$.

The competition area in large systems, including economic and social ones, may be kept in a local domain simply because of the Markovian character of the process.

In the niche, the new but not yet established quality is protected against extinction for a limited period of time. After winning the competition in a small group, the new technology may infect the whole system. In this way, the stochastic effects open up new channels for the evolutionary process and may deeply influence the perspectives of economic systems.

Finally, we express our belief that the deep and not only formal analogy between biological and technological processes which has been discussed already by many authors, may be very fruitful in the development of mathematical models of technological change.

Part III: Modelling the Evolution of Economic-Technological Systems

8 Evolutionary Dynamics in Technological Systems: A Multi-layer Niche Approach

Aura Reggiani and Peter Nijkamp

Introduction

Multi-layer niche structures

The economy is essentially always characterized by a mixture of different discrete technologies, both with respect to their time of adoption and to their type. This view suggests that a more appropriate framework for studying the economics of technical change than an equilibrium one would resemble the sort of ecological dynamics of distinct interacting species and the evolutionary one of the appearances and disappearance of species familiar to modern biologists (Silverberg 1992: 151).

In a recent article, Silverberg (1992) points out that an alternative view on the neoclassical approach to technical change (based on aggregate, shifting production functions) is the so-called 'biophysical' perspective which regards each technology and product as a species engaged in some sort of population dynamics. In particular, he underlines that the principles of mathematical biology, which are strictly connected with the functioning of dynamical systems, self-organization and evolution, seem highly relevant in analysing key problems in the economics of technical change. For example, the logistic function (see also Marchetti and Nakićenović 1979) 'provides a highly versatile technique for resolving the effects of sequences of innovations competing for a particular economic niche' (Silverberg 1992: 152).

The relevance of the formal-interpretative aspects of the logistic function has also been emphasized by Nijkamp and Reggiani (1992a; 1993a) in their analysis of the relationships between competition and stability in a spatial dynamic system. A step further is then the use of niche theory – based on logistic functions – for analysing the evolution of a self-organizing system, in which the entry of new competitors generates new dynamics (see also Nijkamp and Reggiani 1992b; and the next two sections below). In other words, the evolutionary 'niche' envelopes can map out the process of replacement of old by new systems along structured

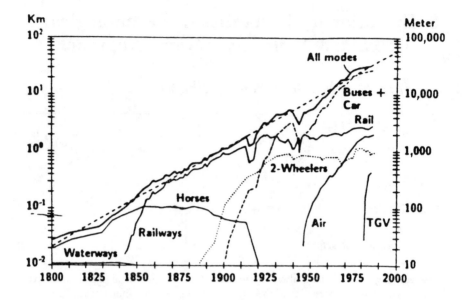

Figure 8.1 Growth of mobility, France.
Source: Grübler *et al.* (1992: 3)

development trajectories. A clear example in this context is the dynamics of transport systems where older systems – made obsolete through technological advance and economic development – are gradually substituted by new ones which are better capable of adapting themselves to continuously changing social, economic and environmental boundary conditions (see Grübler *et al.* 1992). An empirical analysis of this evolution process can be found in the historical scenarios of mobility growth sketched by Grübler *et al.* (1992) (see Figure 8.1).

Figure 8.1 shows that a transport-technology system is a complex multi-layer system, in which each subsystem (the niche envelope) interacts with the others at different levels of structure (or capacities of the system). Thus, the expansion of a particular technological system/niche reaches – at a certain time period – limits in terms of market saturation, social acceptability, environmental constraints, and so on.

It is also interesting to note how the complementarity-substitution effect in transport infrastructures is directly linked to evolutionary processes in other systems – such as the energy system – which reflect in a similar way techno-economic paradigm shifts (see Figure 8.2).

The above patterns also show that new technologies are not adopted

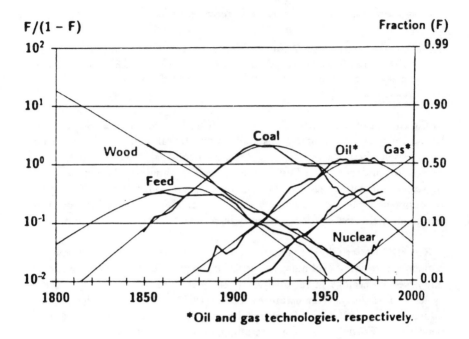

Figure 8.2   Primary energy substitution, USA.
Source: Grübler *et al.* (1992: 13)

instantaneously, but that their diffusion takes different amounts of time which obviously vary among countries, economic sectors, or social classes.

Starting from the above considerations, we propose here an appropriate analytical framework for studying the evolutionary dynamics of technological systems, in particular the multi-layer niche approach. In particular, we will focus our analysis on the interdependencies between the capacities of the niches, besides the dynamic competition of the niches themselves. In other words, we suggest that the capacities are 'nested-time' capacities, in the sense that for each niche the related (time-dependent) capacity level is the result of sub-capacity levels (for example, production, cost, social, energy or environmental limits) embracing a chain of sub-niches. In this context, it is clear that a fundamental role is played by environmental carrying capacity, which can be considered as the 'main' limit for the technological system.

In the next sub-section we will analyse – in the spirit of the above remarks – a general three-layer system, in which the main actors are man and environment.

Economic and environmental systems: a hierarchical evolutionary approach

There has been much recent debate concerning the nature of environmental systems. Much of this arises from the recognition of the increased interaction between man and nature, and of the ascendancy of the former leading to the modification of the latter (Bennett and Chorley 1979: xi).

In the context of man–nature interactions, it is clear that the complex interface between man and environment poses difficult analytical problems – in particular the question whether man, and hence the economic-social system, is separate from nature, for instance, by adjusting the natural environment behaviour within constraints of natural laws to his individual goals and purposes. Economic–environmental interdependence and evolution are also represented in laws from evolutionary theories developed recently in ecology/biology as well as in economics.

Recently, Rosser (1991) has made a plea for a dialogue between economic and ecological theories of evolution. In particular, he pointed out that economics was influenced by ecology in the analysis of complex dynamic phenomena, such as cycles – first analysed in nature by Lotka (1920) and Volterra (1931) – and bifurcations and chaos – discovered by May (1976) in his studies of insect populations. Furthermore, it is interesting to observe that the vivid debate on the nature of evolution, between gradualism (continuous evolution), as advocated by Darwin (1859), and saltationism (discontinuous evolution), as advocated by Wright (1931), was later joined by economists. On the one hand, we may claim Marshall (1920) as the greatest admirer among economists of Darwin for accepting the proposition that the 'struggle for existence' explains the evolution of market structure and that human society gradually and continuously evolves (gradualism in evolution). On the other hand, we may refer to Schumpeter (1934), who believed that the 'very essence of economic development lies in the discontinuities engendered by the innovative activities of entrepreneurs' (Rosser 1991: 208). Positioned in between the two streams of theories (for a wider review, see again Rosser 1991), Boulding (1978) argued for a mix of continuous and discontinuous processes in which instability – even though rarely – plays a significant role by generating discontinuous events. Starting from these recent discussions as well as from the considerations offered in the previous subsection, we will consider here the hypothesis that economics and environment are two evolutionary complex systems, with the possibility of both continuous and discontinuous processes interacting with one another at different levels of structure (or capacities of the system).

We will consider, in particular, as an interesting example, the dynamic relationships between transport systems and environmental systems, by adhering to the dynamic interdependence illustrated in Figure 8.3, where the time-

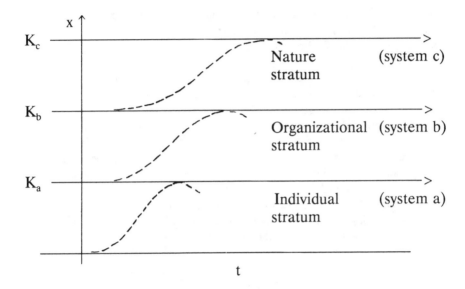

Figure 8.3   The dynamic relationships 'economics – environment': a multi-layer structure.

dependent variables K_a, K_b, K_c represent the related capacity of the three systems a, b, c shown as logistic functions. Note that the economic system has been subdivided into two choice levels (micro and macro) determined, respectively, by a 'generalized' carrying capacity of the two systems (indicated as a and b).

In Figure 8.3, we suppose the emergence of a higher level of structure which altogether leads to the emergence of greater complexity or to the 'progressiveness' of the evolution. However, it should be noted that in our hypothesis the three capacity levels K_a, K_b, K_c are not fixed, but may vary as state variables over time. This means also the possibility of generative feedback processes or systems overlapping – in other words, the emergence of the possibility of explaining 'devolutionary' dynamic processes.

It follows that the evolution of each system can be considered as the result of the competition between different subsystems within the main system, leading to a self-organization process. Such a process can easily be modelled by means of a multi-layer structure based on a recent and increasingly popular approach to competition analysis in ecology and social sciences: niche theory. The fundamental concepts of niche theory can be found in Nijkamp and Reggiani (1992a). Thus, a brief sketch on niche formulation will be given in the next section (with more emphasis on its applications in social and economic sciences). A simulation experiment, based on a two-layer niche structure, in the field of the transport technologies will then be presented.

Evolution of a System by Means of 'Niche' Chains

In general, niche theory deals with optimal adjustment or survival processes in dynamic systems with limited resources (see, for example, Pianka 1978).

Starting from an analysis carried out by May (1973), we recall here that niche theory can be embedded in standard competition models whose potential has recently been advocated for geography and economics (see Nijkamp and Reggiani 1992b; 1993a; 1993b). In particular, we will utilize here the prototype model of several competing populations studied by Lotka (1925) and Volterra (1931) and interpreted on the basis of niche theory by May (1973):

$$\dot{x}_i = x_i (k_i - \sum_{j=1}^{m} \alpha_{ij} x_j) \qquad (8.1)$$

where x_i is the population of species i ($i = 1, 2, \ldots, m$), the constant k_i represents the suitability of the environment for the ith species (for example, carrying capacity) and the competition coefficients α_{ij} measure the overlap in the utilization functions of the resources. It should also be noted that the extension of the Volterra scheme of type (8.1) based on the Pearl–Reed equation (see, for example, Sonis 1991; 1992) is also efficient in this context.

Equation (8.1) is not only a standard model in ecology, but has also been applied elsewhere, even without an explicit reference to niche theory. For example, interpreted simply as a competition system, it was used by Johansson and Nijkamp (1987) in their study on urban and regional development with competing regions.

It is interesting to note (see Smith 1974) that for the system of type (8.1) (for both a continuous and discrete time specification) the equilibrium – if it exists – is either stable or unstable, but in either case non–oscillatory. However, in a recent analysis (see Nijkamp and Reggiani 1993a) the possibility of irregular behaviour emerging in the presence of a 'chaotic' evolution in the system has been demonstrated. An interesting step from this latter analysis is consequently the introduction of the niche concept in such a competition system.

It is clear that from equation (8.1) many particular cases can arise, for example, the well-known prey–predator system. In this context it is also interesting to observe that from a general equation (8.1) also the concept of 'ecological evolution' emerges, as described by Allen (1988b: 19): 'The important point is

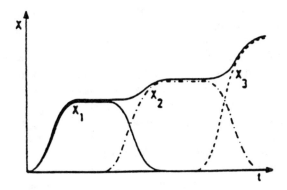

Figure 8.4 Niches occupied successively by species of increasing effectiveness.
Source: Nicolis and Prigogine (1977: 457)

that "evolution" implies some changes of form, character or behavioural strategy, which affect the manner in which individuals perform in capturing prey, reproducing and avoiding death'. Thus, in Allen's view a new population type – a mutant or an innovation – leads to evolution as presented in equation (8.1), an evolution interpreted as change of form and character (see also Nicolis and Prigogine 1977).

In this framework equation (8.1) may be applied to socio-cultural and economic evolution (where the population dynamics can be extended to urban and regional development, economic activities, diffusion of ideas, transport systems, and so on) in which learning mechanisms, innovations or technological changes exist. In other words, we are facing a choice situation with different strategies which can be adopted or rejected by surrounding 'populations'.

Equations based on formulation (8.1) have been applied, for example, to urban dynamics (see Allen and Sanglier 1981; Camagni *et al.* 1986) where each centre's growth path is subject to successive bifurcations which are linked to the appearance of new economic functions as well as to the pace of general technical progress. According to these authors, if the species x_i are interpreted as economic functions, then new species $x_2, \ldots, x_n$ – with respect to the previous species x_1 – are the new economic functions competing with the previous niche (or niche chain). In particular, an evolutionary model of type (8.1) can be interpreted in the framework of the self-organization of systems (that is, the inner dynamics which drives them to reconstitute themselves in new structures) (see Prigogine 1976), where the new 'competitors', or new 'species', may be considered in terms of ecological fluctuations. These fluctuations continue and replace the old population when the new species have a better capability of exploiting the same resources, or the 'ecological' niche (see Figure 8.4).

An interesting example of the process described in Figure 8.4 is provided by the evolution of technological innovation, where the new series are represented by new technological products (or, in general, 'new technological paradigms'). But just as in ecology, each technology which replaces an old one is not capable of doing the same, but generally also generates new opportunities (see Jantsch 1980). Empirical examples of the above process have been carried out, for instance, in the substitution of transport infrastructures and energy systems as shown in the opening section of this paper (see Figures 8.1 and 8.2).

It is noteworthy that system (8.1) — which represents a *hierarchy* of levels of self-organization — is also an autopoietic system, that is, one whose function is primarily geared to self-renewal (or self-production) — see Maturana (1970) and Maturana and Varela (1975).

It is thus clear now that, from a modelling point of view, the competition coefficient α_{ij} in equation (8.1), which represents the measure of niche overlap, plays a fundamental role in the evolution of a 'self-organizing' system, since its value generates the possibility of extinction or coexistence of species. In the next section we will consider the indigenous dynamics of such a system by examining the particular case of the evolution of two species, focusing the attention on the role played by the competition coefficient α_{ij}.

A Transport/Environment Model for Mobility

Introduction

In this section we will analyse the specific case of three competing niches in transport systems behaviour, starting from the theoretical analysis developed in the previous sections. In particular, given the hypothesis of a multi-layer dynamic structure as introduced above, we aim to investigate the relationships between stability and complexity for such a structure (for a definition of static/dynamic complexity in a network, see Nijkamp and Reggiani 1993c). In other words, we want to examine — in the case of unstable dynamics for the key elements (capacities or modes) — the (related) emerging impact on the whole system.

The above niche methodology can be applied to each type of transport network given a certain segment (or area or country) for different technological opportunities to be chosen.

We will consider in our model the case of three competing modes (car, railway and air travel) with reference to mobility flows. We will specify formulation (8.1) in a discrete-time version, since the relevant types of data are often discrete in nature.

A two-layer model

For the case of three competing species, system (8.1) in discrete form can be reduced to (for $x_1 = x$, $x_2 = y$ and $x_3 = z$):

$$x_{t+1} = x_t \left(K_{1,t} - \alpha_{11} x_t - \alpha_{12} y_t - \alpha_{13} z_t\right)$$

$$y_{t+1} = y_t \left(K_{2,t} - \alpha_{21} x_t - \alpha_{22} y_t - \alpha_{23} z_t\right) \qquad (8.2)$$

$$z_{t+1} = z_t \left(K_{3,t} - \alpha_{31} x_t - \alpha_{32} y_t - \alpha_{33} z_t\right)$$

where x represents the *road* mode, y the *air travel* mode and z the *rail* mode. The variable k refers to the total capacity of the mode in a given period, including the capacity growth in the relevant period as a result of new investments. This means essentially that the capacity variable can be influenced by the investments as a control variable; clearly, this has implications for the competitive position of each of these modes.

The competition coefficients α_{ij} represent, in a 'niche' interpretation, the measure of niche overlap over time. We will assume for the sake of simplicity that $\alpha_{12} = \alpha_{21} = a$; $\alpha_{13} = \alpha_{31} = b$; $\alpha_{23} = \alpha_{32} = c$; $\alpha_{11} = \alpha_1$; $\alpha_{22} = \alpha_2$; $\alpha_{33} = \alpha_3$. It is noteworthy in particular that, when the competition coefficient α_{ij} is equal to zero, we have no competition (or no common resources), while for $\alpha_{ij} = 1$ x_i and x_j completely overlap. Partial overlap is consequently expressed by the condition $0 < \alpha_{ij} < 1$.

Thus our competition system (8.2) can easily be rewritten as follows:

$$x_{t+1} = x_t \left(K_{1,t} - \alpha_1 x_t - a y_t - b z_t\right)$$

$$y_{t+1} = y_t \left(K_{2,t} - a x_t - \alpha_2 y_t - c z_t\right) \qquad (8.3)$$

$$z_{t+1} = z_t \left(K_{3,t} - b x_t - c y_t - \alpha_3 z_t\right)$$

Next we assume – as indicated in the first section of this paper – that the effective capacity of the three modes may be actually constrained by the external environmental costs of transport, not only by the social costs of their own mode but also by the social costs of competing modes (all of them are competing in terms of use of scarce environmental resources). Thus the actual capacity of all modes may be varying over time, until a threshold level is reached that is determined by the environmental cost constraint on each transport mode.

Consequently, by taking into consideration the principles of Figure 8.3, condensed in a two-layer model, we will assume a new level of organization in which the capacities K_1, K_2, K_3 of the three modes are also competing for scarce environmental amenities. The relating model then reads as follows:

$$K_{1,t+1} = K_{1,t} (C_1 - \beta_1 K_{1,t} - e K_{2,t} - f K_{3,t})$$

$$K_{2,t+1} = K_{2,t} (C_2 - e K_{1,t} - \beta_2 K_{2,t} - g K_{3,t}) \qquad (8.4)$$

$$K_{3,t+1} = K_{3,t} (C_3 - f K_{1,t} - g K_{2,t} - \beta_3 K_{3,t})$$

where C_i is the maximum threshold level of environmental costs for each mode i ($i = 1,2,3$).

The next step is to test by means of simulation experiments the sensitivity and the stability of this two-layer environment transport mode model.

Simulation experiments

In this sub-section we will investigate the behaviour of the nested model (8.3)–(8.4) by regarding, in particular, the conditions and relationships causing (in)stability between the variables K_1, K_2, K_3, x, y, t and C_1, C_2, C_3.

We will first start our presentation of simulation experiments for stable behaviour, that is, for values of C_i that lead to stability of the model results. We will use the following starting values:

$$C_1 = 2.9 \qquad C_2 = 3 \qquad C_3 = 2.5$$

with the following values for the competition coefficients:

$$\alpha_1 = 0.05 \qquad \alpha_2 = 0.05 \qquad \alpha_3 = 0.05$$
$$a = 0.01 \qquad b = 0.05 \qquad c = 0.05$$
$$e = 0.1 \qquad f = 0.5 \qquad g = 0.3$$
$$\beta_1 = 1 \qquad \beta_2 = 1 \qquad \beta_3 = 1$$

The related simulation experiments have been carried out using the well-known STELLA simulation programme for dynamic systems. We obtain the stable relationships for both the three modes and the three capacities shown in Figures 8.5 and 8.6.

In particular, it can be seen from Figure 8.6 that the above parameter values lead to a stable configuration in which the modes 'car' and 'rail' turn out to become the winners in the long run, followed by the mode 'air travel'.

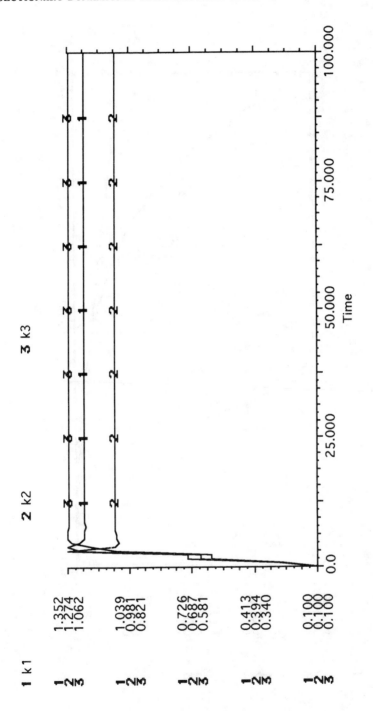

Figure 8.5   Stable behaviour for the capacities of the three modes.

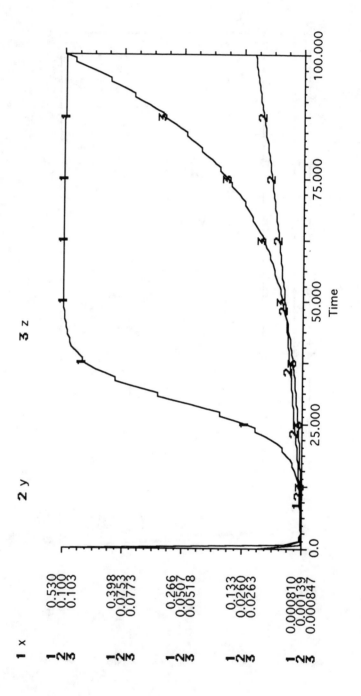

Figure 8.6   Stable behaviour for choice among the three modes (car, air travel, railways).

By now increasing the values of C_i as follows:

$$C_1 = 3.5 \qquad C_2 = 3.8 \qquad C_3 = 3$$

and by keeping the other parameters equal, we can next observe the emergence of a 'chaotic' behaviour for the capacities (see Figure 8.7) corresponding to oscillations in the mode choice (see Figure 8.8).

Concluding remarks

In the present paper we have identified a conceptual-theoretical framework for describing the dynamics of transport technology substitution/complementarity leading to dynamic man−environment relationships. Starting from a general multi-layer approach stemming from empirical analysis as well as from ecologically based theories, we defined a two-layer model (based on niche theory) constrained by the capacity (varying over time) of the two-layer system. The model was − for spatial mobility behaviour − simulated for the particular case of three competing modes (car, rail, air), that were nested with respect to the competition of the three capacities concerned and limited by a final threshold determined by environmental costs (or social costs, in general).

Simulation experiments showed the direct link − in terms of (in)stability − between the nested variables, so that (un)stable values for the choices of the capacities correspond to (un)stable values of the modes. The model, in this two-layer niche formulation, also shows an extreme sensitivity to parameter values, notably competition coefficients and carrying capacities.

The present example represents a first step toward a broader research direction in which further layers of capacity may be identified within these two principal layers in a network-tree structure. A first new step in this context would be a subdivision, on the one hand, of the first layer into two levels of choice (micro and macro) determined, respectively, by the carrying (technical) capacity of the modes and by the investment capacities determined by modal decision-makers. On the other hand, the 'cost-capacity' level can also be subdivided into three further sublevels (safety costs, 'purely' environmental costs and operating costs), whose hierarchy also varies over time.

Obviously, this multi-layer model may lead to n additional hierarchical levels interacting with one another in a nested parallel form (as, for example, in the case of energy substitution). Consequently, the formulation of the model in n layers may also lead to more difficult research issues, such as computational problems, scale problems and stability analysis. In this framework a parallel computing approach or a neutral network approach would certainly be useful.

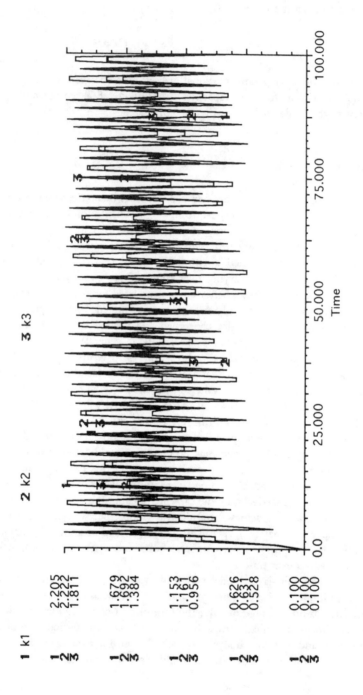

Figure 8.7   Oscillating behaviour for the capacities of the three modes.

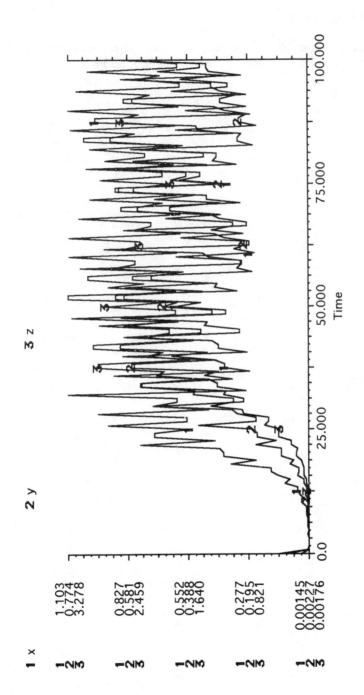

Figure 8.8 Oscillating behaviour for choice among the three modes.

Acknowledgement

The present chapter has been developed in the framework of Italian CNR – Progetto Finalizzato Trasporti 2 – contract no. 92.01943.PF74.

9 Entrainment in a Disaggregated Economic Long-wave Model *et al-*

Christian Kampmann, Christian Haxholdt, Erik Mosekilde and John D. Sterman

D40 , C62

Introduction

The world economy appears to alternate between long periods of relative affluence and periods of stagnation and economic hardship. Most scholars agree that periods of prolonged depression occurred in the 1830s and 1840s, from the 1870s until the 1890s, in the 1920s and 1930s, and from about 1974 until the present (Bieshaar and Kleinknecht 1984; van Duijn 1983). The Russian economist, N.D. Kondratieff (1935), was the first to draw attention to the repetitive character of this phenomenon and to relate it to essential forces in the capitalist economy. Schumpeter (1939) advanced the hypothesis that technological changes lead capitalist systems to go through phases of growth interspersed with periods of 'creative destruction' of capital, to make way for new technologies.

Empirical studies have furnished evidence that innovations (Mensch 1979), and even political and social values (Namenwirth 1973; Weber 1981), are correlated with these long-term movements in the economy. Although most economists still take a rather agnostic stance concerning the existence of long waves (Mansfield 1983; Rosenberg and Frischtak 1983), the slowdown in economic growth during the last two decades and the inability of conventional policies to restore the postwar prosperity have promoted renewed interest in the field.

Why do major depressions seem to recur at regular intervals of 30–70 years? Some authors have sought to explain periods of severe depression such as the 1930s as the simultaneous downturn of several essentially independent cycles (see, for example, Long 1940). If the economy were completely linear, its total behaviour would be the superposition of the separate modes, and the coincidence of downturns in each cycle would indeed produce a large depression. However, such an explanation leaves unanswered a number of basic questions. If the economy is linear, why do the individual sectors of the economy adjust their changes in employment and production so as to produce a coherent motion of the economy as a whole?

We believe that, to explain this fact, one must acknowledge that most of the relationships that bind elements of the economy together are highly nonlinear. For instance, there is a nonlinear constraint in the fact that nominal interest rates cannot be negative. Likewise, output is constrained by capacity, goods inventories cannot be negative, and so on. Moreover, psychological effects that guide decisions are likely to be nonlinear in nature.

The significance of these nonlinear links is their ability to create coherence in the overall behaviour of the system. Modern theory of nonlinear dynamics suggests that the different cyclical modes can become entrained through the process of mode-locking, whereby the periods of the interacting modes adjust to one another to attain a rational ratio (see, for example, Jensen et al. 1983; 1984). One mode, for instance, may complete precisely one cycle each time the other mode completes precisely three cycles.

This type of interaction is well documented in physical, biological and technical systems (see, for example, Colding-Jørgensen 1983; Glass et al. 1986; Mosekilde et al. 1990). A classical example is the synchronization of the rotational motion of the moon to its orbital motion, which is the reason why the moon always shows the same face towards the Earth. Other well-known examples are the synchronization of the circadian rhythm of most living organisms to the shift between day and night, the synchronization of clocks hanging on the same wall, and the synchronization of menstrual cycles between women living in close contact. It seems likely that similar phenomena are responsible for synchronizing the individual sectors of the economy to create the overall macro-economic cycles (Forrester 1977). Despite its obvious significance, however, nonlinear entrainment between economic sectors has so far received little consideration.

Roughly speaking, mode-locking occurs because the nonlinear structure of the interacting parts of a system implies forces that 'nudge' the parts of the system into phase with one another. In the case of the synchronization of adjacent clocks, for instance, each clock has an escapement mechanism, a highly nonlinear mechanical device, which transfers power from the weights to the rod of the pendulum. When a pendulum is close to the position where the escapement releases, a small shock, such as the faint click from the release of the adjacent clock's escapement, is enough to trigger the release. Hence, if the clocks are very close to being in phase, this interaction draws them still closer.

In a series of papers, we have analysed how mode-locking and other nonlinear dynamic phenomena arise in a simple, nonlinear model of the economic long wave (Mosekilde et al. 1992; Sterman and Mosekilde 1993). The model explains the long wave as a self-sustained oscillation arising from instabilities in the ordering and production of capital. An increase in the demand for capital leads to further increases through the investment accelerator of 'capital self-ordering', that is, by the fact that the capital sector depends on its own output to build up its stock of productive capital. Once a capital expansion is under way, self-reinforcing processes sustain it beyond its long-term equilibrium, until nonlinear interactions finally allow production to catch up with orders. At this point, however, the economy has considerable excess capital, and the feedback loops reverse, forcing capital production to remain below the level required for replacements until the excess has been fully depreciated and room for a new expansion created.

The concern of the present paper is the simple model's aggregation of capital into a single type. The real economy consists of many sectors employing different kinds of capital in different amounts. Parameters such as the average productive life of the capital produced and the relative amounts of different capital components employed may vary from sector to sector. In isolation, the house-building and infrastructure-capital industry may show a temporal variation significantly different from that of, for instance, the machinery industry. What circumstances lead more realistic, multi-sector models to behave in a similar fashion to the aggregate one-sector model, and what circumstances produce more complicated dynamic behaviours? To address this question requires a detailed look at the mechanisms that couple different sectors in the economy together, and a study of the implications of this coupling for different parameter values.

An early study by Kampmann (1984) took a first step in this direction by disaggregating the simple long-wave model into a system of two or more capital-producing sectors with different characteristics. Kampmann showed that the multi-sector system could produce a range of different behaviours, at times quite different from the original one-sector model.

The present paper further investigates these results, using a two-sector model. One sector might represent the construction of houses and infrastructure-capital components with very long lifetimes while the other could represent the production of machines, transportation equipment, computers, and so on, with much shorter lifetimes. In isolation, each sector produces a self-sustained oscillation with a period and amplitude determined by the sector's parameter values. However, when the two sectors are coupled together through their mutual dependence on each other's output for their own production, they tend to synchronize or lock together with a rational ratio between the two periods of oscillation.

We study how the mode-locking occurs under the influence of two factors: the difference in the average lifetime of capital produced by each sector, and the degree of linkage between the sectors. One would expect that a significant difference in capital lifetimes would, *ceteris paribus*, lead to more complex fluctuations which may well differ substantially from the original 50-year cycle. Conversely, a stronger coupling between the sectors should lead to more uniform behaviour, akin to that of the original single-sector model.

The following section describes the structure of the disaggregated model. Apart from the obvious modifications needed to extend the model to more than one sector, and except for a few alterations in parameter values and function specifications, which we felt were appropriate for a more detailed study, the disaggregated model is equivalent to Sterman's (1985) original model. The simulation results of our model are presented in the third section of the paper. In accordance with the results of the forced one-sector model (Mosekilde *et al.* 1992), the two-sector model exhibits both mode-locking, period-doubling bifurcations, and deterministic chaos. However, the details of the phase diagrams for the two models differ significantly. Finally, we consider the implications of the study. Being primarily exploratory and experimental in nature, many of our conclusions from the study are suggestions for extensions of the work. In particular, the role of a price system and of limited substitution between capital components in shaping the behaviour is an important future area of exploration.

The model

As mentioned above, the model contains a few minor modifications to Sterman's (1985) original model, apart from the extensions needed when going from more than one sector. A more extensive description of the model and a comparison with the original model can be found in an earlier version of this paper (Haxholdt *et al.* 1993).

The model describes the flows of capital components from ordering to final discards in two capital-producing sectors. Each sector uses capital from itself and from the other sector as the only factors of production. The sector receives orders for capital from itself, from the other sector, and from the consumer goods sector. Orders are backlogged until capital is produced and delivered.

The model consists of ten ordinary differential equations, corresponding to ten state variables, namely the capital stock of each type in each sector (2×2), the production capital on order (the 'supply line' of capital) of each type in each sector (2×2), and the total order backlog in each sector (2×1). The state variables are indicated by capital letters.

Each sector $i = 1,2$ maintains a stock K_{ij} of each capital type $j = 1,2$. The capital stock is increased by deliveries of new capital and reduced by physical depreciation. A stock of capital type j depreciates exponentially with an average lifetime of τ_j. A key parameter, which is varied in the simulation studies below, is the difference $\Delta\tau$, in average lifetimes of the two capital types. Capital output is distributed 'fairly' between customers, that is, the delivery of capital type j to sector i is the share of total output from sector j, x_j, distributed according to how much sector i has on order with sector j, S_{ij}, relative to sector j's total order backlog, B_j. Hence,

$$\dot{K}_{ij} = \frac{x_j S_{ij}}{B_j} - \frac{K_{ij}}{\tau_j} \qquad (9.1)$$

$$\dot{S}_{ij} = o_{ij} - \frac{x_j S_{ij}}{B_j} \qquad (9.2)$$

where o_{ij} is sector i's new orders for capital from sector j.

Each sector receives orders from both capital sectors, o_{ii} and o_{ji}, and from the consumer goods sector, g_i. It accumulates these orders in a backlog B_i which is then depleted by the sector's deliveries of capital x_i. Hence,

$$\dot{B}_i = (o_{ii} + o_{ji} + g_i) - x_i \qquad j \neq i \qquad (9.3)$$

Each sector's output x_i is limited by its production capacity c_i. The capacity in each sector is assumed to be a constant-returns-to-scale Cobb–Douglas function of the individual stocks of the two capital types, with a factor share, $\alpha \in [0,1]$, of the other sector's capital type and a share $1 - \alpha$ of the sector's own capital type, that is,

$$c_i = \kappa_i^{-1} K_{ii}^{1-\alpha} K_{ij}^{\alpha} \qquad j \neq i \qquad (9.4)$$

where κ_i is a constant capital–output ratio. The parameter α thus determines the degree of coupling between the two sectors. In the simulation studies, the value of this parameter is varied between 0, indicating no interdependency between the sectors, and 1, indicating the strongest possible coupling where each sector is completely dependent on capital from the other sector.

The output from sector i, x_i, depends on the sector's capacity c_i, compared to the sector's desired output x_i^*. If desired output is much lower than capacity, production is cut back, ultimately to zero if no output is desired. Conversely, if desired output exceeds capacity, output can be increased beyond capacity, up to a certain limit. Hence

$$x_i = f\left(\frac{x_i^*}{c_i}\right) \cdot c_i \qquad (9.5)$$

where

$$f(0) = 0; \ f(1) = 1; \ \lim_{r \to \infty} f(r) = 1.1; \ f(r) > r \text{ for } 0 < r < 1 \qquad (9.6)$$

Sector i's desired output x_i^* is assumed to be the value that would allow firms in that sector to deliver the capital on order B_i with the (constant) normal average delivery delay δ_i for that sector. Hence,

$$x_i^* = \frac{B_i}{\delta_i} \tag{9.7}$$

Sector i's desired orders for new capital from sector j, o_{ij}^*, are assumed to consist of three components. First, *ceteris paribus*, firms will order to replace depreciation of their existing capital stock, K_{ij}/τ_j. Second, if their current capital stock is below (above) its desired level k_{ij}^*, firms will order more (less) capital in order to remove the discrepancy over time. Third, firms consider the current supply line S_{ij} of capital and compare it to its desired level s_{ij}^*; if the supply line is below (above) desired, firms order more (less) in order to increase (decrease) the supply line over time. In total,

$$o_{ij}^* = \frac{K_{ij}}{\tau_j} + \frac{k_{ij}^* - K_{ij}}{\tau_i^K} + \frac{s_{ij}^* - S_{ij}}{\tau_i^S} \tag{9.8}$$

where the parameters τ_i^K and τ_i^S are the desired adjustment times for capital stock and the supply line, respectively.

Actual orders, however, are limited to be non-zero (no cancellation of orders) and the fractional rate of expansion of the capital stock is also assumed to be limited. These restraints are accounted for through the expression

$$o_{ij} = (K_{ij}/\tau_j)\, g\left(\frac{o_{ij}^*}{K_{ij}/\tau_i} \right) \tag{9.9}$$

where

$$g(1) = g'(1) = 1; \quad g''(1) = 0; \quad \lim_{r \to \infty} g(r) = 6.0; \quad \lim_{r \to -\infty} g(r) = 0 \tag{9.10}$$

Note that $g(r)$ has a 'neutral' area around the steady state point, $r = 1$, where actual orders equal desired orders, which in turn equal current capital depreciation.

The desired capital stock, k_{ij}^*, is assumed to be proportional to the desired production level x_i^* with a constant capital–output ratio. Thus, it is assumed in this initial work that there is no substitution of the two capital types in the ordering decision, only in capacity. Hence,

$$k_{ij}^* = \kappa_{ij}\, x_i^* \tag{9.11}$$

where κ_{ij} is the capital–output ratio of capital type j in sector i.

In calculating their desired supply line, s_{ij}^*, firms are assumed to take account of the current delivery delay for each type of capital. Their target supply line is the level at which the deliveries of capital, given the current delivery delay, would equal the current depreciation of the capital stock. The current delivery delay of capital from a sector is the sector's backlog divided by its output. Thus,

$$s_{ij}^* = \frac{B_j}{x_j} \times \frac{K_{ij}}{\tau_j} \qquad (9.12)$$

Finally, the orders from consumers to each sector, g_i, are assumed to be exogenous, constant and equal for both sectors. The latter assumption is not without consequence, since the relative size of the consumer demands for the two types of capital can change the dynamics of the model considerably (see Kampmann 1984). This issue should be investigated in further work.

The capital–output ratios and average capital lifetimes are formulated in such a way that the aggregate equilibrium values of these parameters for the system as a whole remain constant, equal to their values in Sterman's (1985) original model, where the average lifetime of capital was 20 years and the capital–output ratio was 3 years (see Haxholdt *et al.* 1993). Furthermore, parameters in the decision rules were scaled to the average lifetime of capital produced by that sector. This means that, when there is no coupling between the sectors ($\alpha = 0$), one sector is simply a time-scaled version of the other. We felt that this approach was the cleanest way to investigate the coupling of two oscillators with different inherent frequencies.

Figure 9.1 shows a simulation of the limit cycle of the one-sector model. Even with the modifications we have introduced, the behaviour of our model is virtually indistinguishable from that of the original model (Sterman 1985). With the above parameters, the equilibrium point is unstable, and the system quickly settles into a long-term cycle with a period of approximately 47 years. Each new cycle begins with a period of rapid growth, where desired output significantly exceeds capacity. The capital sector is thus induced to order more capital from itself which, by further swelling order books, fuels the upturn in a self-reinforcing process. Eventually, capacity catches up with demand, but at this point it far exceeds the equilibrium level. The self-ordering process is now reversed, as falling orders from the capital sector lead to falling demand, which further depresses the capital sector's orders. Consequently, output quickly collapses to the point where only the exogenous goods sector places new orders. A long period of depression follows, where the excess capital is gradually depleted, until capacity finally reaches demand. At this point, however, capacity is below its equilibrium level, and the cycle is ready to start anew.

Simulation results

To understand some of the phenomena that can arise from interaction between different capital-producing sectors in a disaggregated economic long-wave model, we have performed a series of simulations with the two-sector model described above. In spite of its simplicity, this model contains a considerable number of

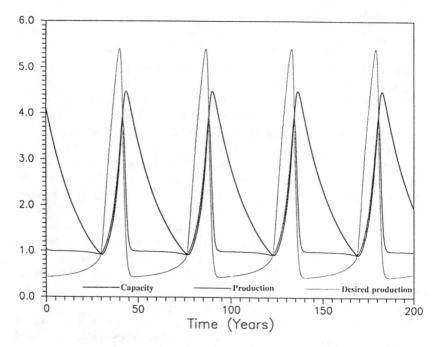

Figure 9.1 Simulation of the one-sector model. The steady-state behaviour is a limit cycle with a period of approximately 47 years. The plot shows the production capacity, the actual production and the desired production of capital equipment, respectively. All variables are shown on the same scale.

parameters which might differ from sector to sector. In the present study, we vary the difference in capital lifetimes, $\Delta\tau$, for different values of the coupling parameter, α. As described in the previous section, we have scaled all other parameters with the capital-lifetime parameters in such a way that, for no coupling between the sectors, they are simply time-scaled versions of the original one-sector model. In the simulations that follow, sector 1 is always the sector with the longest lifetime of its capital output, corresponding to such industries as housing and infrastructure, while sector 2 has the shortest lifetime parameter, corresponding to machinery, computers, and the like.

Introducing a coupling between the sectors will, apart from linking the behaviour together, also change the stability properties of the individual sector, taking the other sector as exogenous. Thus, a high value of the coupling parameter, α, implies that the strength of the capital self-ordering loop in any sector is small. In the extreme case $\alpha = 1$, neither sector will order any capital from itself. If the delivery delay of capital from the other sector is taken as

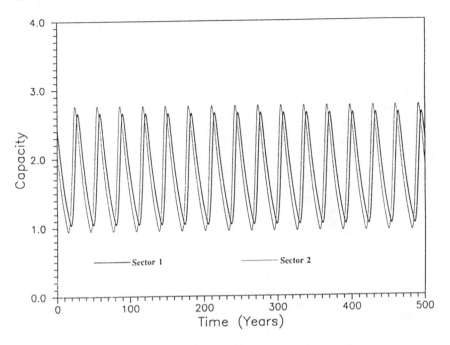

Figure 9.2 Synchronization (1:1 mode-locking) in the coupled two-sector model. The graph shows the capacity of the two sectors as a function of time in the steady state (after transients have died out). The difference in capital lifetimes, $\Delta\tau$, is 6 years (that is, the lifetime of capital types 1 and 2 is 23 and 17 years, respectively). The coupling parameter, α, is 0.25 here and in Figures 9.3–9.5. Due to nonlinear coupling, the two sectors are locked into a single cycle. The two sectors complete an equal number of cycles, that is, the mode-locking is 1:1.

exogenous and constant, the behaviour of the individual sector changes to a highly damped oscillation. Indeed, a linear stability analysis around the steady-state equilibrium of the individual sector shows that this equilibrium becomes stable for sufficiently high values of α. As will become evident below, this stability effect of the coupling parameter has significant effects on the mode-locking behaviour of the coupled system.

As long as the two sectors have fairly similar parameters, we expect synchronization (or 1:1 frequency locking) to occur, that is to say, we expect that the two sectors will adjust themselves to one another and exhibit a single aggregate economic long wave with the same period for both sectors. The same may be true for sufficiently high coupling strengths, irrespective of differences in sector parameters.

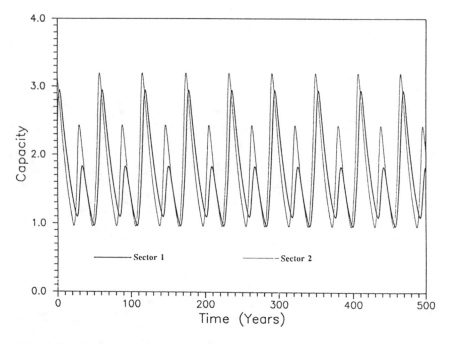

Figure 9.3 Period doubling (2:2 mode-locking) resulting from increased lifetime difference. As $\Delta\tau$ is increased to 9 years, the uniform cycle is replaced by an alternating pattern of smaller and larger cycles so that the total period is doubled. As in Figure 9.2, α = 0.25. The two sectors still complete an equal number of cycles, that is, the mode-locking is 2:2.

As an example of such synchronization, Figure 9.2 shows the outcome of a simulation performed with a difference in capital lifetimes between the two sectors of $\Delta\tau = 6$ years and a coupling parameter $\alpha = 0.25$. It shows that the two sectors, although not quite in phase, have identical periods of oscillation. The larger excursions in production capacity are found for sector 2, which is also the sector that leads in phase. Sector 2 is the sector with the shorter lifetime of its capital product, and this sector may thus be identified as the machinery industry. $\Delta\tau = 6$ years corresponds to a lifetime for machinery capital of 17 years and a lifetime of houses and infrastructure of 23 years.

If, with the same coupling parameters, the difference in capital lifetimes is increased to $\Delta\tau = 9$ years, we observe a doubling of the period. The two sectors now alternate between high and low maxima for their production capacities. This type of behaviour is referred to as a 2:2 mode. It has developed out of the synchronous 1:1 mode through a period–doubling bifurcation (Feigenbaum 1978).

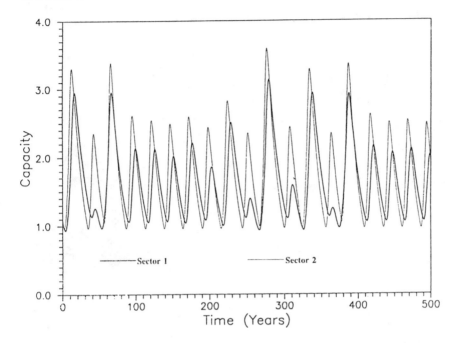

Figure 9.4 Chaotic behaviour. As $\Delta\tau$ is increased further, the model exhibits a progression of period doublings, which at some point become infinitely dense. Just beyond this point, as here where $\Delta\tau$ is 10.7 years, the behaviour is chaotic. (As in Figures 9.2 and 9.3, $\alpha = 0.25$.) The model shows no regular periodic behaviour, and initial conditions close to each other quickly diverge so that, in practice, the behaviour is unpredictable. Note that the behaviour nevertheless remains similar to the original uniform cycle, except that the individual cycles vary greatly in size.

The 2:2 solution is illustrated in Figure 9.3. Again, both the temporal variations of the two production capacities and the corresponding phase plot are shown. In the phase plot, the stationary solution now performs two loops before closing precisely on itself. We conclude from this simulation that the presence of two capital-producing sectors with different parameters can lead to a period-doubling, a phenomenon that cannot develop in the aggregated one-sector model without external forcing.

As the difference in lifetimes is further increased, the model passes through a Feigenbaum cascade of period-doubling bifurcations (4:4, 8:8, etc.) to reach chaos at approximately $\Delta\tau = 10.4$ years. Figure 9.4 shows the chaotic solution existing for $\Delta\tau = 10.7$ years. Calculation of the largest Lyaponov exponent (Wolf 1986) confirms that the solution in Figure 9.4 is chaotic. We conclude that deterministic

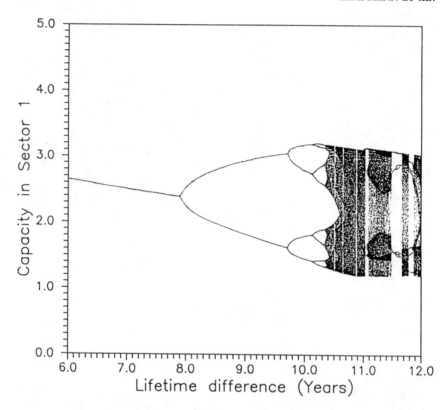

Figure 9.5 Bifurcation diagram for increasing lifetime difference and constant coupling. The diagram shows the local maxima attained for the capacity of sector 1 (the longer-lived capital producer) in the steady-state behaviour for varying values of $\Delta\tau$. The parameter α is held constant at 0.25. For a given $\Delta\tau$, a single capacity value indicates a uniform limit cycle; two values indicate a period doubling with a smaller and larger cycle. In chaotic regions, the number of local maxima is infinite since no individual cycles are identical.

chaos can arise in a macro-economic model which in its aggregated form supports self-sustained oscillations, if the various sectors, because of differences in parameter values, fail to synchronize.

A more detailed illustration of the route to chaos is provided by the bifurcation diagram in Figure 9.5. Here, we have plotted the maximum production capacity attained in sector 1 over each cycle as a function of the lifetime difference $\Delta\tau$. The coupling parameter α is kept constant and equal to 0.25.

Inspection of Figure 9.5 shows that the 1:1 frequency locking, in which the production capacity of sector 1 reaches the same maximum in each long-wave upswing, is maintained up to $\Delta\tau \cong 8.0$ years, where the first period-doubling bifurcation occurs. In the interval 8.0 years $< \Delta\tau < 9.7$ years, the long-wave upswings alternate between a high and a low maximum. There then follows an interval up to approximately $\Delta\tau = 10.1$ years with 4:4 locking, an interval with 8:8 locking, and so on. In the chaotic regime, we find periodic windows deriving from the 1:1 solution, such as the 10:10 and 7:7 solutions existing around $\Delta\tau = 11.6$ years and $\Delta\tau = 11.85$ years, respectively.

However, in these intervals, other stationary solutions may exist as well, and these solutions may be reached from different sets of initial conditions. The phase diagram in Figure 9.6 gives an overview of the dominant modes for different combinations of the lifetime difference $\Delta\tau$ and the coupling parameter α. The zones of mode-locked (that is, periodic) solutions in this diagram are referred to as Arnol'd tongues (Arnol'd 1965). Besides the 1:1 tongue, the figure shows a series of 1:n tongues, that is to say, regions in parameter space where the buildings industry completes precisely one long-wave oscillation each time the machinery industry completes n oscillations. Between these tongues, regions with other commensurate wave periods may be observed. An example is the 2:3 tongue found in the area around $\alpha = 0.15$ and $\Delta\tau = 12$ years.

Similar to the 2:2 period-doubled solution on the right-hand side of the 1:1 tongue, there is a 2:4 period-doubled solution along part of the right-hand edge of the 1:2 tongue. It is likely that similar phenomena may be found along the edges of the 1:3 and 1:4 tongues, and so on, producing a fractal, self-similar structure. However, at present we have not yet investigated the structure in detail.

The phase diagram in Figure 9.6 also reveals that the synchronous 1:1 solution extends to the full range of the lifetime difference, $\Delta\tau$, for sufficiently high values of the coupling parameter, α. We believe that the cause lies in the stabilizing effect of high values of α on the individual sectors. When α is sufficiently large, the equilibrium of the individual sectors becomes stable, when the delivery delay and demand from the other sector is taken as exogenous. For reference, two curves have been drawn in Figure 9.6, defining the regions in which one or both of these individual equilibria are stable: For a given value of the lifetime difference, values of α above the curve result in a stable individual sector equilibrium.

As α increases, the overall behaviour is more and more derived from the coupled capital self-ordering feedback, and less and less from the autonomous self-ordering mechanism in each individual sector. Thus, for high values of α, there is less competition between the two individual, autonomous oscillations, and therefore less prevalence of the normal mode-locking phenomena.

For large differences in capital lifetimes and low values of α, the short-lived sector (sector 2) completes several cycles for each oscillation of the long-lived sector (sector 1). However, as α is increased, the short-term cycle is reduced in amplitude, and, for sufficiently high αs, it disappears altogether, resulting in a synchronous 1:1 solution.

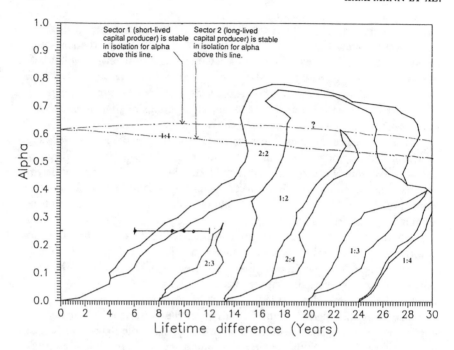

Figure 9.6 Parameter phase diagram. The diagram summarizes the steady-state behaviour of the two-sector model for different combinations of α and $\Delta\tau$. A region labelled '$p{:}q$' indicates the area in the parameter space where the model shows periodic mode-locked behaviour of p cycles for sector 1 and q cycles for sector 2. (However, other solutions may coexist at the same point in the diagram, depending on the initial conditions of the model.) The question mark indicates that the details of the diagram are still under exploration. In particular, regions of chaotic behaviour have not yet been outlined in detail. The dashed curves across the diagram indicate the value of α above which each sector in isolation (with the other sector treated as exogenous) becomes stable and the cycles are created solely by the interaction of the two sectors. This effect implies that, for large α, synchronous behaviour becomes more and more prevalent. Finally the line $\alpha = 0.25$ and $6 \leq \Delta\tau \leq 12$ years locates the region examined in the previous figures.

The locally stabilizing effect of high values of α creates a complicated distortion of the Arnol'd tongues in Figure 9.6. For instance, Figure 9.6 reveals that both the 1:1 region and the 2:2 region are folded down above the other regions for high values of $\Delta\tau$.

Moreover, it appears that the phase diagram contains other routes to chaos than through period-doubling bifurcations. In particular, the region between the 2:2 tongue and the 1:2 tongue should be explored. We have not yet been able to delineate in detail how the 1:2 tongue ends at high coupling strengths.

In the continuation of the study, we intend to chart the Arnol'd diagram in more detail. In particular, the areas of high coupling strength are likely to contain overlapping solutions which cannot be uncovered with a simple simulation approach. The more detailed analysis will involve tracing the boundaries of each tongue into the region of overlap.

Conclusions

The present paper represents work in progress and the results are necessarily incomplete. In particular, the details of the phase diagram in Figure 9.6 remain to be explored. However, even at this preliminary stage, we can draw implications for both the validity of the simple long-wave model and for economic theory in general.

By employing only a single capital-producing sector, the simple long-wave model represents a simplification of the structure of capital and production. In reality, capital is composed of diverse components with very different characteristics. We have focused on the difference in the average lifetime of capital, and it is clear from our analysis that a disaggregate system with diverse capital components exhibits a much wider variety of fluctuations. For strong and moderate degrees of coupling this has the effect of merging individual cycles into a more uniform coherent cycle. Moreover, the period of individual cycles remains in the 50-year range, although the amplitude may vary greatly from one cycle to the next. The synchronized behaviour of the two–sector model thus retains the essential features of the simple model. On the other hand, it is not clear whether realistic parameter assumptions would fall within the region of synchronization.

However, our analysis has relied only on the coupling introduced by the input–output structure of capital production and has ignored the many other sources of linkage. The most obvious links are created by the price system. If, for instance, one type of capital is in short supply, one would expect the relative price of that capital to rise. To the extent that sectors can substitute different types of capital in their production, one would then expect demand for the other, relatively cheaper, capital components to rise. Thus, an imbalance in one sector would more quickly spread to other parts of the economy, and it is likely that the overall motion of the system becomes more coherent. (We have performed a few preliminary simulations of a version of the model that includes a price system, and these simulations show a strong tendency for synchronization.) In this connection, the degree of substitution between capital types in the production function may well be an important factor: one would expect high elasticities of substitution to yield more coherent overall behaviour. The next step in our work would therefore involve introducing relative prices and different degrees of substitution.

In light of the coupling effect of the price system and of other macro-economic linkages (for example, the Keynesian consumption multiplier), one would therefore expect disaggregate capital systems to show a coherent long-wave motion for a wide range of parameter values, and the basic validity of the simple one-sector model seems intact. Thus, the fact that the simple model aggregates capital into a single commodity does not give cause for doubt about the theory. More important modifications may arise when one explicitly considers other factors excluded from the model, such as labour, wages and interest rates. Thus, an important future step will be to extend the simple long-wave model to include other macro-economic linkages.

Another, more immediate extension of our study would involve looking at more than two sectors. It is far from self-evident how a many-sector system would behave. On the one hand, a wider variety of capital producers would introduce more variability in the behaviour and, hence, less uniformity. On the other hand, as the system is disaggregated further, the strength of individual self-ordering loops within sectors is reduced to near zero (the α parameter approaches 1), and overall cycles arise exclusively from the interaction between sectors. This, as we have seen, would tend to lead to more uniform behaviour. The results from earlier studies with more than two sectors (Kampmann 1984) indicate that the former effect is likely to dominate, that is, the system behaviour becomes less regular.

For economic theory in general, our results hopefully demonstrate the importance of studying nonlinear coupling in the economic system. The intricacies of such phenomena suggest that there is a vast unexplored domain of research in the area of economic cycles, and that results from such studies may well prove counter-intuitive and, hence, generate new insights into the causes and cures of business cycles. We believe that nonlinear entrainment plays a much larger role in shaping economic cycles than the correlations from common external random shocks on which much of mainstream business cycle theory relies.

10 Managing Uncertainty in Complex Systems: Financial Markets

Peter M. Allen and Hoon K. Phang

D 81   G20

Introduction

Innovation and change make the details of the future uncertain, and our capacity to innovate and respond provides a way of surviving nevertheless. The conclusions of a preceding chapter in this volume (Allen) were that although rational, causal models of systems represent an instantaneous description of how the system is working at a particular time, because they are necessarily incomplete, the system structure will evolve over time, as new variables, mechanisms and values emerge. This evolution was also seen to be necessarily unpredictable to some degree, although mathematical models have been developed which can successfully generate an evolutionary tree, and can be used to examine the mechanisms that allow adaptability and evolutionary change (Allen 1988b; 1990; Allen and Lesser 1991).

A range of applications of these ideas has been developed over the years, ranging from urban and regional evolution, through fisheries models and ecology to economics and financial matters. What they show is that evolution both leads to, and is driven by, the presence of micro-diversity in populations and groups. Nature's way of dealing with the uncertainty of the future is to have a diverse population of parallel strategies enjoying differential success over time. The key element in their long-term survival is the capacity to continue to generate microscopic diversity, even when for a particular period, the 'best possible' strategy seems to be clear. Following the pioneering work of Nelson and Winter, it is clear that technology change and economic evolution work on similar principles, and that the survival of companies in a particular sector requires that they perform reasonably efficiently, but also that they constantly test the possible rewards arising from modified products and different production techniques. This paper will focus on the implications of these general ideas of 'evolutionary drive' for decision-making and trading strategies in the context of financial markets.

Intelligence and learning in a financial market

Financial markets offer us an interesting and archetypal example of a complex system. There is a macroscopic level – for example for a variable like 'price' – and there is also a microscopic level of the many different actors attempting to anticipate changes in price, and searching for effective strategies to do this. But, despite this, the financial market is characterized by the 'centrality' of the activity of buying and selling, and in this way avoids the greater complication of a spatial market system. It therefore provides a simpler, homogeneous environment for study whereby prices comprise the most important observable.

As mentioned above, the traditional paradigm of understanding in this arena has been built around the concept of equilibrium and the rational expectations theory. Also, because probability calculus was adopted as the mathematical basis of financial theories, it was not surprising that price distributions were assumed to be 'normal'. General equilibrium theory and the 'efficient market' hypothesis portray changes in the market as being due to external factors represented as a *random walk* (Osborne 1964; Muth 1961; Fama 1970). The appropriateness of this approach has since been fiercely debated partly because of the adoption of simplifying assumptions about the way investors behave and the correspondence of the resulting analytic framework to reality. Although statistical inference was able to provide a vast array of modelling and research tools, the limitations imposed by the underlying assumptions clearly underestimated crucial and complex mechanisms that endogenously drive events within the financial system.

The subsequent realization that equilibrium forms only a partial view and indications of the existence of *instability* through market crashes has motivated the search for alternative paradigms. Nonlinear dynamics, in particular *chaos theory*, has inspired many in their research (Day 1983; Grandmont and Malgrange 1986; Chen 1988; Kesley 1988; Savit 1988; 1989; Peters 1989; 1991a; 1991b; Scheinkman and LeBaron 1989; Blank 1991; Hsieh 1991; Larrain 1991). In order to apply the mathematics, one needs to identify, as a first step, the existence of nonlinearities as well as chaotic behaviours in the time series concerned. Interestingly, most analytical results indicated that nonlinearities and chaotic behaviours do indeed exist marginally in most cases.

Although deterministic chaos itself is a very interesting phenomenon and has given rise to much exciting research, the implications of the earlier paper in this volume (Allen) are that differential equations are in any case an inadequate description of the evolution of such systems, and that the underlying micro-diversity of actors needs to be taken into account explicitly. In reality, the strategies used by different actors are also 'produced' within the system and local variations are constantly testing the effects of possible modifications. Here we shall examine the evolution of successful strategies in the 'possibility space' of trading rules.

Rational analysis is the traditional scientific approach to problems, and it can deal successfully with a system which is knowable, providing that we know what it is that we would like to minimize or maximize, and of course we would only be able to know what would be good 'objectives' if we knew and understood the system. But in contrast, evolution shows us how to deal with a system that cannot be known completely, and for which, in consequence, we cannot formulate clear goals.

In a particular financial market clearly all the participants cannot focus on a single optimal strategy, because if this were so then if someone wanted to buy nobody would want to sell! The stable functioning of a market can only result from the establishment of diverse, varied and changing strategies which are complementary to each other. As was discussed elsewhere (Allen, this volume) such systems represent a new domain of organization beyond the 'mechanical' where the strategies of traders are mutually interdependent, the system has many possible responses to perturbations and where survival is related to the *capacity to change*. An important feature of this capacity to change is that it involves suboptimal behaviours, imperfect information, mistaken inferences and the power of creativity.

Let us consider financial markets from these points of view. At first it seems quite clear that our objective is to make profits over some particular time scale, and that therefore rational analysis of the 'system' is what is required. But, of course, everyone wants to make profits and therefore to buy 'cheap' and sell 'dear'. So, the real difference between the players in the market concerns what they believe about the future value of what they buy or sell. Indeed, for one player to buy what another sells implies that they almost certainly believe opposite things about the future movement of its price, or possibly that they are operating on different time scales. The important point, however, is that there are many ways in which one can arrive at a view concerning whether a stock should be bought or sold and at what price.

Trading strategies are quite naturally the subject of constant discussion and debate within financial circles. Mostly, positions and views are held as a result of personal history and experience and beliefs about how the world works. But, of course, trading strategies concern the *future*, that is, they are about actions which should be taken in order that the future will be influenced in a certain way. And this, in turn, implies that we are seeking a strategy which can give good results despite the fact that we *cannot* know *the* future, because there are in fact different possible futures. When some trends in the markets become apparent, the traders will then react to this, and by their actions change what subsequently will occur in reality. This implies that markets will always drive themselves to the *'edge' of predictability* and therefore we should try to understand and learn to manage the processes of change rather than predict future prices.

Thus, it becomes quite clear that in order to deal with the 'unknown' future successfully, or at least sustainably, diversity and adaptability in the strategies adopted are most important, rather than finding the single 'optimal' strategy. Systems that simultaneously modify the macro-structure as well as the nature of the underlying micro-components require more than the usual 'mechanical' solutions that had been so excessively prescribed in the past. *Intelligence* in managing such systems, financial markets in this case, depends very much on the capacity to change and the time scale of this adaptability is vital in determining success and sustainability. Similarly, the role of diversity should be emphasized for fear of falling into the positive feedback trap, in the event where success overshadows linkages to the external environment and subsequently, overlooking the need to persist in the exploration of the continuously changing strategy space.

A self-adaptive trading model

In order to examine these issues, we have developed a trading model, and, using ideas inspired by the evolutionary approach, made it self-adapting. A popular and relatively elementary mechanism, the *moving average* method, was chosen to produce the appropriate trading signals. Despite the proliferation of analytical methods used in practice, the moving average is one of the simplest, yet most versatile and widely used of all technical indicators (Murphy 1986). Because of the way it is constructed and the fact that it can be easily quantified and tested, it is the basis for many mechanical trend-following systems in use today.

A moving average calculates the mean of the most recent values of an ongoing time series. It has to be decided over how far back (usually in days) the moving average will extend. The body of data to be averaged moves forward with each new trading period. The period to be used is a nominal number that is subjective to each individual user and it is this number that, more often than not, determines the success of a strategy that employs the method.

Essentially, moving averages are calculated every day, and since these are figures based on the last *n* available measurements, the line formed by connecting these averages will lag the actual price line, which will cross it whenever a trend reverses. It is this crossing phenomenon that is taken to indicate a change in price trend, and hence a moment to buy or sell the commodity in question. The moving average is a follower, not a leader. It never anticipates, it only reacts. The manner of interpretation really depends on each individual and it is both the selection of the period *n* and the timing of each transaction that command the success of such a strategy. If the price of a commodity traces out a fluctuating path, moving unpredictably through peaks and troughs, then providing that the up and down trends can be detected early enough, profit can be made by applying the moving average method. It usually signals a change in trend when the price curve cuts the moving average curve. However, this method can also go astray if the price produces a 'spike', cutting the moving average curve and then immediately cutting it in the opposite direction. Such an event will result in losses − not just because of buying high and selling low, but also due to trading costs.

A *bandwidth* can be added to this method to act as a precaution against unnecessary trades. This is a measure above as well as below the calculated moving average curve. Trades are signalled not when the moving average curve cuts the original price curve, but when it breaks through the band both sides of the price curve. This reduces the number of instances when 'spikes' would have initiated a false trade.

For this particular problem therefore, we can define the 'possibility space' for the evolutionary/learning process. It is the space of all possible strategies. Figure 10.1 illustrates the two-dimensional strategy spaces of the nickel futures contract taken at different time intervals based on the moving average period and bandwidth parameter. The variability in the landscape caused by pay-offs changing at different parts of the curve captures succinctly the problem that a static strategy will face if used throughout the period. The unevenness shows that a particular strategy has good and bad patches and, unless adaptability is introduced, the strategy will not be sustainable.

Basically, the self-adaptive concept entails the division of the historical period into several equal sections, which we will call x. To start the simulation, the strategy first selects for the 'best' moving average period n, and best bandwidth, from a potential array of parallel strategies over section x based on the criteria set. This period n is then used in the trading simulation for the next period y. At the end of period y, the strategy looks back at that point in time into a period of x duration before and performs the selection process again. The trading simulation is then repeated for the next period y and so on. Therefore, the value of n and the bandwidth used will differ from one period y to another and it shows the changes in volatility, caused possibly by changes in world events, in the relevant markets' underlying fundamentals, or changes in other actors' strategies.

Besides selecting for the 'best' strategy from an array of *parallel strategies*, the model also investigates for the appropriate time scales in which the strategy can most ideally operate. x is really the length of time period in which one believes that the *current prevailing dynamics* persists. On the other hand, parameter y denotes the *persistence time* of the collective dynamics found in the period x before. In other words, a good strategy found in a period x will be used in the coming y period as that is the time horizon in which the prevailing dynamics of the market is found to persist. The entire process is then repeated to establish the new strategy that will work in the dynamics of the next period, and the same throughout the whole historical period.

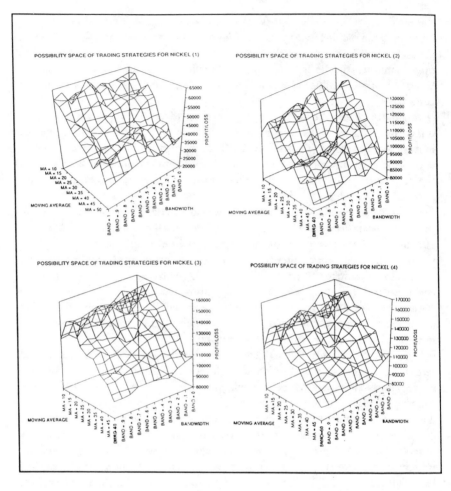

Figure 10.1   The landscape of returns experienced by different strategy parameters over different periods.

The trading model includes things like commission charges incurred in executing trades, fluctuations in exchange rates as well as slippage costs when transactions were not carried out at the expected price as a result of delays in communicating trades to the trading floor. These factor bring a sense of reality to the simulation results obtained.

Discussion of simulation results

Simulations on two types of price time series were carried out using this model. The first group consists of *real* time series data gathered from financial markets, while the second were *generated* time series. The latter were generated from random as well as chaotic equations, and thus are driven explicitly by the respective mechanisms.

First, we will discuss the results of trading in the real market environment. These time series span a spectrum of futures contracts – metals, soft commodities, a financial index and currencies – each over a total of 44 months to the 31 December 1991 (see Table 10.1). The results showed that without using any information from the future, a remarkable level of profit was possible.

The characteristics of the various time series had a significant impact on the use of strategies at different times, which indicated that the model was indeed adjusting to changing conditions. This concept, with the strategy *coevolving* with changing dynamics in the markets, clearly corresponds to the basis of the evolutionary framework.

In addition to trading on real time series, we have also used different mathematical formulae of randomness or chaos to generate 'artificial' time series: biased and unbiased random walks, logistic chaos, and the Lorentz and Rossler equations. The simulation results displayed an improvement over the static strategy similar to that obtained for the first group of real time series. Only a minority of four out the 18 time series produced worse results. Unlike the real time series, where noise is present, these generated time series are purely driven by the underlying generating mechanisms used. Random walks of various kinds as

Table 10.1   Types of futures contract time series

Metal	Gold
	Nickel
	Aluminium
	Copper
Soft commodities	Cocoa
	Coffee
	Sugar
Financial futures	Financial Times Stock Exchange 100 Index
Currencies	US dollar/sterling
	US dollar/DM
	US dollar/Swiss franc
	US dollar/yen

well as chaotic equations were used to generate these price time series. This simulation exercise reveals the evolutionary concept's capacity to deal with time series that are supposedly unpredictable.

By being able to deal successfully with an unknown future, the trading model developed has shown its resilience to unpredictability. The potential diversity of strategies captured in the model lies in the form of 50 or so variations of moving average method. By reinforcing the successful strategy, the model adapts to changing price dynamics and in the process produces better performance. Thus, the model shows us that the evolutionary approach has the capacity to deal successfully and sustainably with an unknown future. From this, intelligence is not the ability to achieve optimal performance in the short term but the capacity to know how and when to change strategy. In systems where events are dependent on the strategies of surrounding populations, continual modification of views and a process of imperfect learning are the only form of intelligence.

As an interesting aside, the model can be extended to study further the effects of positive feedback by channelling the impact of trading activities directly on to price returns and the subsequent altered course of events.

Portfolio management

In addition to the model described above, the different commodities and currencies trading have been combined in a 'self-adapting' portfolio system. In this, the recent success of trading in different commodities affects the number of lots that are traded. This trading can be either long (buying what you do not have) or short (selling what you do not have), and all that matters is that the trading success over the last period affects the weighting of the 'attractivity' of the commodity. In addition, we have a measure of the accumulated 'reliability' of a particular commodity or currency, and this, too, plays a role in the weights accorded. If our trading system is not working well in copper, for example, then the losses will lead to the system reducing the number of lots traded, while if it is doing well, the inverse will occur. We also have a parameter, which the user is free to choose, which determines the 'strength' of the portfolio management. If it is set to zero, then whatever the trading has been like, there is an even spread of investment right across the portfolio. If the value is set high, then the fund is strongly concentrated in the contracts that have been performing well.

In order to give some idea of the potential performance of this kind of 'evolutionary intelligent' model, the portfolio gains for the period over the past 15 months range between 50% annual rate of return with no portfolio management, and 140% annual rate of return with strong management (Figure 10.2).

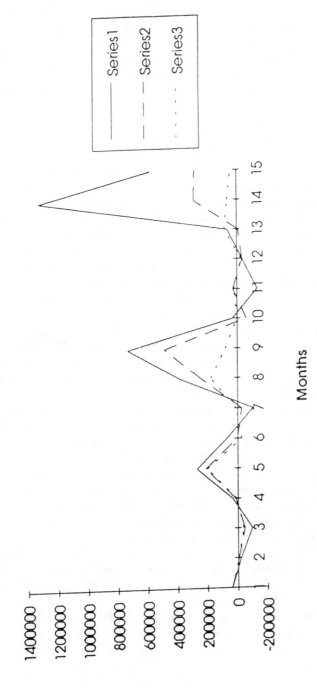

Figure 10.2 The successive (not cumulative) trading gains and losses over the 15 months. Series 1 has a management strength of 100, series 2 of 30 and series 3 of 0.

General discussion

In this and earlier papers, it has been shown that the evolution of complex systems is a process that goes beyond the 'mechanical' paradigm. Instead of the system being viewed as a 'point' moving on a trajectory in some fixed landscape of attractors, we see not only that is the landscape itself generated by the actors in interaction, but also that the system itself can never be reduced to a 'point' in phase space because of its internal variability and the information flows concerning other behaviours, strategies or technologies. The macroscopic description in terms of differential equations is an approximation to reality, within which there is an underlying microscopic diversity, which explores the stability of the 'taxonomy' that has led to the choice of variables in the model. Not only is this micro-diversity itself important, but equally vital are the processes which provide and maintain this diversity, processes of 'error-making' and imperfectly transmitted rational views and information at the individual, microscopic level, which confers creativity and seeming intelligence on the system as a whole.

Because of creativity and learning, the only *certainty* in an evolutionary system is *uncertainty*. At any particular instant imperfect information concerning 'what to do' is inevitable if the system is creative, and naturally creativity is in turn inevitable if the individual, micro-level components do not know exactly what they should do for the best, and indeed what factors define 'best'. Long-term success is not just about improving performance with respect to the external environment of resources and technology, but also is affected by the 'internal game' of a complex society. The 'pay-off' of any action for an individual cannot be stated in absolute terms, because it depends on what other individuals are doing. Strategies are interdependent.

Ecological organization is what results from evolution, and it is composed of self-consistent 'sets' of activities or strategies, both posing and solving the problems and opportunities of their mutual existence, as a result of varying views and initiatives which, when positive feedback outweighs negative, leads to a new feature in the system. Value is assigned afterwards as a '*post-hoc* explanation' rationalizing events by pretending that there was some pre-existing 'niche' which was *revealed*, although in reality there may have been a million possible niches, and just one in particular arose.

The future, then, is not contained in the present, since the landscape is fashioned by the explorations of climbers, and adaptability will always be required. Intelligence is the 'cognitive' response to this demand, and the problem we face is that of making successful rather than unsuccessful adaptations over time.

How, then, can we learn in an uncertain world? The answer is through the 'evolutionary approach'. The weighting attached to different possible visions of the world and hence to possible strategies must be reinforced or diminished according to their relative success. Our financial model demonstrates that, even in chaotic systems, although short-term 'learning' is impossible, our trading model can still make a profit, since this is equivalent to learning in a statistical, longer-term sense. Because the chaotic attractor is fixed, in our examples, the adaptive system can find parameters which trade successfully. If, on the other hand, the chaotic system were changing over time, then it would perhaps be more difficult to succeed, and in fact, the chaotic attractor would change if any significant actors succeeded in 'learning' which parameters were successful. This is what was meant earlier by saying that the system runs itself on the edge of predictability. The contest then is between actors with different 'speeds' of learning, so that money can be made even in a chaotic system, provided that one continues to learn and adapt.

Technological change provides evidence of just this kind of evolutionary process. It both drives and is driven by the differential selection of diverse micro-behaviours, rewarding firms that can generate, identify and use new knowledge, and spurring others on to try to do better. Instead of focusing only on the physical manifestations of a successful technology or strategy, after it has occurred, we need to understand the underlying processes that allow adaptability and learning within an organization. In the financial example discussed here, it was possible to run all strategies of a certain kind in parallel, and to allow a portfolio of them to evolve over time. Clearly, this suggests a similar approach for technological evolution, where several strategies need to be simultaneously present, and a balanced portfolio needs to survive in order to deal effectively with future uncertainties. This concerns the balance between individual freedom and managerial control both within firms and across sectors of the economy, as well as their information-gathering capacities, the ability of societies to generate 'useless' (until now) information and make it potentially available, and the receptivity and adaptiveness of organizations. The new understanding of the evolutionary process therefore shows us the severe limitations of the idea of 'best practice' and 'cost-cutting' as a universal strategy, showing us instead the value of a 'portfolio' approach to life, since survival is ultimately more important than efficiency.

Acknowledgement

This work was partially supported by Toppan Moore Systems Limited (Japan). We are grateful for the support of NASA, and also of the Open Society Fund of New York.

Part IV: Contributions from the Sociology of Technology

11 Academic–Industry Relations: A Sociological Paradigm for Economic Development

Henry Etzkowitz

030

010

Introduction

What are the necessary and sufficient conditions to produce a self-sustaining chain reaction of high-technology firms, a Cambridge phenomenon or a Route 128? It has become a central issue of economic development policy, an article of faith based upon some historical fact, that linking research universities to a source of private or state venture capital will result in the formation of new firms. Scientists and engineers have become capitalists even as science and technology becomes a more central element of production, as important as labour or financial capital (Webster and Etzkowitz 1991).

The stage theory of economic development, in which countries must all go through the same series of steps in lock-step order, has been superceded. What has emerged instead is a set of relationships among universities, industry and government. Universities, even those left behind as isolated entities from a colonial era, are being reorientated towards their local economy. As more countries see scientific research as a key to economic development, science policy has become tied to technology policy and both of these have become instruments of economic development. This has led to government policies to encourage academic–industry ties in industrialized and industrializing countries (capitalist or former socialist), at the national and regional levels, in the First, Second and Third Worlds (Parker 1992).

Evolutionary paradigms and Schumpeterian analysis provide us with a methodology for viewing technological change as a causal factor of economic development rather than as a residual category. While the evolutionary model offers a means to account for technological change, it tends to view new developments as random occurrences which are then 'selected' and capitalized upon (Nelson and Winter 1982). Evolutionary economics, of course, recognizes the importance of analysing revisions, in purpose and organizational structure of institutions such as universities, companies and governments, for understanding processes of technological change. While not all of these events are the result of human internationality, a significant historical proportion are. This paper shows the importance to technological change of identifiable individuals and groups that have marshalled resources to realize well-thought-out plans for institutional change. Moreover, in time, incremental initiatives and reforms can bring about a qualitative shift in purpose that merits a more far-reaching designation. The emergence of academic relations with industry and of technology transfer as an explicit university mission, in the late twentieth century, is an academic revolution as potentially far-reaching as the one that made research an academic goal during the late nineteenth century.

Academic–industry relations and technological change

Economists typically view land, labour and capital as the primary sources of economic productivity. Technological change has been a component of a 'residual' variable consisting of what could not be explained by the three traditional factors of production. After the Second World War, economists began to view technological change as an important factor in the creation of economic productivity. A strong relationship was identified between the amount of resources committed to research in an area of technology and the rate of technological advance. Thus, the amount of expenditure for research and development was identified as the best indicator of technological change. But this finding left unanswered the question of just how technological change takes place. Three major hypotheses have been set forth to address this question: the self-generation of technology; economic demand exercised through the market-place; and organizational innovations by governments, corporations, social movements and universities.

One argument is that technology drives itself through a cumulative and self-generating dynamic (Rosenberg 1976: 110). Thus, the imbalance between a highly productive machine is one part of a manufacturing process and a less productive machine in another part of the same process is a strong incentive to the development of new techniques. For example, 'Ray's flying shuttle led to the need for speeding up spinning operations; the eventual innovations in spinning in turn created the shortage of weaving capacity which finally culminated in Cartwright's introduction of the power loom' (Rosenberg 1976: 112). Other examples of imbalance among interdependent processes that led to technical advance include bicycle manufacture, steel production and rifle ordnance. However, these instances of one highly productive component in a technological complex stimulating innovations elsewhere in an interdependent system occurred only after the key element in the technology was already established. Thus, metal-forming tools for bicycle manufacture and the Bessemer process of steel production were already widely used before they created an imbalance that stimulated innovation in related technical areas. However, the Bessemer process itself only slowly replaced previous processes of steel production even though it was more efficient and available. Thus, while the thesis of technical imbalance helps explain the creation of additional advances once the basic element of a new technology is in place, it does not explain the origination of new areas of technology.

A second argument is that technological progress is the result of the economic demand for new products by potential users, leading corporations to fund research to develop them in the expectation that profits will result. Economic demand is a plausible explanation of the direction of technological change in those areas of the economy in which market forces predominate. However, in industries in which a few corporations predominate or in areas where the government provides most of the funds for research and development, such as military and health technologies, the market is less important than organizations and their actions.

The third argument is that organizational innovations drive technological change. These include such diverse phenomena as the transformation of patent protection from an individual to a corporate right, as well, allowing technology to be suppressed (Stern 1956); national economic development projects, such as canals and railways, that advanced civil engineering in the nineteenth century; academic involvement in the development of military technologies in the twentieth century (Groueff 1967); the impetus of social movements, such as that of space-flight enthusiasts in early twentieth-century Germany and the United States (Bainbridge 1976) and the reopening of mature technologies to technical advance by the environmental movement. The interaction between universities and industry produces inter-organizational innovations.

The rapid growth in new and traditional forms of linkage between industry and universities is the basis of an emergent sociological paradigm for economic development. Future economic growth is dependent not simply on a new cycle of innovation but on a new structure for innovation that ties basic and applied research ever more closely together. Although the locus of academic–industry relations has shifted in recent years to basic research disciplines such as solid-state physics and molecular biology, exemplars of the relationships between science and business can be found in chemistry in the mid-nineteenth century (Etzkowitz 1983) and in pharmaceutical science even earlier (Gustin 1975).

Academic–industry relations were institutionalized in the late nineteenth century along with the creation of new scientific disciplines derived from the solution of industrial problems. Richard Nelson has called attention to the rise of electrical and chemical engineering out of lines of applied research and technological development (Nelson, this volume). For example, in the early twentieth century William Walker, an MIT professor, invented 'unit operations', the basis of chemical engineering, in cooperation with the Arthur D. Little Consulting firm with which he was also affiliated. The unit-operations concept provided chemical companies with a reliable means to improve their production processes and gave academics a methodology for conducting research and training students in the monitoring and control of chemical manufacturing. Cooperative programmes, established by universities and companies for students to work in industry as part of their academic training, provided a framework for cooperation between the two spheres (Servos 1980). A similar interaction between university and industry took place in electrical engineering (Wildes and Lindgren 1985). Thus, chemical engineering and electrical engineering exemplify one model of university—industry relations: analysis of industrial problems by researchers based in engineering schools and technological universities.

Arguing that engineering schools represent the primary academic site for relationships with industry, Nelson also notes the appearance of the biotechnology industry from academic research in molecular biology as an alternative, anomalous development. The development of industrial companies from basic academic research in biology and from molecular modelling in chemistry represents a second model of university—industry relations: formation of firms by researchers exploiting the technological and commercial implications of their discoveries. In the 'applied' model of university—industry relations there is a movement from technology to the emergence of a discipline; in the 'basic' model there is a movement from the science to a technology and resulting products. In molecular modelling and molecular biology the new industries arise as the basic research scientists become the technical people and entrepreneurs: the biotechnology and chemical software firm founders. In the former case, the academic sector came out of the analysis of industry production problems; in the latter, the industrial sector arose out of the implications of university research findings. In either format, academic leadership was crucial to both industrial and disciplinary innovations.

If these two models constituted the universe, academic—industry relations would consist of two linear models going in opposite directions: from product development to academic research and vice versa. However, there are developments not encompassed by the two linear models such as new basic research questions arising out of changing requirements for product development and, more conventionally, 'spin-off' activity from applied research. To take account of processes that go beyond the two linear models, we need a spiral model with feedback loops at different points: going from basic research to product development, from product development to creating new lines of research, and things happening in the middle as well.

Although the linear model has been declared dead, the conduct of basic research in isolation from practice persists as an ideal and the goal of arranging transfer of technology across strongly defended university boundaries is very much alive. Despite disclaimers of disbelief in the 'linear model' of science, with its one-way flow from basic science through applied science to technology and the market, many academic scientists still uphold this model and continue to justify expansion of support for basic research as an isolated enterprise. Others of their colleagues undertake various tasks simultaneously, engaging in fundamental and applied investigations as part of the same research programme. Examples of basic research scientists establishing or participating in industrially related centres and even firms, while remaining committed to and involved in fundamental investigation, abound. For example, at Harvard, Mark Ptashne participated in the organization of Genetics Institute Inc. while maintaining his academic laboratory; and Walter Gilbert left his position in the Biology Department to found Biogen Inc., returning later to his academic position.

A 'spiral model' of interaction in both directions, with cooperative arrangements between university and industry at various stages of research, development and innovation, has yet to be fully accepted, despite the existence of numerous instances. The invention of the transistor has been seen as the outcome of the development of notions of strategic basic research in semiconductor physics at Bell Laboratories (Nelson 1962). Glass research, a highly applied field tied to incremental product development in industry, has been opened up to investigation of basic issues. This has come about through governmental requirements for 'clean' production processes as a result of pressures from environmental movements in the USA and Germany (Etzkowitz 1992c).

This last example indicates that academic-industry relations cannot be seen only in terms of the complex interactions between two institutional spheres, with fairly strict boundaries between them. In our model, thus far, we have taken account of only university and industry. Government at various levels is, of course, also an important force in science-based economic development. This is the case even in countries such as the USA and the UK that have strong ideological restrictions on the role of government in the economy. Indeed, the development of university-industry relations in these countries has been strongly influenced by governmental actions at the national level that have often served as a 'hidden industrial policy' substituting for direct interventions that were too controversial to be undertaken (Etzkowitz 1990). In other countries, multinational entities such as the United Nations, the World Bank and the European Union have been the prime movers in establishing initiatives to link universities and industry for purposes of economic development (Parker 1992). At the regional level, coalitions of business, political and academic leaders have been influential in developing strategies and forming new institutions, such as venture capital firms and incubators, to link the spheres (Etzkowitz 1993). Thus, our analysis of university-industry relations must include government as well, and model the interactions among the three spheres.

Academic Revolutions

Contemporary interactions among university, industry and government are the outcome of two academic revolutions. The first was identified by Jencks and Riesman (1968) as the introduction of research into the university. In the late nineteenth and early twentieth centuries the university began to be transformed from an institution for cultural preservation and transmission of knowledge into an institution conducting research as well. Many universities in European countries still operate as teaching institutions, research having grown up in separate institutions. In the United States a different course was taken in the late nineteenth century in part because there were insufficient funds to set up independent research institutes (Oleson and Voss 1979). A few independent centres of research, such as the Carnegie Institute in Washington, were founded, but for the most part it was found that the way to begin research inexpensively was to give small amounts of funds to professors who used them to reduce their teaching load and to hire students to help with their research. An academic model emerged in which research was combined with teaching. This innovation took forethought and leadership; it also generated controversy over the mission of the university. Several university presidents, including Gilman of Johns Hopkins and Harper of Chicago, were the 'entrepreneurs of institutional innovation'. They championed the idea of setting up a university that combined research with teaching.

Although involvement with industry has revived the debate over the role of the university in society, the issues raised also derive from long-standing tensions among teaching, research and service (Hounshell 1980; Weiner 1982). Many of these tensions had their roots in the remarkable growth of academia during the late nineteenth and early twentieth centuries. This era was characterized both by a differentiation of functions into separate institutions (land grant and liberal arts colleges) and by an integration of functions (graduate education, research and undergraduate teaching) in universities. Thus, research was tied to graduate education in the United States rather than segregated in independent institutes (Geiger 1986). We see parallel lines of development at present: the building of specialized technological universities such as Rensselaer Polytechnic Institute and Georgia Tech upon industrial ties and the integration of industrial ties and economic development functions, along with research and teaching, into liberal arts research universities such as Columbia and Stanford.

In the course of the late nineteenth-century academic revolution, much of the internal content of academia was reshaped as graduate education and research were incorporated into the academic enterprise (Jencks and Riesman 1968). Nevertheless, the traditional tasks of undergraduate education were left in place, although it was no longer the primary function of all schools. As new universities were founded, and teaching institutions transformed into research universities, these institutions continued to educate undergraduates. No university, even among those most committed to research, was able to eliminate undergraduate education and a school such as Clark, founded without an undergraduate college, soon added one (Veysey 1965). If they could have found a way some might have dropped teaching at the undergraduate level, but such students were needed to help pay for the larger enterprise and, as graduates, become wealthy persons who could endow the university. The dual goals of research and teaching have remained in coexistence in US universities, even when undergraduate education is subordinated to graduate education and research.

The first academic revolution introduced dual roles into academia, transforming professors from teachers of youth, who would not likely remain in academia, into disciplinary specialists as well. Whereas earlier professors often covered many areas of knowledge in their teaching, their successors engaged in creating knowledge in a special field and passing it on in mentor relationships to aspirants to their specialty. Conflicts emerged over the balance between teaching and research as some professors sought to reduce their undergraduate teaching responsibilities in order to concentrate on research and graduate education. For example, just after the turn of the century, Stanford University was visited by controversy over whether a professor's research involvement merited relief from teaching obligations. Was not a conflict of interest the inevitable result of the attempt to do both? (Jordan 1906).

A second academic revolution currently under way is making economic development a function of the university in addition to teaching and research. The internal impetuses for the changing role of the university include: the industrial activities of individual academics in forming firms, which take on a collective force as they become increasingly commonplace; the organizational initiatives of academic administrators in establishing procedures and administrative offices for university–industry relations; and conflict-of-interest controversies over linkages with industry, often leading to the formulation of explicit policies regulating and legitimating such ties.

Of course, the US university has traditionally maintained a service function ranging from programmes of continuing education to technical assistance to agriculture and industry at the land grant universities. Research universities, however, typically confined their public contribution to the national level in the form of provision of professors as temporary members of government or as advisers. Similarly, relations with industry were typically maintained through consultancies to national corporations. The new phenomenon is the involvement of research universities at the regional and local levels in interaction with industry and government for the purpose of assisting economic development. This policy is made possible by the gestation of new academic structures such as centres, incubator facilities and research parks (Etzkowitz and Peters 1991; Etzkowitz et al. 1994).

The industrialization of the university has taken place as firm-like entities have grown up within academia. The availability of significant research funding from foundations, in the 1920s and 1930s, and from government, from the 1940s, allowed group research projects to be organized. To this day the professor is called an individual investigator, even though he or she is surrounded by graduate students, post-doctoral fellows, technicians, research administrators and secretaries. In addition to intellectual contributions, the head of this firm-like organization has the responsibility to find the funding, manage the personnel and publicize the research results. Once the group grows beyond six to eight persons the professor is typically forced to withdraw from the laboratory and become a research administrator. When a discovery is found to be commercially viable, it is not a great leap for the entrepreneurs of these 'quasi-firms' to become the heads of actual firms (Etzkowitz 1992a). The tasks are not that different from what they have already been doing. Indeed, investigators typically liken the experience of running a research group to that of a small business. The organizational responsibilities of a professor at Yale have been compared to those of a managing director of a medium-sized corporation.

The development of the professorial role in engineering and the experimental sciences into that of an organizational leader of a quasi-firm is one part of the transformation of the university. Another aspect is the creation of intersections between university, industry and government. In the late nineteenth century most US universities developed in accordance with an ideology of pure research, set forth by physicist, Henry Rowland, in his presidential address to the AAAS. The land grant universities charted an alternative course in support of agriculture. In Boston, a university was established to integrate basic and applied research in support of industry. The anomalous institution, of course, is the Massachusetts Institute of Technology.

The Massachusetts Institute of Technology

The document on which the Massachusetts Institute of Technology was based, detailed the appropriate relationship among research, education and industry. It was drafted by an institutional innovator, William Barton Rogers, who eventually became MIT's first president. The plan was written in 1846 but MIT was not founded until 1861. During the intervening period Rogers moved from Virginia, where he was unable to find a source of support in a rural area to start a technological university, to Boston, then the high-technology centre of the United States. In Boston he met industrialists, business and civic leaders whom he convinced to support the founding of a technological university. He also attained government support to get MIT chartered as a land grant institution.

Rogers's concept was not simply for a polytechnic institute of applied research but for an institution which would incorporate basic research in association with applied research and the development of technology. At the time, he was unable to amass sufficient resources to realize the entire plan. Thus, MIT was basically a teaching institution for engineers in the late nineteenth century. During that period, research was initiated by hiring consulting engineers from industry as professors. Upon joining the university, they did not give up their consulting practices but continued to interact with industry. By the 1920s, some of their students, such as Vannevar Bush, took this consulting role one step further. When a firm rejected an idea invented by one of its employees, Bush and his associates formed a new firm. This was the first step to the development of an industrial sector surrounding the university.

Firms then began to grow up out of MIT from the early twentieth century onwards. Some observers have identified the firm formation process, including the Route 128 complex which grew up after the Second World War, as an outcome of the military laboratories set up at MIT during that era (Dorfman 1983). However, the firm formation process was under way before the war. The infusion of military-related government funding of research expanded the process of firm formation to handle contracts for the government but it was not the initiator of this dynamic. There is a similar story to be told about Stanford, where Silicon Valley did not appear magically from the groves of fruit trees in Santa Clara county.

A notion of 'spontaneous generation' has been used to suggest that these industrial developments at MIT and Stanford are unique processes that cannot be duplicated (Dorfman 1982). In fact, as organizational phenomena, they are eminently duplicable. Institutional innovation is not a random occurrence; it is typically the result of a carefully thought-out plan and an extensive organizing campaign.

The next stage in the development of MIT occurred during the 1930s. The institutional innovator and entrepreneur was Karl Compton, the president of MIT. He set forth a national plan for putting science to work during the Depression. When this plan was rejected at the federal level, he tried again at the local level in Massachusetts through participation in a regional organization of politicians, academic leaders and business persons. The idea that arose from Compton's efforts to utilize the strengths of the region was to transform research going on in the university into the development of new firms. Implementation of this strategy was interrupted by the Second World War. However, immediately after the war Compton and his colleagues put forth a plan to found a venture capital firm. This institutional innovation joined together the business expertise of the Harvard Business School with MIT's technical expertise. Capital was obtained from financial institutions and universities to found American Research and Development Corporation in 1946, the model and progenitor of the venture capital industry (Etzkowitz 1993).

A series of institutional innovations linked MIT to industry through consultation, firm formation, an industrial liaison programme and contracts. These formats allow firms to interact with the university, both intellectually and commercially. Until 1980, MIT, Stanford and the land grant schools were unique in their extensive relations to industry. At that point, the rest of the US research university system, dependent primarily for research funds on the federal government during the post-war era, was realigned by government initiative.

Science and Industrial Policy

An expanded role for the federal government in science-based economic development was originally proposed by the Carter administration during the late 1970s debate over 'reindustrialization'. However, the US government was unable to arrive at a format to fund industrial research directly due to ideological opposition. In 1980, to achieve that result, the universities were used as a surrogate to infuse industry with new research. The rules governing intellectual property rights emanating from federally funded research at universities were changed; research results from federally funded grants were left to the universities. On the one hand, universities were required to make an effort to commercialize research as a condition of receiving federal funds; on the other hand, they were given the incentive of earning money from their technology transfer efforts. Almost immediately a new administrative structure appeared within the universities. Heretofore, very few universities had offices to patent and license research; in a few short years virtually every university with significant sponsored research has established such an office.

Apart from these indirect measures, only limited steps were taken towards an industrial policy during the 1980s due to opposition to government playing a more direct and specific role in the economy, other than through taxation and monetary policies. Industrial policy was further held in abeyance by the Reagan – Bush administration's strong belief in *laissez-faire* economics. Despite ideological reservations, there were a few notable exceptions. For example, in the mid-1980s, a government-supported industrial research consortium, Sematech, was established at the request of the semiconductor industry to assist US firms in meeting international competition. But this was viewed as an exception to the rule. When Craig Fields, an administrator at the Defense Advanced Research Projects Agency, attempted to extend the activities of this agency into civilian technologies in the early 1990s, he was fired by the Bush administration. Fields soon reappeared as an innovative head of the Microelectronics and Computer Technology Corporation, another exceptional industrial consortium (*Technology Access Report* 1992).

Despite a plethora of experiments a comprehensive national science, technology and innovation policy, complemented with sufficiently funded programmes, does not exist. There are, however, a series of variegated elements of such a policy and programmes, ranging across military, health, small business and basic research agencies. In the Clinton administration, these linkages among university, industry and government are being gradually put together into an economic development policy. At the state level, regardless of political ideologies, governors and legislatures have taken the lead in assisting a high-technology firm formation process to help create jobs. Large corporations, especially in the pharmaceutical area, have used contract mechanisms to fund newer lines of university research, which might become useful to them, in exchange for patent rights. In the computer industry more informal arrangements have arisen, as was traditional in the chemical industry. Often firms give a relatively small amount of money to a professor to support research in order to keep an eye on alternative research areas in case the company's internal effort fails. In the biotechnology area many professors have taken the lead as firm founders themselves. These phenomena are spreading throughout the university research system.

In other parts of the world similar developments are taking place. Given different institutional backgrounds, these processes take different courses. For example, in eastern Europe institutional arrangements, under socialism, consisted of a series of concentric circles, with government surrounding and industry and the university inside. In this setting there were formal structural relationships between research institutes and industry for ideological reasons. The intelligentsia were expected to support the working class but in a system largely lacking industrial innovation there was little need for that research to be put to use. With the collapse of socialism, the institutional sectors are moving apart from each other. Government has reduced its funding of the research institutes. If the research institutes are to survive they must secure funds from foreign industry or attempt to set up their own industrial sector. Many of the institutes are beginning to develop small 'filial firms' that stay within the research institutes for a period of time before moving out. In the United States, when an employee leaves to start a new firm there has typically been a quick and total separation often accompanied by a lawsuit over intellectual property rights. More recently, some large firms have been helping to start new companies, retaining a portion of equity as recompense. National laboratories and government agencies, such as the Department of Energy, have declared that technology transfer is their mission. These are some of the processes that are generating technological change and a new mode of economic development.

Interaction among universities, industry and government is taking place world-wide, irrespective of the previous level of economic development. Virtually every country that has a university, whether it was founded for reasons of education or prestige, is now attempting to organize knowledge-based economic development. Usually this takes place by finding a niche where research can be connected to a local resource. For example, in Finland it takes the form of applying computer technology to the forestry industry. In Mexico the United Nations is the institutional innovator, setting up a centre (the Centro para la Innovación Tecnológica) at the National Autonomous University (UNAM) in Mexico City to make contracts between the university and industry. Sometimes there is a lack of fit between research done locally and local industry; results may then be sold abroad and the production may move as well. This happens in the United States and internationally, with similar controversies over national interest, free trade and the role of the university as a source of disinterested expertise (Etzkowitz 1992b).

Conclusion

In the 1930s Karl Compton and his colleagues at the Massachusetts Institute of Technology recognized that New England possessed research resources to a greater degree than the rest of the United States and sought to capitalize this regional resource, just as if it were a harbour or mineral deposit. If existing companies, whether national or local, were not interested in or capable of commercializing emerging technologies then new companies would have to be formed. Through their role in the formation of American Research and Development Corporation, MIT, the Harvard Business School and the Boston financial community helped create the venture capital industry. Through years of discussions with the business and financial communities, committee work, publicity and institution formation, Compton and his colleagues translated the academic wealth emanating from New England's first industrial revolution into a new wave of economic development. A partnership among university, government and industry created a regional pattern of economic growth based on science and technology that has since been emulated throughout the world.

The interaction between MIT and business leadership led to a shift of economic development strategy from a sole focus on remedying geographical deficits through reducing taxes and improving transportation infrastructure to utilizing institutional resources such as research and development facilities to facilitate the formation of new high-technology enterprises. Following MIT's lead, Engineering Dean and Provost Frederick Terman initiated a strategy of technically based regional economic development in northern California in the 1940s, building up Stanford's engineering and science departments to have a critical mass of technologists to interact with industry (Leslie 1993). The founders of the Research Triangle in North Carolina used a variant of the tactic of building a high-technology infrastructure in the 1950s, successfully influencing the location decisions of several government laboratories and regional branches of national science-based corporations (Hamilton 1966). Creating a research base for formation of firms has since become the centrepiece of state government economic development strategies throughout the United States (Dougherty and Etzkowitz 1993).

Local strategies vary, depending upon the intensity of the research base and the nature of existing industrial development. Regions with a low level of research tend to concentrate on building up their research capacities, by encouraging the development of research at 'teaching' universities and by attracting company and governmental laboratories. For example, by attracting funds from the National Science Foundation during the 1960s, then available to improve second-rank universities, the University of Colorado at Boulder was able to improve its science departments. Over time the university became home to a number of leading researchers, some of whom became entrepreneurial scientists during the 1980s and established their own firms. Other areas, with a declining industrial base, have established research centres at local universities to improve the technology of mature companies.

Universities and industry, heretofore relatively separate and distinct institutional spheres, are assuming tasks that were formerly largely the province of the other in the development of new technology. As the university becomes more dependent upon industry and government, so have industry and government become more dependent upon the university. In the course of the 'second academic revolution' a new social contract is being drawn up between the university and the larger society, in which public funding for the university is made contingent upon a more direct contribution to the economy. To the extent that universities become more entrepreneurial, there will be even more than the traditional tension between research and teaching. As the university crosses traditional boundaries through linkages to industry, it must devise formats to make its multiple purposes compatible with each other. So far the university has been an ingenious innovator: mixing disciplinary departments with interdisciplinary centres, and encompassing critical disciplines such as environmental science with economically relevant fields such as materials science.

The university is also increasingly becoming a self-generating institution, instead of an eleemosynary one economically dependent upon others. The generation of economically relevant research allows the university an increasing social space in which to negotiate the terms of its relationship to the larger society. Thus, university–industry linkages may not necessarily subordinate the university to other institutional areas of society. The degree to which academic–industrial collaboration jeopardizes the role of the university as a source of disinterested expertise must be examined. It is also possible that as universities add economic development to teaching and research, they will assume a new form even as those schools which added research to teaching, from the mid-nineteenth century, became a different type of university. The spectre of academic decline may actually turn out to be an augur of renascence.

12 Non-equilibria Dynamics and the Sociology of Technology

Gertrud Blauwhof

In calling attention to differential productivity growth and technical change, evolutionary economics has initiated a shift from an equilibrium to a non-equilibrium perspective on economic development. With the questioning of the equilibrium thesis macro-economic dynamics and institutional analysis also became more prominent in economics; following Keynes, for instance, what was true for the individual economic actor was no longer necessarily true for all, and thereby micro-economics lost some of its importance (cf. Galbraith 1987). In sociology, on the other hand, debates between action-orientated and system- or structure-orientated approaches date back to the early days of the discipline, while the recent rise of constructivist analyses marks the increasing recognition by sociologists of non-equilibria dynamics.

This paper contrasts evolutionary economics with a constructivist example of the non-equilibrium turn in sociology. The case in point, namely the sociology of translation, is chosen because, like evolutionary economics, it combines a concern for technology with an evolutionary perspective. Additionally, comparing evolutionary economics with a constructivist approach allows us to address the question of how to relate theories of firm behaviour with theories about network properties.

An analytical comparison of evolutionary economics and the sociology of translation forms the core of this paper. In order to ground this comparison, it is preceded by an introductory section that sketches the main concepts and the overall line of reasoning of both approaches, and which, accordingly, should be taken as a kind of 'functional history'. The concluding section of the paper will argue, among other things, that the micro−macro debate and the corresponding analytical problem of firms versus networks emerges naturally from evolutionary perspectives: due to certain intricacies of dynamic analyses, theoretical reflections on the evolution of complex systems necessarily branch into perspectives that will highlight either the construction or the re-construction and adjustment of such systems.

Evolutionary economics and the sociology of translation: two summaries

Historically speaking, evolutionary economics emerged against the background of neoclassical economic theory (see, for example, Sahal 1981). Neoclassical economics assumes, among other things, that firms maximize (expected) profit and that industry and economy as a whole are in (moving) equilibrium (Nelson 1981). Furthermore, by consequence of these assumptions, the neoclassical tradition couples a rationalistic outlook on firm behaviour with a transparent understanding on the economy which, presumably, is characterized by certainty, stability and complete information.

In recent years both these assumptions have been called into question. For example, both Simon ([1947] 1965) and scholars in the Behavioral School in economics (Cyert and March 1963) have challenged the maximization thesis and replaced it by the notions of optimizing and satisfying, and by a concern for search and learning processes. The equilibrium thesis, on the other hand, was questioned by Schumpeter ([1943] 1976) and Alchian (1950), among others, and both proposed an evolutionary approach instead. Schumpeter ([1943] 1976), for instance, called attention to the importance of new products and production modes for economic development, and to the ways in which established economic practices adjust to such changes. More specifically, the argument put forward was that the interaction between the two processes of creation and adjustment – marked as the process of 'creative destruction' – induced nonlinear dynamics in economic development. While Schumpeter ([1943] 1976) highlighted the entrepreneur and his visions, Alchian (1950) called attention to the 'decisions and criteria dictated by the economic system'. In maintaining that realized rather than expected positive profits form the mark of economic success and viability, Alchian (1950) stressed the importance of an 'ex post survival criterium'. And since imitation and rule-following behaviour among firms exemplified such 'selective adoption' processes, economic evolution should, so it was argued, be understood probabilistically.

With hindsight Nelson and Winter (1977; 1982) appear as the turning-point in the emergence of evolutionary economics as a distinct line of research. Much like Schumpeter, these authors maintain that productivity growth and, in particular, inter-industry productivity differences are key issues in economics which, in order to be addressed, require analyses of innovation and technical change. Furthermore, while underwriting an evolutionary perspective, they buttress such an outlook by drawing on Simon ([1947] 1965) and on the Behavioral School and, accordingly, by a concern for search and learning processes (cf. Nelson and Winter 1982: 40ff.). An evolutionary approach thus emerged which – contrary to the neoclassical assumptions of maximization and (moving) equilibrium – emphasized the importance of uncertainty and imperfect information, of routines, heuristic search processes and optimizing behaviour, and of non-equilibria.

Key concepts in Nelson and Winter (1977; 1982) are those of 'variation' and 'selection': 'variation' designates the emergence of new technologies out of search processes at the level of the firm, while 'selection' denotes the relative weight of technologies over time as resulting from, for example, the (im)possibility of imitation and/or expansion and the effects of existing institutional structures. Like Schumpeter ([1943] 1976), the model thus also turns on the two processes of creation and adjustment. Furthermore, corresponding to its concern for routines and heuristic searches, the model stresses the need for a micro-economic foundation. To this purpose it takes the decision rules employed by firms as a basic operational concept (see, for example, Nelson and Winter 1982: 14), as a result of which there emerged a probabilistic and 'evolutionary theory of the capabilities and behaviour of business firms operating in a market environment' (Nelson and Winter 1982: 3). Furthermore, while discursively acknowledging the importance of feedback loops among 'variation', and 'selection', such interactions were analytically bracketed for the sake of developing 'conformable sub-theories' (Nelson and Winter 1977: 49).

In later years research in evolutionary economics followed a number of paths. Stochastic evolutionary modelling, for example, received increasing attention (see, for example, Jiménez Montaño and Ebeling 1980; Silverberg 1988). Likewise, processes affecting either the actual or expected relative weights of new technologies were investigated further; this, in turn, spurred interest in the significance of institutional structures (national and/or sectoral) and their comparative differences for technological development (Freeman 1988; Nelson 1988). It also resulted in the introduction into evolutionary economics of concepts such as the 'technological paradigm' (Dosi 1982; 1984) and the 'technological guidepost' (Sahal 1981; 1985). Furthermore, a concern with 'how it actually happened' generated extensive empirical research and the study of the interactions between creation and adjustment processes (Teubal 1979; Pavitt 1984; Saviotti and Metcalfe 1984; Abernathy and Clark 1985; Clark 1985; Barras 1986; Van den Belt and Rip 1987; Bodewitz et al. 1988; Robson et al. 1988).

Along with the substantive insights generated by these studies, the analytical bracketing of interaction between 'variation' and 'selection' gradually broke down, and by the late 1980s the notion of 'increasing dynamic returns' (Arthur 1988b; 1990) entered the vocabulary of evolutionary economics. While marking the (re)appearance of a nonlinear perspective on the evolution of technology, the notion of 'increasing dynamic returns' called attention to the ways in which various forms of interaction between the generation and the adoption of new technologies result in feedback loops, in self-amplification, and in nonlinear dynamics. (One well-documented example of a positive feedback-inducing process concerns 'learning by experience' ('learning-by-doing', 'learning-by-using); see, for example, Rosenberg (1976). As learning progresses, it may result in, for example, improvements in design, enhanced technological versatility, market stimulation, accelerating processes of standardization, and scale economies (Zuscovitch 1986). Or, in 'modern' terminology, because of such feedbacks technologies may drift into 'lock-ins' and irreversible states signifying differential weights and the hampering or elimination of further competition (Arthur 1988b).)

By suggesting that nonlinearity originates in the interaction between 'variation' and 'selection', the notion of 'increasing dynamic returns' generated yet another new concept, namely that of 'complex nonlinear systems' (Allen 1988b). It also carried a question: when 'complex nonlinear systems' involve interactions among, for example, producers, users, universities, and so on, what should be taken as the corresponding unit of analysis? Something like 'national systems of innovation' (Lundvall 1992)?

The sociology of translation

The sociology of translation emerged during the 1980s in the area of science and technology studies. In brief, this area, by that time, had experienced the following changes. In the 1950s and 1960s Mertonian sociology of science prevailed, which, in sustaining the Popperian distinction between a 'context of discovery' and a 'context of justification', understood science primarily as a rational and autonomous realm devoid of social interests and progressing through accumulation (see, for example, Merton [1942] 1973). By characterizing science in terms of incommensurable paradigms shouldered by groups of practitioners, Kuhn (1962) tore both these assumptions to shreds. Next a relativist approach emerged, namely the 'sociology of scientific knowledge' (SSK), which set out to demonstrate the 'social construction of scientific knowledge' empirically (Bloor 1976; also Collins 1985). Among other things, it highlighted the importance of uncertainty and of group-based search rules (similar to Wittgenstein's 'forms of life') in the constitution of scientific knowledge. Furthermore, to make its case the SSK approach singled out the natural sciences as its area of research, and thereby engineering and technology moved into focus. In particular, by the mid-1980s constructivist analyses of technology took off in the form of the 'sociology of translation' (Callon 1980; Callon and Latour 1981) and the 'social construction of technology' (Pinch and Bijker 1984; Bijker *et al.* 1987). The primary objective of these analyses was to demonstrate how technology becomes (socially) constructed, and this objective meant, among other things, that precedence would be given to descriptive empirical research and to case study research.

In the case of the sociology of translation, the starting-point in understanding the construction and the emergence of technology concerns the two processes of association ('the primary mechanism') and attribution ('the

secondary mechanism') (Latour 1987; 1988). In brief, the sociology of translation considers both mechanisms as emerging from action and, in particular,
from action governed by uncertainty. Each action, so it is argued, associates a
particular set of elements and thereby attributes a particular quality to these
elements. Given uncertainty and incomplete information, however, such
attributions can only form projections in need of testing, and the sociology of
translation thus maintains that the accomplishment of action depends on the
success of such tests, or, in other words, on the question of whether the
projected qualities acquire substance as well as form.

In terms of empirical research the foregoing is elaborated as follows (see, for
example, Callon 1986a; 1986b; 1987; Callon et al. 1986; Latour 1987). First, since
action, in the case of science and technology, commonly takes the form of raising
problems, a 'problematization' (that is, a discourse) is taken as the starting-point
and the unit of analysis of empirical research. Furthermore, since a 'problematization' represents an actor's perspective on a situation, it is also denoted by the
term 'actor-world', that is, a set of intentionally associated elements that — in the
shape of a 'heterogenous network' — literally forms the actor's vision (and if
acknowledged by others, the actor itself). Second, in order to reduce uncertainty
and to certify a vision, all elements of a 'problematization' need to be tested and
aligned, and the procedures invoked to that purpose are called 'translation'
processes. Third, if such 'translation' processes are successful, they are said to
lead to the 'enrolment' of each of the elements of the initial problem: each
element, at that instance, has been made to act as envisaged and thus plays its
role. Furthermore, as a result of achieving 'enrolment' the network as a whole
'stabilizes', and is said to invert from a vision into an operation or, alternatively,
from a projected form into a form that carries substance. Such a form is denoted
by the term 'intermediary' (Callon 1992). Fourth, since substances are understood
to exist only through attribution, they are considered to become obsolete if not
associated continuously by renewed action, and this, in turn, is taken to involve
another problematization whereby an 'intermediary' is 'mobilized' and brought
into circulation anew.

In terms more familiar to economists, this amounts to the argument, first, that
technologies emerge — potentially at least — through an actor's vision (for
example, an invention). Second, that the realization of this vision presupposes all
kinds of tests whereby problems are resolved and certainties created, and whereby
the different components of a project (production facilities, potential consumers)
are mutually aligned. Third, that successful searches and alignments lead to
innovation (understood as market introduction), and to the inversion of a plan
into an artefact. Fourth, that the endurance of achievements and consequently the
diffusion of innovation, depends upon the circulation of 'intermediaries' (sales
representatives, advertising, and so on) and, in particular, upon the acknowl-
edgement of intermediaries by, for example, buying. Moreover, once bought but

never used, an innovation still loses significance, and therefore diffusion depends on the incessant repetition of attribution through renewed action and association, that is, on the recurrence of 'translation' and 'stabilization'.

In concluding this outline of the sociology of translation the following should be noted. First, the sociology of translation takes a discourse – understood as a network of heterogenous entities upon which different qualities are bestowed – as its unit of analysis. For example, such a discourse (or communication network) initially has the form of a vision, then changes its form into an innovation, and still later may change its form into, for example, the nation-wide treatment of disease X with apparatus Y, or the industry-wide production of aircrafts following the DC-3 exemplar.

Second, corresponding to its concern for a dynamic framework in which entities carry no other qualities but the ones attributed to them empirically, the sociology of translation dismisses a priori distinctions and analytical categories ('social', 'technical', 'economical', 'political', 'natural', and so on). Instead, it suggests that since attributions and thereby qualities change with time and place, the analyst should 'follow the actors in their construction processes'.

Third, the sociology of translation suggests that the empirical repetition of 'translation' and 'stabilization' introduces recursion and feedback loops into the dynamics of a network. In particular, due to repetition 'intermediaries' may 'normalize' and become symbols (for example, money; actor Q as the embodiment of company W) and this, in turn, is taken to accelerate the circulation process (Latour 1987; Callon 1992). In terms of network structure, furthermore, repetition is taken to initiate a process of 'irreversibilization' characterized by increasing convergence and boundary formation. More specifically, inflexibility may progress so far empirically that, notwithstanding the second remark made above, certain networks may be characterized as 'techno-economic networks', that is, as networks in which the communication process turns on a scientific pole, a technical pole and a market pole (Callon 1992).

Reflecting upon the summaries

Does the sociology of translation indeed represent an evolutionary and non-equilibrium perspective on technology, and is a comparison with evolutionary economics justified? The summary suggests affirmative answers to both questions; for example, the two concepts of 'translation' and 'stabilisation' reveal a concern for non-equilibrium dynamics and, in particular, suggest an alternation among non-equilibria states and temporary instances of stabilization and equilibria. Similarly, the emphasis on 'translation' and on testing in particular is comparable to the concern of evolutionary economics for search processes. More specifically, both approaches stress the significance of uncertainty and of incomplete information; and this concern leads to an interest in trial and error, testing and decision-making procedures, and search and learning processes in general. Furthermore, in terms of their analyses of technological development these concerns give rise to the following general correspondences. First, both analyses understand technological development as a path-dependent process in which the coupling between discrete events (as accomplished by, for example, testing and learning) induces feedback loops and nonlinear dynamics. Second, both suggest that as a consequence of uncertainty and incomplete information, technological development involves processes of alignment, adjustment and interaction among, for example, scientists, engineers, producers and users. Third, both suggest that beyond a certain stage the dynamics of technology involves two types of process: local searching and learning processes, on the one hand, and internal or self-referential loops (for example, 'technological paradigms', 'mobilization'), on the other.

An analytical comparison

In order to establish whether and how evolutionary economics may benefit from sociology, a more thorough analysis is needed. This section presents an analytical comparison which focuses on the following issues: primary research questions; units of analysis; analytical perspectives; main arguments; and main concepts. Furthermore, having delineated the respective positions, the question of how to account for them will be raised.

First, concerning primary research questions, it may be observed that evolutionary economics aims to explain why 'variations' emerge and why certain subsets are 'selected' and allowed further development. The sociology of translation, on the other hand, focuses on the question of how technologies emerge and how they diffuse, and aims to describe these processes.

Second, in both lines of research the units of analysis vary accordingly; because of its micro-economic concerns evolutionary economics takes industry as an aggregate of firms and identifies the firm as its basic operational concept. The sociology of translation, on the other hand, takes a discourse (that is, a communication network) as its unit of analysis.

Third, each line of research entails a corresponding and therefore different analytical viewpoint or perspective; in asking for the origins of, for example, interindustry productivity differences, evolutionary economics tends to approach the issue of technological development from the perspective of hindsight, that is, from an a posteriori perspective. The sociology of translation, on the other hand, asks the analyst to follow the process whereby technology is constructed, and thereby opts for an a priori perspective that views technology as emergent.

Not surprisingly, the former differences also reflect themselves in the main argument of each approach and, accordingly, in its main concepts. Put generally, evolutionary economics maintains, first, that the initial spectrum of innovations may be accounted for in terms of firm-specific search processes, and second, that this variety is diminished by either the directive and conditioning qualities of metaheuristics (for example, 'technological paradigms') or by means of firm-specific potentials for imitation and expansion and sector-specific institutional structures (for example, market versus non-market), or by both. Furthermore, the notions of 'variation' and 'selection' represent its key concepts and signify the two strands of its analysis. The sociology of translation, on the other hand, highlights the relational and constructive aspects of technological development and maintains, first, that the development of technology involves the mutual adjustment and alignment of the various components of a project, and second, that success is based upon the stabilization of mutual roles and definitions. Furthermore, its key concepts are the notions of 'translation' and 'stabilization', each of which, again, captures a particular aspect of a bipartite argument.

It may thus be argued that differential firm positions and structural differences serve as the explanatory variable of evolutionary economics, while relations and, in particular, the form of the relations being established serve as the explanatory variable in the sociology of translation. Table 12.1 summarizes the comparison.

An analytical comparison, by its very nature, leaves little but the skeleton of an analysis. For example, next to its concern for firms evolutionary economics has most certainly called attention to the importance of sector- and nation-specific institutional structures in understanding selection processes (see, for example, Nelson 1988; Freeman 1988; Lundvall 1992), and to the importance of disciplinary or speciality-based metaheuristics (Dosi 1982; 1984). Similarly, next to its focus on discourse the sociology of translation has recently reinstated actors – in their capacity as 'intermediaries' – as part of its analysis (Callon 1992). However, in neither case do these concerns seem to have had much of a bearing on, for example, the unit of analysis, the analytical perspective or the principal concepts.

The analytical comparison of the two approaches therefore suggests that beyond a common concern for an evolutionary and non-equilibrium-orientated analysis of technological development, the two approaches have next to nothing in common. However, a reflection on these findings should prevent too hasty conclusions. Why, for example, do two approaches, both of which claim to study technology, differ in their units of analysis? Why does the one highlight 'variation' and 'selection' processes while the other stresses 'translation' and 'stabilization'? Are these differences perhaps related to their common concern for a dynamic perspective on technology? Answers to these questions have to come from an analysis of how each approach has constructed its research agenda, and to such an analysis the remainder of this section will be dedicated.

Table 12.1 Analytical comparison of evolutionary economics and the sociology of translation.

	Evolutionary economics	Sociology of translation
Primary research question	Why do 'variations' emerge and why is a subset 'selected'? (i.e. *why* do technologies develop in particular ways?)	How are 'actor-worlds' constructed and how do they gain stability and endurance (i.e. *how* do technologies develop?)
Unit of analysis	Firm	Discourse (i.e. communication network)
Analytical perspective	Mainly a posteriori ('hindsight')	a priori (e.g. 'follow the actors in their construction processes')
Main argument and concepts	'*Variation*' generated through local search processes; '*selection*' through conditioning effects of metaheuristics (e.g. 'technological paradigm'), firm-specific potentials for imitation and expansion and/or sector-specific institutional structures	'*Translation*' process certifies and aligns elements of a problem or 'actor-world'; if successful 'translation' results in '*stabilization*' and inversion (e.g. plan → (arte)fact)
Explanatory variable	Differential firm *positions*, i.e. structural differences	Form of *relations* being established

Reconstructing research agendas

As noted above, both approaches took as their starting-points a concern for uncertainty and search processes and a concern for a dynamic analysis of technology. Furthermore, in the case of evolutionary economics the problem of differential productivity growth was also a major concern, whereas in the case of the sociology of translation constructivist considerations led to a concern for action. Given these building-blocks, how did each line of research proceed?

In brief, in the case of evolutionary economics the attempt to understand the 'productivity puzzle' appears to have defined both its point of reference and its analytical perspective: certain empirically established sectoral productivity differences, in constituting the issue in question, came to serve as point of reference in evolutionary economics, and this, in turn, called forth an a posteriori perspective. After all, in questioning the origins of certain historical phenomena, the analyst has little choice but to adopt the perspective of hindsight. However, the attempt to develop a dynamic perspective then created the following situation. If technology is taken to be dynamic and historically evolving, it follows that time makes a difference; however, by its commitment to the 'productivity puzzle', evolutionary economics had also committed itself to an a posteriori perspective, so where is this difference to be found? The question obviously leaves but one answer, namely that of locating 'variation' in the past. Furthermore, by consequence of this configuration of an a posteriori perspective coupled with a concern for the dynamics of technology, evolutionary economics was logically compelled to propose the notion of 'selection' next to that of 'variation': without envisaging a difference between the past and its point of reference, it would have violated its assumption of development and evolution; but given this assumption, it had to propose a selective process because without reduction the difference fades again. Moreover, by coupling an a posteriori viewpoint with a dynamic perspective, the economy then came to be understood as moving towards an equilibrium state (see, for example, Nelson and Winter 1977: 48); but in contrast with the sociology of translation, evolutionary economics proposes no concept to denote such a state (for example, 'stabilization'). (It may be noted that had evolutionary economics sustained the alternative assumption, that is, that the economy gravitates towards disequilibria, it would have delegitimized the significance of the 'productivity puzzle' and questioned its own research agenda.) Furthermore, empirical research supported the above outlook because an a posteriori perspective, unfortunately, cannot but privilege those developments which continue to exist up to the point in time occupied by the analyst. Both conceptually and empirically, the coupling of a dynamic perspective with an a posteriori viewpoint thus led to a tendency to privilege continuity, and this, in turn, found its wording in terms like 'basic design', 'technological paradigm', 'regime', and so on, or, alternatively, in the criticism that evolutionary economics exhibits a tendency towards determinism (Bijker et al. 1987).

In the case of the sociology of translation, on the other hand, the attempt to develop a constructivist analysis of technology carried both a dynamic and an a priori perspective. After all, the very idea of constructivism involves the assumptions that, first, time makes a difference, and second, that this difference is to be found in the future; otherwise there is nothing to construct. In opting for constructivism the sociology of translation was thus led, first, to take the process of construction as its unit of analysis, and second, to take its origins, that is, a human actor, as its point of reference (as exemplified in its methodological recommendation to 'follow the actors'). Third, it was led analytically to adopt an a priori perspective in which technology is seen as emerging. Moreover, the reason to conceptualize the process of construction (that is, its unit of analysis) in terms of discourse also appears to have been induced by its constructivist concerns. Constructivism, after all, hinges on the assumptions of uncertainty, mutual non-transparency, and incomplete information; otherwise the world is already in place. Given these assumptions, however, it then follows that action cannot be taken to be operative at the moment it is issued but, instead, has to be understood as a projection in need of affirmation and, accordingly, in need of interaction. Yet how else should one understand interaction but in terms of communication and, in particular, in terms of discourses that perhaps may turn operative and material at some point in the future?

Thus constrained by its own concerns, the sociology of translation proceeded – logically speaking, that is – on a path like that of evolutionary economics yet in the opposite direction: it proposed the notion of 'stabilization' to denote a different state *vis-à-vis* its point of reference, and that of 'translation' to denote the process of transition in between these two different states. Furthermore, just as evolutionary economics suggests a transition towards equilibrium, so the sociology of translation suggests a transition towards 'stabilization', but with one important difference: while evolutionary economics suggests that its point of reference is characterized by equilibrium, the sociology of translation suggests that its point of reference is characterized by heterogeneity and disorder. But just as evolutionary economics provides no concept to denote equilibria, so the sociology of translation provides no concept to denote non-equilibria (for example, 'variation'). Furthermore, empirical research has again sustained this particular outlook because a constructivist and particular an a priori perspective cannot but carry an image of incessant disorder and heterogeneity; each action, after all, defines new problems to be solved and new goals to be achieved. Both conceptually and empirically, the coupling of a dynamic perspective to an a priori viewpoint thus privileges discontinuity and change, and fosters an image which the sociology of translation – quite opposite to evolutionary economics – has been repeatedly accused of, namely an image of voluntarism (see, for example, Amsterdamska 1990).

Dynamic analyses

What does the former imply for evolutionary analyses that aim to highlight, for example, the dynamics of technology? Put abstractly, the problem involved in such analyses appear to include the following. Perhaps the most basic assumption that comes with a dynamic perspective is that time matters – the assumption of evolution and historical development. However, if yesterday's technology is presumed to be different from today's or tomorrow's, it then follows, first, that a dynamic perspective poses an abstract difference between two instances in time; and second, that it poses a duality between disequilibria (change) and equilibria (continuity), because the one without the other refutes the assumption of development. After all, mere continuity implies statics, yet its presence goes unnoticed by lack of contrast, whereas mere change implies flux yet its presence, again, goes unnoticed when not opposed to non-change. Furthermore, while this duality, in both analyses, expresses itself in the presumed movement towards 'stabilization' and equilibrium (note that the alternative assumption suggests a continuous movement towards chaos and thereby refutes evolution!), a dynamic perspective therefore also implies, third, that a point of reference is required in order to specify the difference that history makes empirically. Fourth, it also implies that either disequilibrium be attributed to a point of reference and equilibrium to the future (emergence), or that equilibrium be attributed to a point of reference and dis-equilibrium to the past (reorganization, restriction and adjustment).

Evaluating the comparison

What are the implications of this analysis for evaluating the results of the analytical comparison, and for assessing the relation between evolutionary economics and the sociology of translation?

The analysis suggests that the observed differences between the two approaches (see Table 12.1) should be understood as a consequence of opting for a dynamic analysis of technology yet — given different disciplinary research traditions and intellectual concerns — choosing different points of reference. More specifically, the analysis in fact suggests that the emergence of two perspectives is logically implicated in the very attempt to develop a dynamic perspective on technology, because the specification of development hinges on the duality of continuity and change and, in particular, on the denoting of a point of reference.

In terms of substantive insights, the problem of having to denote a particular point of reference gives rise to analyses in which the strengths of the one appear as weaknesses in the other and vice versa. For example, while evolutionary economics has called attention to the importance of metaheuristics (a 'technological paradigm'), the sociology of translation in fact provides the appropriate unit of analysis (a discourse) and an argument that accounts for the evolution of metaheuristics — that is as another case of repeated attribution by association and, in particular, as another case of condensation due to the repeated circulation of 'intermediaries'. Similarly, while the sociology of translation has called attention to the importance of action, construction and heterogeneity, it in fact loses sight of these concerns empirically because the process which it studies, by virtue of its continuation, incessantly condenses and supplants heterogeneity with homogeneity. Again, in this case evolutionary economics actually provides the corresponding analytical category (the firm as economic actor) just as it provides an argument that accounts for the emergence of variance.

However, the issue is not that both approaches have never called attention to the significance of the questions and the arguments posed and proposed by the other line of research, because they have. For example, in suggesting that the direction of a translation process emerges from the juxtaposition of its elements (Callon 1986a), the sociology of translation not only raises an issue similar to the main research question of evolutionary economics, it even suggests that this problem is to be understood in terms of differential weights due to the circulation of 'intermediaries', that is, in terms of 'variation' and 'selection'. However, the reason why an issue like the direction of technological development escapes systematic specification in the case of the sociology of translation, is that its a priori perspective prevents it from ever observing anything but emergence. Similarly, while evolutionary economics has repeatedly called attention to the relational dimension of technological development, the problem of how technologies develop nevertheless escapes systematic analysis. The reason, in this case, is that its a posteriori perspective prevents evolutionary economics from seeing any relations other than those which have been accomplished successfully.

The discussion may easily be extended over all dimensions of Table 12.1, but the point to note is that each line of research carries a dimension which is discursively acknowledged but which nevertheless escapes systematic analysis and which, paradoxically, is equivalent to the research question of the other approach, its unit of analysis, its main argument, and so on. Thus formulated, however, the analytically unarticulated and latent dimension in each approach also corresponds to its major concerns, and this, in turn, points to yet another problem which (dynamic) analysis cannot escape from, namely that in developing a line of research, the guiding concerns – by virtue of what they stand for – serve as a point of reference and thereby escape further questioning (cf. Luhmann 1984).

In terms of evaluating the comparison, this leads to two conclusions. First, analytically speaking, both approaches carry a latent dimension which corresponds to their guiding concerns. Second, in having acknowledged this dimension discursively, each approach is to be regarded as an appreciative yet partial perspective.

Conclusions

What are the implications of this analysis for understanding the evolution of technology? If granted, it leads to the following conclusions.

First, if, as has been argued, the problem of having to denote a point of reference foredooms a dynamic analysis of technology to fall apart into two perspectives, it then follows that evolutionary economics may benefit from sociology by acknowledging the importance of 'translation' and 'stabilization' processes and, in particular, by acknowledging the referent of these two concepts, namely, a discourse or a communication network. Furthermore, if communication networks are acknowledged as the referent of an evolving technology, it then also follows that the notion of 'complex nonlinear systems' should be taken to refer to communication networks and, in particular, to communication networks that are self-referential, operationally closed and potentially self-organizing.

Second, if the former argument is accepted, it follows that the Schumpeterian distinction between creation and adjustment, or the more recent distinction between 'variation' and 'selection', in fact represents a problem of different referents: while the creation phase has the economic actor as its referent, the adjustment and reallocation phase should be taken as having a communication system as its referent. More specifically, it would then also appear that the debate concerning the relative significance of micro- and macro-dynamics – as exemplified in, for example, Schumpeter's ([1943] 1976) concern for the entrepreneur versus Alchian's (1950) concern for the economic system – represents yet another instance of the duality between continuity and change and, in particular, another example of denoting different points of reference in evolutionary analysis. It may be expected, furthermore, that analyses of either creation or adjustment processes will appear paradoxical to one another just as the sociology of translation and evolutionary economics appear paradoxical to one another (cf. Zuscovitch 1986).

Third, if theoretical reflections on complex nonlinear systems branch into appreciative yet partial semantics, it then also follows that the hypothesis of self-organization (see, for example, Luhmann 1984) is crucial to further research, because empirically such systems appear either as emerging (in an a priori perspective) or (in an a posteriori perspective) through 'selection', that is, as an instantiation of an otherwise virtual system (Giddens 1984). More specifically, when framed in terms of the evolution of complex systems, both evolutionary economics and the sociology of translations should then be valued as analyses each of which highlights different 'sub-routines' (Simon 1973) of the same system, namely, construction and re-construction. While evolutionary economics is concerned with understanding the macro-state of an (emerging) complex system, the sociology of translation is concerned with micro-variation. It also follows that the evolution of complex systems should be understood in terms of the association of communications, that is, in terms of coevolution, and, in particular, in terms of covariations each of which in itself represents a selection among possibilities. More specifically, while 'selection' should be taken to refer to the acknowledgment of variation by a communication system, 'stabilization' should be taken to refer to the reorganization of such a system in view of increased complexity due to 'selection' (Leydesdorff 1993b).

Fourth, in terms of empirical research, the discussion points to the importance of sectoral analyses for further elaborating the dynamics of complex systems. The sectoral level, after all, not only represents the linchpin between micro-variation and macro-dynamics but also may be expected to represent the locus of nonlinear dynamics. More specifically, following Simon (1973), the idea of a 'loose coupling' of nearly decomposable systems may perhaps serve to bracket either the low frequencies at which macro-dynamics operates or, alternatively, the high-frequencies of micro-economic behaviour. Analytically, the one approach corresponds to taking the nodes of a network (for example, firms) as the unit of analysis, whereas in the other case the network itself forms the unit of analysis.

Fifth, while the substantive value of the sociology of translation for evolutionary economics is dependent upon the research questions that evolutionary economics will raise in the future, the Schumpeterian notion of 'creative destruction' unquestionably suggests that both perspectives are important, at least to the evolution of complex systems. Since the dynamics of such systems seem to move beyond our analytical capacities, however, future research may be expected to depend on the articulation of expectations based on self-organization theory, and this, in turn, points to what is perhaps the ultimate message of sociology, namely that these expectations cannot but remain dependent on our own distinctions and, in particular, on the point of reference we denote in order to give meaning to our constructions.

Acknowledgements

I would like to thank Ehud Zuscovitch for calling my attention to the paradoxes in Schumpeterian theory, and Arie Rip for valuable comments on earlier drafts of this paper. I am also grateful to Gene Moore for correcting my English; whatever inconsistencies that have remained are mine.

13 The Evolution of Technology: A Model of Socio-ecological Self-organization

Mary E. Lee

The paradigm that is moving both the 'natural' and the 'social' sciences away from models built upon assumptions about input and output, externalities, and optimal equilibrium states is that of self-organization. As Silverberg (1988) notes, this paradigm switches the focus of analysis from discrete states of equilibrium between 'internal' and 'external' forces to intrinsic nonlinearities that have potential cumulative effects in terms of the collective behaviour of the system. Recently, new methods of testing for 'hidden structures' of nonlinear dynamics in economic data (Brock *et al.* 1990) have strengthened the argument for the applicability of this paradigm to modelling systems in which human behaviour is a component of structure.

My major focus in this paper is to place the dynamics of technology into the larger context of a 'socio-ecological' system of hierarchical self-organization − a context in which these dynamics can be better interpreted. Science and technology have traditionally been defined as functional economic 'sectors' in which human activities are goal-referential to understanding nature and the uses of nature in fulfilling human preferences and needs. Technology is assumed to be driven by these preferences and needs, which in turn drives 'adaptive upgrading' via competitive selection of the most efficient consumption of non-human resources and this, in turn, ultimately drives human evolution. The challenges to this traditional conceptualization are well known (cf. Rosenberg 1982; Nelson and Soete 1988). The self-organization paradigm provides a preliminary basis for a model of 'socio-ecological' evolution in which technology can be described as a local resource transfer process that both effects and is affected by the configuration of resource conditions at other levels.

General hierarchy theory and models of evolutionary change

The concept of 'hierarchical' self-organization offers an alternative to conventional evolutionary models of system behaviour. But the concept of hierarchies has a controversial history; it has appeared in a number of different disciplinary contexts and has differing semantic connotations within these contexts (Wicken 1992; Young 1992). Following the lead of Young (1992), I need to make the distinction here between a 'domination' hierarchy that is a culturally dependent value-ranking and an 'actualization' hierarchy of processes that evolve towards ever more complex levels of operation. Domination hierarchies have to do with human values about the distribution/allocation of resources and therefore can place constraints on system behaviour (Stinchcombe 1983). Actualization hierarchies, however, are the result of ongoing, interdependent processes in which operational dependency relationships among system components are present. Such hierarchies delineate the 'structure' of a system as a function of these processes. A better understanding of actualization hierarchies is necessary to move towards a better understanding of the structuring effects of domination hierarchies. Unless otherwise specified, I discuss the operation of actualization hierarchies in the remainder of this paper.

In conventional models of 'systems' evolution, 'external' conditions provide the parameters for system behaviour. The elements of such models consist of abstract units that have invariant properties. Properties and parameters are not only invariant but also always independent of one another. However, in a hierarchical model, parameters are determined not by externalities, but by other component levels of the system. Properties and parameters are no longer independent. Not only do component units refer to each other, their constituting relationships themselves are subject to change. This means that it is not possible to derive any description of invariant constituting relations, such as a finite-state equation, to model system behaviour (cf. Kampis and Csanyi 1991).

A basic problem in modelling self-organization is formulating a model that, while causally 'closed' in that it requires no explanatory structures that are exclusively and independently exogenous, is effectively 'open' in that it allows of 'outputs' that are of greater complexity than 'inputs'. Closed systems are, by definition, self-organizing. But a closed system admits of neither inputs nor outputs, again by definition. Further, problems abound in differentiating a 'system' from its 'environment'. The axiom of systems theory that a system cannot be more complex than its environment (Pondy and Mitroff 1979) does not clarify the differentiation issue: is a 'social system' more or less complex than its 'environment'? It would be difficult to argue that society is either 'structurally' or 'functionally' more complex than its environment (cf. Nicolis 1986).

The 'structure' of actualization hierarchies, as used here, refers to time-conditional configurations of the dependent and interdependent processes that sustain ongoing system operation. What is often referred to as a 'system' is actually a hierarchical level of operation within a vast open system of self-organizing processes. If no exclusively and independently exogenous processes are hypothesized to affect system behaviour, the system is by definition self-organizing. Levels of operation within the system are hierarchically ordered by the complexity of the processes that sustain ongoing system activity. This complexity arises through a series of differentiating transformations such that some transformation processes are asymmetrically dependent upon prior transformation sequences. The asymmetrical dependency of these processes outlines a logic for differentiating between levels of system operation.

Such levels of operation are 'nearly decomposable' (Pattee 1973, pp. 129–56; Simon 1973; Nicolis 1986) levels of system structure. Each higher-order level is a 'product' of interaction at lower levels. Such 'products' have emergent properties quite distinct from lower-level elements. A hierarchical order results such that system 'structures' are bounded by their own self-referential 'processes'. These hierarchical levels have been described as 'a complex of successively more encompassing sets' similar to a set of Chinese boxes (Grobstein 1973: 31). Behaviour differs between these levels. Behaviour will also differ within levels over discrete periods of time. The primary processes of change in this self-organizing system are transformation processes and feedback processes (Nicolis 1986). Further, the processes that delineate the structure of the system are irreversible, that is, change within the system is cumulative over time and the system cannot return to a state described by its 'initial' conditions. In fact, one can generally predict that, over time, new hierarchical levels will arise. Elements of higher-order levels exhibit distinctive properties that emerge from the cumulative, irreversible effects of operations at lower-order levels.

The dependencies and interdependencies of these processes can be modelled to describe how microscopic events evolve into hierarchically ordered, macroscopic structures of time-conditional probability distributions.[1] The apparently uncoordinated interaction of microscopic elements leads to emergent macroscopic properties that can be represented by a small number of order parameters that summarize the net result of complex system feedbacks and dependencies (Silverberg 1988). Higher-order operations tend to reduce the transformative complexity of the sustaining lower-level processes such that, from a starting set of initial conditions of dimensionality N, the system 'locks in' at a much more compact state that has lower dimensionality (Nicolis 1986). In other words, macro-state configurations feed back into the micro-state variance – there is therefore a 'layered' process of change.[2]

Time-conditional configurations of transformative processes are essential features of evolutionary theory in all areas of inquiry. Collective properties of these transformative processes should be describable as moments of a probability density function that substitutes for the microscopic dynamics (Nicolis 1986). As noted, a hierarchical level is determined by the number, location, complexity, and the degree of operational interdependence among components that maintain flexibly bounded, ordered relationships among themselves. Probabilities that any *specific* macro ordering of relationships between individual components will obtain can be calculated using a generalizable formula for entropy,[3] such as the Kolmogorov–Sinai equation used by Nicolis (1986) and Kaneko (1991). Relationships between components can be expressed as transitional probabilities in a tree diagram and, further, as Markov and semi-Markov chains (Nicolis 1986: 42–5) or as a coupled map lattice (Kaneko 1991) that models the distribution of states.[4]

Levels in the system are formed and broken down in relation to perturbations of boundary values provided by behaviour at levels above and below. In other words, if the heretofore stable reference state of another level becomes unstable, the relationship of components at the level being considered might be forced to rearrange to accommodate the new referent 'control' parameters. At any given hierarchical level, the operations that relate components within that level may, over time, sequentially bifurcate from steady state to steady state with no attendant change in the nature of the dynamical variables involved. However, when changes take place in operations that relate *levels*, the nature of the dynamical relationship of variables in the level being considered will also change.

A preliminary model of technology and evolutionary change

What is the most basic unit of evolution? In other words, can I identify these transformative processes and what is transformed by these processes? Freese (1988) posits that the basic process of evolutionary change in both 'ecosystems' and 'social systems' is the 'resource transfer'. In Freese's model, resources must be thought of as 'transformables', rather than as 'consumables'. Resources are anything – tangible or intangible – that interactants use to sustain interaction (Freese 1988: 102). Thus, the basic unit of change, according to Freese, is the 'resource transfer group' (RTG) that is constituted by this interaction. The resource 'interactants' that constitute RTGs may be individual or 'corporate' collectives, such as molecules, organisms or firms.

The RTG is conceptualized as the smallest autonomous component of system operation that could serve as the basis of self-organized evolution at all levels. Types of resources, means of transfer, rates of transfer, and transfer redundancy are essential to Freese's (1988: 76–7) definition of an RTG, so that an RTG can be defined as a relationship between at least two interacting entities such that, over time, the same resource is repeatedly transferred by the same means at the same rate.

RTGs concatenate to form 'chains' or 'lattices' of resource dependency configurations that define a basic transition matrix. Interrelationships between RTGs comprise self-organizing hierarchies; irreversible change accrues from the cumulative use and transformation of resources through a seemingly endless process of bundling and transferring. As the system transforms resources, some transformations are inherently asymmetrical and cannot revert to an earlier form. New interactions appear when prior interaction sequences are superceded and cannot be restored because the resources on which they depended have been permanently altered (Freese 1988: 70). Resources combine and recombine as the products of resource interaction are added back into the system as 'augmented' resources; augmentation is said to occur with the appearance of a resource interaction that is 'new' to a particular level of the system (Freese 1988: 68). Resource augmentation in turn affects the augmentative development and depletion of resources throughout the system. Rather than 'adapting' to changes in 'external' conditions, units are adapting to dependency changes between other units of the same system. As a system evolves, there are thresholds of change beyond which entirely different resource conditions and resource configurations emerge. Thus, adaptation is a process of continual 'self-selection'.

This defines serial differentiation (Freese 1988: 68, 72), which describes how variation within a unit converts to variation between units over time. Serial differentiation is continuous, it is a property of microscopic interaction that converts to macroscopic diversity, complexity and organization in which system structures are continually redesigned by the effects of their own interactions (Freese 1988: 83). Serial differentiation is not a direct function of the behaviour of interactants, but rather a property of their interaction; other resource variables are implicated in system behaviour. As resources are increasingly transferred they are increasingly transformed. Augmentation derives from the autocatalytic effect of system interaction on system resources. The continual addition to a subsystem of its own interaction affects the augmentative development and depletion of resources throughout the system. Since resources are interconnected in entire chains of resource transfers, the interaction effects of these additions reverberate throughout the system. As augmentative interactions appear, resource configurations change and the system 'evolves'.

Living organisms themselves contribute to the evolutionary process of serial differentiation. Their own sustenance activities change, by resource augmentation and depletion, the conditions which sustain life. If I concede, as does Freese (1988: 116), that social interactions are continuations of resource transfers at lower-order levels that emerge at a higher-order level because of the additional resources that social interactions transfer, then cognitive resources and the higher-order 'social' resources which they sustain are just such augmentations in evolutionary history. An emergent property of the augmentation 'human cognition' is 'goal-seeking' behaviour.

In society, actors' order-defining interpersonal interaction organizes, structures and facilitates resource transfers (Freese 1988: 102). As Luhmann (1989) recognizes, human cognition operates upon data from whatever it defines as the 'environment'. This produces information about interactions within and between each lower- and higher-order structure. Humans perceive the effects of resource interactions at all levels and human cognition generates information that is reflexive to previous beliefs, values and prescriptions for corporate human action – the cognitive stuff of which ideologies and the domination hierarchies that allocate 'rights' of resource transfer are made. These cognitive states then, in turn, have both feedforward and feedback effects on the subsequent structuring of resource transfer processes (cf. Leydesdorff 1992).

It is, however, the micro-level transfer of both tangible and intangible resources, as opposed to the form of interpersonal interactions *per se*, that leads to the coupling and decoupling of various resource groups: 'any social entity whose [only] raw material is interpersonal interaction is not viable . . . any structure of social relations, which is order defining, has to be connected to some structure of resource transfers, which is action-sustaining' (Freese 1988: 105). In brief, intangible ideas about the right to transfer goods and services must be underpinned by the actual transfer of these goods and services from one resource interactant to another. Without the actual transfer, ideas about allocations of rights to transfer could not be sustained. But these ideas, themselves, become additional resources that are transferred among resource interactants. These ideas thus become a part of the system of resource transfers, and can therefore impose constraints on system behaviour in terms of subsequent resource transfers.

Suppose I define 'technology' as human ideas about the use of available resources. I could therefore consider these ideas as an element of a particular class of a higher-order cognitive resource that I will call 'representational' (Knorr-Cetina 1981; Leydesdorff 1992). That is, knowledge is the result of cognition operating on observation to differentiate, define and map 'non-self' resources as well as being a resource available for transfer in and of itself in the form of a reconstructed representation of that experience. Now, assume that such cognitive resources are transferred locally among human interactants by a variety of communicative mechanisms. To the extent that certain ideas about the use of resources actually sustain resource interactions within and among various human RTGs, they become, to use Luhmann's (1989) term, 'coherent'. To the extent that these cognitive resources become bundled with other resources, to use Bijker's (1993) terms, they would be integral elements in a 'socio-technical ensemble'. To use Granovetter's (1985) terminology, technological ideas become 'embedded' in a 'system' of 'economic action'. Or, as Freese (1988) would say, they become essential strands within entire bundles of resources that 'flow' within and among various resource groupings. Given this definition, technology would not only sustain human interaction at the microscopic level within resource groups, but bundled with other resources technology would also sustain larger configurations of resource dependencies. Thus, I am interested not only in the local groups in which individuals transfer cognitive resources, but also in the higher-order configurations that transfer 'bundled' resources. Further, let me

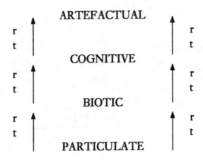

rt = resource transfers

Figure 13.1   The base resource array.

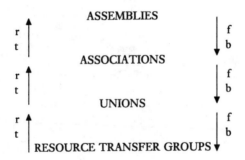

rt = resource transfers
fb = feedbacks

Figure 13.2   Intermediate hierarchies.

propose that the transfer and bundling of resources by humans produces another set of resources: artefacts.

Consider the basic dependency structure of the resource set depicted in Figure 13.1. Each level is dependent on the lower-order levels in that it is a proper subset of all possible resource combinations at the preceding level. Each higher-order subset pictured in Figure 13.1 is the product of resource transfers at lower-order levels, producing augmented resources that have emergent properties quite different from other resource combinations in the preceding set(s). Think of each set as an 'array' of resources that are available for bundling and transfer to all higher levels. Now consider a further hierarchical organization *within* levels, as proposed by Freese (1988) and shown in Figure 13.2.

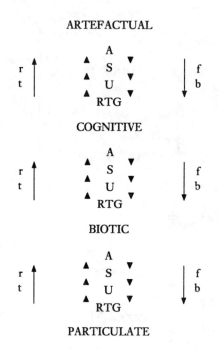

ARTEFACTUAL

COGNITIVE

BIOTIC

PARTICULATE

A = assemblies
S = associations
U = unions
RTG = resource transfer groups
rt = resource transfers
fb = feedbacks

Figure 13.3   Overall structure of the system.

'Entailment' (White and McCann 1988) structures in these intermediate hierarchies (Figure 13.2) form as resources are transferred between interacting entities. Since the transfer of resources among one transfer group is related to the resource transfers of other groups through common 'connectors', some groupings will form subsets of other groupings.[5] Asymmetrical connections between associations, however, form assemblies such that some assemblies are of a higher order than others. Let there be any number of component groupings at each hierarchical level. Ordered assemblies would be 'loosely coupled' at a global level of operation. Given this, the overall structure of the system can be depicted as in Figure 13.3.

Now, to simplify discussion, let me say that the resource set shown in Figure 13.1 is the 'base array' of resources, remembering that the 'particulate' set is the superset for all subsets. Let me further stipulate that each set provides a finite (though perhaps inconceivably large) number of 'primary' resources. These resources sustain the activities of a finite number of RTGs and, therefore, intermediate hierarchies of unions, associations and assemblies at any given point in time. Some resource transfer activities produce resource augmentations and, therefore, new types of resources available for transfer. For example, there are a finite number of particulate resources (according to many physicists) that sustain the production of atoms, molecules, elements, stars, star systems, and so on. The number of ways in which this finite number of particulate resources could possibly *combine* into differing states throughout time would approach infinity. Correspondingly, there is a finite number of cognitive states that sustain the production of rituals, languages, cultures, societies, and so on, among humans. Again, the number of possible combinations of these resources, over time, approaches infinity. RTGs draw upon primary resources provided in a base array, bundle those, and transfer them to form higher-order unions, associations, and assemblies. The number of all possible resource combinations, over time, would also approach infinity.

With the resource array and the components of intermediate transfer hierarchies in place, I have the necessary and sufficient conditions to maintain a system of self-organization; these conditions are the ability of a system to simulate an 'environment' as well as to simulate parts of itself (cf. Nicolis 1986). The *coupling* of all levels via specific resource transfers and feedbacks, however, serves to limit behaviour and therefore the number of possible system states. The coupling between any two levels can be described by a joint probability function[6] that makes explicit the mutual information contained in each level. The behaviour at each level will be limited by the actual interactions among RTGs as well as by the dynamics of the higher-order groupings. At each hierarchical level, the states of levels above and below act as bounding conditions for the behaviour of variables in the level under consideration. Each resource set in the base array, along with its concomitant intermediate hierarchies, would be a 'nearly decomposable level' (NDL) of system structure. Additionally, each level within any given intermediate hierarchy would be an NDL. The problem of modelling macroscopic evolution thus becomes one of describing the *coevolution* of two or more levels.

Given this model, rather than a relatively autonomous social 'subsystem', 'sphere' or 'sector', technology becomes a particular subset of cognitive resources that: are transferred locally within and among various RTGs; are bundled with other resources to form augmented resources and higher-order structures within intermediate hierarchies; sustain (or not, at any given time) entire chains or lattices of resource transfers; and produce an emergent level of artefactual resources and, therefore, another source of feedback to lower-order levels.[7]

Relevance of theories of mathematical chaos to the proposed model of socio-ecological evolution

The model sketched above and the possibilities for mathematical description of the model are, of course, highly speculative. But the proposal allows me to think about the coevolution of technology and cognition, which are ultimately connected to coevolutionary relationships between cognition and other aspects of the larger 'environment'. If the hierarchical dynamics exhibited by differing dimensionalities in mathematical chaos (cf. Baier and Klein 1991; Morrison 1991) are consistent with levels of operation within a hierarchically self-organized system, the transfer of resources between RTGs, and therefore the appearance of resource augmentations, should behave stochastically, introducing elements of chance into the system. Because RTGs connect to form unions and action among unions is transitive, autopoietic effects are localized at the level of unions. Proceeding from steady state to steady state will not change the nature of the variables within a hierarchical level. But cross-correlational effects of the stochastic operator should manifest at higher levels when the system 'chooses' between equipossible states (Nicolis 1986: 207–15). Because resource transfers taking place in differing levels have correlative correspondence, when fluctuations in a coupled level exceed a certain variance threshold, the effects will propagate over time to the level under consideration.

The sensitivity to initial conditions that characterizes chaotic dynamics occurs in bounded continuous flows or successions of discrete states in which nonlinear parameters give rise to exponential divergence in neighbouring states. Successions of state descriptions, when modelled in phase space, may exhibit 'basins of attraction' that represent the system's 'preference' for the organization of micro-states into a specific range of macro-states. Two-space projections reveal a 'tree' pattern of bifurcations, representing the 'history' of state changes. As Arthur (1988b) and Opschoor (1991) have shown, efficiency and equilibrium, as classically defined in economics, have little to do with selection of a path of behaviour that leads to such state lock-ins. As summarized by Prigogine and Stengers (1984: 170): 'The mixture of necessity and chance constitutes the history of the system.'

For example, when RTGs choose between two or more equipossible 'strands' of 'downstream' resources, that choice may, through stochastic operators, effect a 'decoupling' at the association level. That decoupling will produce a feedback effect to lower levels. According to both theory (see, for example, Prigogine and Stengers 1984) and experimental simulations (Kaneko 1991), although the transformation processes are probabilistic, the feedback effects are *deterministic*. If a fluctuation at one level produces a symmetry-breaking effect in operations *between* hierarchical levels, the nature of variables at both levels will change. Macroscopic states can impose inherently unstable constraints on behaviour at microscopic levels. Thus, each NDL outlined in the preceding section has the potential to produce self-organized 'criticality' (cf. Bak and Chen 1991).

To develop such a model fully, one would need to be able to specify a function that describes the relationship between rates of microscopic behaviour, i.e. RTG activation/degeneration, resource augmentation, and resource depletion. According to theory, these rates would differ for each NDL, with lower-order levels behaving asynchronously in relation to higher-order levels (cf. Silverberg 1988; White 1990). Such a function might be similar to the logistic equation, which appears to model closely a number of population processes. Kaneko (1991) employs the logistic function in his simulation of a globally coupled system of interacting nonlinear elements in a 'hyperchaotic' systemic state.

The coupling of components that are each chaotic, in themselves, produces a high potential for the system to exhibit what Kaneko (1991) calls 'fully developed spatiotemporal chaos', which seems to be structurally stable for the entire system at almost all initial conditions. His simulation shows that, despite the chaotic behaviour within components, the overall system can remain surprisingly stable. The effects of localized, transient chaos can be 'extinguished' by propagating to a coupled higher level, so that the overall effect is smooth statistical behaviour. The system displays a further characteristic, a tendency towards producing two 'conflicting' patterns of behaviour: serial differentiation and mean-field reduction of dimensionality. Kaneko (1991) notes that this model exhibits behaviours in common with existing models of neutral dynamics and optical networks, speculating that the same dynamics might describe hierarchical self-organization in such diverse processes as turbulence, evolutionary history, cognitive differentiation, and even society itself.

However, while the overall system may remain stable, chaotic dynamics could dramatically change the local structure of resource transfers. When those dynamics propagate between levels, even if 'localized' at those levels, behaviour at those levels may be altered dramatically, especially over relatively brief, discrete periods of evolutionary time. This will be especially true as one 'moves up' the hierarchy to 'social' levels of the system. At the level of society, human resource transfers can effectively 'speed up' rates of resource augmentation because of the number and the nature of resources that are transferred among human RTGs. On the other hand, ideologies that allocate the 'right' to transfer resources tend to 'homogenize' resource transfer configurations, effectively reducing the dimensionality of the actualization hierarchy at intermediate levels. These 'conflicting' patterns of system behaviour are produced by: elements of chance in the operational transition of specific resource transfer configurations; and feedback effects from higher-order resource transfer configurations that effectively 'lock in' the state of the system, even if that state is inherently unstable and 'far from equilibrium'.

Summary

While entirely speculative in terms of its ability consistently to predict the behaviour of a system that includes human action as an element, the preliminary model outlined above is consistent with current theory and evidence about the nature of evolutionary processes. Lack of adequate data is a major drawback to developing such a model. If data sources could be developed and the model further specified, the following implications would in my view benefit subsequent research in the area of technology and evolutionary change. First, if the evolution of physical, biological and social orders can each be modelled as irreversible, self-organizing processes, barriers to interdisciplinary research are weakened. Second, since 'augmentation' is an effective measure of 'adaptation' (as Freese suggests), we can define what 'counts' as adapted without using input—output models of 'technical advance' (see, for example, Stoneman 1983) as a standard for comparing the adaptation of 'developed' and 'underdeveloped' economies. Third, by eliminating the dualistic dichotomies usually drawn between 'biological' and 'social' processes of change, we can begin to analyse irreversible outcomes arising from the interaction of human social arrangements and the 'non-human' resources upon which they ultimately depend. Last, by understanding the underlying dynamics of 'actualization' hierarchies, we can better discern the effects of 'domination' hierarchies in human societies. If specific feedbacks at each level could be identified and modelled, the 'deterministic' effects of specific resource configurations could be better predicted.

Notes

1. For example, if we let the configuration of structural units in state space be the N-dimensional vector $\mathbf{x}$ at time t, given the probability density function $P(\mathbf{x};t)$, we can derive a macroscopic equation that describes the evolution of the transition matrix. The general form of this model is:

$$\frac{d}{dt}<\mathbf{x}> = f_1\,[<\mathbf{x}>;\mu]$$

   where f_1 is a nonlinear polynomial (Nicolis 1986: 44).
2. I am indebted to a personal communication from Loet Leydesdorff for this wording.
3. There is much discussion about the appropriateness of various measures of 'thermodynamic' versus 'informational' entropy for describing various types of phenomenon. I do not claim an invariant system-wide property of thermodynamic conservation; although this property may hold at certain levels of the hierarchy, it will not at others. I therefore accept a more generalizable interpretation of entropy as a measure of the probability of obtaining any specific macro-state given a particular number of

micro-states. More in-depth discussion of this argument can be found in Weber *et al.* (1988), Bailey (1990) and Dyke (1992).

4. While Nicolis (1986) uses Markov chains to describe transitions in informational states, Markov chains also provide the basis for modelling cumulative effects of the availability of scarce resources as 'opportunity chains' (Weissburg *et al.* 1991), which is probably a better example for the current discussion. However, perhaps the best model for the system under discussion is provided by the lattice coupling map described by Kaneko (1991), as algebraic properties of lattice structures provide certain modelling advantages (cf. Hamilton 1982; Morrison 1991).

5. For example, X is *not* related to Y when one resource transfer has occurred between X and Y; rather X is related to Y if and only if at least one interactant who transfers resources to X also transfers resources to Y. This interactant is a 'connector'. Set–subset relationships are identified by considering each of the $[N(N-1)/2]$ possible pairs among the interactants and calculating the percentage of asymmetrical relationships and the correlations of pairs. Suppose that interactants A, B and C each transfer resources to X; A, B, C and D each transfer resources to Y; and B, C and D each transfer resources to Z. Then X 'entails' Y since those who transfer to X are a 'subset' of those who transfer to Y; further, Y 'entails' Z since, in each case, there are no asymmetrical exceptions (cf. White and McCann 1988).

6. Given the two-point probability function $p\left(x_n(i),\ x_{n+t}(i+m)\right)$, and the single point probability function $p\left(x(i)\right)$, the mutual information is (Kaneko 1991: 236):

$$I\left(t,\ m;i\right) = \int \log p\left(x_n(i)\right)\ \mathrm{d}x_n(i)$$

$$+ \int \log p\left(x_{n+t}(i+m)\right)\ \mathrm{d}x_{n+t}(i+m)$$

$$- \int \log p\left(x_n(i),\ x_{n+t}(i+m)\right)\ \mathrm{d}x_{n+t}(i+m)$$

7. I cannot resist noting here that should 'true' artificial intelligence ever be perfected, additional intermediate hierarchies will give rise to yet another level of resources: 'Virtual Artefacts'.

033 *180·92*

14 New Models of Technological Change: New Theories for Technology Studies?

Loet Leydesdorff

What I love best about the calculus is that . . .
it frees us from working with our imagination.

Leibniz (1692)

Can the interaction between evolutionary economics and nonlinear systems theory help us to specify new perspectives for technology studies? How are contributions from economics, sociology, evolution and systems theory relevant to an understanding of the dynamics of technology in society? This question seems urgent at the end of this compilation of contributions from various disciplines. Is the whole more than the sum of its parts?

I shall argue that the theory of complex dynamic systems can guide us in clarifying these issues. The formal theory enables us to proceed from theoretical specification to generalization. Conclusions concerning the further development of technology studies can be drawn on the basis of the emerging paradigm, and normative implications for technology policies can be specified. However, this inference requires a series of reflexive steps.

First, it is necessary to deconstruct the biological metaphor in evolution theory. In *cultural* evolution theory, variation can no longer be considered as a consequence of 'natural' or external selection. Nowadays, both the natural environment and the markets are increasingly changing due to technological developments. However, the assumption of a feedback − or a coevolution − between the selecting macro-system and the micro-variation potentially closes the evolutionary system into a self-referential loop (Maturana 1978). 'Variation' and 'selection' should then be considered as sub-dynamics of the complex system. On the one hand, this change in perspective allows us to envisage that the category which was, for example, specified as the selecting instance at one moment, may have to be respecified as generating variation at a next moment. On the other hand, the respecification of evolutionary categories 'on the fly' has implications for the epistemological status of theoretical specifications. The categorical meaning of the variables is then allowed to change, in addition to possible changes in the values of these variables.

While the discursive interpretation tends to become confused when both the theoretical categories and the values attributed to them change, the algorithmic simulation enables us to identify the various dynamics. By understanding variables as fluxes, one is able to distinguish change in the value of the variables from interactive effects affecting the variables themselves. The specification of theoretical categories, however, requires reflection based on the adoption of a specific – that is, selective – perspective (cf. Hinton et al. 1986). In other words, the 'phenotypical' behaviour of the model system is more complex than its composing ('genotypical') dynamics, while only the latter can be made the subject of substantive theorizing (Langton 1989).

The theoretical systems constitute another layer of complex (reflective) systems on top of the complex social system(s) under study. The various paradigms compete in the effort to understand technological developments by reflexively organizing the complex systems under study. The lack of external standards would make it appealing to compare the explanatory power of the various discourses *within* another self-referential metadiscourse. But is a metadiscourse available that can contain sufficient complexity for the comparison?

The message of the postmodern philosophy of science has been precisely that such a comparison among 'incommensurable' paradigms is no longer possible (cf. Kuhn 1962). The transition from variables in a spatial model to fluxes in an algebraic model, however, provides us with an additional degree of freedom in the discourse, since variables can be considered as instantiations of fluxes. The resulting discourse pays a price for being formal; it only *refers* to substantive specification (cf. Andersen 1992). Nonlinear dynamics, therefore, can be considered as another partial perspective, but one that enables us to formulate an expectation about relations among discourses. In the final sections of this paper, the application of this analysis to technology studies will lead to conclusions both with respect to the subject matter and with respect to the interdisciplinary organization among the contributing disciplines.

The reconstruction of evolution theory

What are the differences between biological and socio-economic theories of evolution? First, there is a difference with respect to the evolving unit of analysis, and second, the difference has epistemological implications. Although philosophers of biology have increasingly been aware that selection is internal to the complex system (see, for example, Eldredge 1985; Freese 1988; Lee, this volume), practising biologists may refer to 'nature' or 'natural' selection without necessarily deconstructing these concepts as theoretical attributions. In evolutionary economics, however, 'selection environments' have been defined more abstractly than observable markets (Nelson and Winter 1977). Therefore, economic selection environments are obviously theoretically constructed, as are the units of variation. Neither the entrepreneur nor the firm, let alone the modern corporation, are 'naturally given', they are the results of a stage of cultural evolution that has been achieved through human history. The analytical categories can no longer be attributed to an unambiguous referent, and consequently the units of analysis themselves are reflexively constructed on the basis of previous understanding, that is, *within* discursive networks (cf. Hesse 1980).

Given that the analytical categories themselves are theoretically constructed, various theories may differ profoundly in terms of their basic assumptions about units of analysis or, in other words, about the systems that are considered central to economic analysis. For example, while some contributions to evolutionary economics have drawn on the theory of the firm, others have argued that technologies or industries are the evolving systems. If one analyst provisionally equates different technologies with different production units, other scholars can provide us with counter-examples for this identification. Thus, cultural evolution theory requires more reflexivity about the evolving unit than biological evolution theory originally contained (Andersen 1992). Both 'selection' and 'variation' are *theoretical* attributions: variations are contained in the hypothesized systems as uncertainty in the distributions, while selections provide the uncertainty with feedbacks (cf. Allen, this volume). Since the processes under study are multi-layered, various interacting dynamics (of variation and selection) can be assumed. More than one selection may operate on a variation, and the various selections may interact. In general, the specification of these relations generates a model.

A feedback can reduce the uncertainty to a skewed distribution, but this selection does not yet transform the uncertainty into a signal (Bruckner *et al.*, this volume). Only if the selecting system is sufficiently stable over time will it additionally be able to distinguish what it recognizes as variation from what is merely noise. Thus, the selecting system additionally preselects the communication by setting boundary conditions to the *relevant* variation (cf. David and Foray, this volume). However, these two negative feedbacks — one from the selection and one from the preselection by the self-referential system — can sometimes be combined into a positive feedforward. When this happens, evolution may begin.

But this is no longer 'natural' evolution; it is rather the specification of an evolutionary model of the system under study which may also happen to be additionally identifiable in terms of events that have actually occurred. Observable history is the special case which happens to occur among ranges of other possibilities that the model can explore (see, for example, Brunner, this volume).

Algorithmic simulation and discursive model specification

As is well known from harmony theory, under specific conditions a system of various dynamics (for example, feedbacks) may begin to resonate. Resonances provide complex systems with strong filters of noise, and therefore they are expected to have survival value (Simon 1969; Smolensky 1986). In the case of a multi-layered system, some subsystems may additionally drift in terms of their relevant resonances, while certain niches may better be shielded against variations in other parts of the system (Reggiani and Nijkamp, this volume). Cycles with different and changing frequencies should be expected. While biological theory has operated with natural units of time like seasons, years, and generations, cultural evolution theory has to specify one or more frequencies (or a spectrum) for each relevant context (cf. Kampmann et al., this volume).

In principle, each additional context introduces an infinite number of possible interactions. Without substantive specification – that is, assumptions – the problem is usually non-computable. As noted, theoretical reflection is based on choosing a perspective: each specification operates as a selection device among other selection devices. The various theoretical specifications condition one another in the model system. By running the model, one may discover that in some regions the systems under study are inherently unstable. Whether stable solutions can be found remains an empirical question. Note that observable stability is the special case where action and counter-action balance. At other times, so-called 'strange' or oscillating attractors can be shown (Greiner and Kugler, this volume; cf. Semmler 1986; Boldrin 1988). Thus, running a model provides us with insights into the potential dynamics of the nonlinear system. While one may be able to find a local optimum in a simple model by trial and error, one needs to program stochastic variation into the complex system in order to have the computer explore the model's state space for local or global optima (see, for example, Rumelhart et al. 1986; Baum 1988; Langton 1989; Allen, this volume). Additionally, one can run the simulation a thousand or more times, and then develop its statistics.

In summary, the relations between modelling and theorizing generate a tension that drives the scientific research process. First, without sufficient specification the number of possibilities becomes rapidly non-computable (cf. Penrose 1989). Second, the appreciation of the results of a simulation requires its reflexive interpretation in terms of a theory. But without a simulation model one is not able reflexively to control the position that is (implicitly) chosen when understanding the complex system under study. Theoretical specifications assume a point of entrance into the state space of the model that they help to specify, and the results of the simulation may allow for theoretical inferences. But the latter have to be tested for their significance, since myriads of other inferences always remain possible.

Substantive theorizing requires a selective perspective, and therefore the theoretical reflections contain *less* complexity than the model system under study. Discursive theories specify sub-cybernetics (cf. Blauwhof, this volume). Note that there is no alternative: substantive theorizing is necessary for the specification of sub-dynamics. Upon theoretical specification of the various sub-dynamics (for example, the market or the dynamics of innovation), probability distributions (variation) and conditional statements (selection) span the complex model in a multi-dimensional space. The specified mechanisms − formalized as equations − condition one another as selective devices. The interaction, however, is by definition nonlinear, and therefore the outcome is foreseeably counter-intuitive from each partial perspective. The model system shows us the 'unintended consequences' that cannot be specified by theorizing (cf. Giddens 1984). Albeit always dynamic, the model system can additionally be considered as *evolutionary* if it is allowed to use variation in order to explore and eventually to change the multi-dimensional space that the theoretical specifications have spanned (see, for example, Allen and Phang, this volume). This may further complicate the theories, but the epistemological constraints on the appreciative understanding remain the same.

Theory feeds into the system *ex ante* for reasons of specification, and *ex post* in order to interpret the results. The results of the simulations require theoretical interpretation in the various traditions in order to improve the specifications in a next round. The discursive interpretation can be functional for the more precise specification of sub-cybernetics, and therefore theorizing may locally improve a model. This intellectual process is by definition discursive. Each theory will claim comprehensiveness, while metatheoretically one expects various reflexive discourses to emerge as competing paradigms. The interaction among the discourses contains more complexity than each of the contributing disciplines, and this is made explicit by running the model. The discourses inform one another by discussing the various simulation results. In response to these interactions the axes of the reflexive discussions may gradually change. New developments in theorizing are made possible by exploiting these gains in creative recombinations (Lee, this volume; cf. Luhmann 1990).

Towards a general theory of complex dynamic systems

Is this hope for combinatorial profits the epistemological end of the road for scientific theorizing? Indeed, it is for substantive theorizing; one has to wait and see what will emerge in terms of new conjectures. But the general theory of complex dynamic systems additionally suggests a procedural expectation for comparing the various combinatorial solutions in a model system. This expectation can be derived from the central hypothesis that all 'entropical' systems self-organize their thermal 'death' (Georgescu-Roegen 1971).[1] The potential 'energy' contained in the initial conditions dissipates through the system as rapidly as possible according to the substantive dynamics of the system. In the complex system this is a complex process, like the whirl when flushing a toilet (Dyke 1993). But the processes are constrained by the selective instances that organize the fluxes (Swenson 1989).

Both substantive and reflexive systems perform 'life' cycles in a hyperspace that includes the time dimension. Formally, time is just another dimension of the complex system. Differentiation is then equivalent to decomposability along the time axis. Self-organizing systems will tend towards differentiation along dimensions which are functional for the survival of the system. Differentiated systems build on and replace the lower-order ones by encompassing them as nearly decomposable sub-cybernetics (cf. Simon 1969). Complex dynamic systems can be compared in terms of their evolutionary 'advancement': the more differentiated they are, the more complexity the system is able to hold. The axes stand perpendicular and the interactions tend to be depressed.

If the higher-order system goes into crisis, the sub-cybernetics becomes less controlled, and thus more active (as a muscle becomes hypersensitive upon its denervation). Eventually, a self-organizing system gives way to another self-organization of the chaos. But the various model systems can be compared in terms of their efficiency in organizing the fluxes of probabilistic entropy that they generate by operating (Swenson 1989). Different solutions refer to different optima, and one can program the model so that it is able to search for and to compare among alternatives (Rumelhart et al. 1986; Anderson et al. 1988).

The reflexive understanding of the results, however, implies a necessary reduction of the underlying complexity by choosing a perspective. The scientific discourses can be considered metatheoretically as cycles in relation to the hypercycle which is run in the model system (cf. Leydesdorff 1993a). But if they are so formalized, no substantive language is left to integrate the various perspectives. While the algebraic understanding in terms of formal models and fluxes initially constituted only another discourse, this formal discourse can be developed into a discourse of a different order than the substantive theories that feed into it. As a hypercyclic model it enables us to reconstruct the complex interactions under study, and to distinguish the relative positions (and weights) of substantive specifications by comparing them in terms of the dynamic analogon of the part of the variance (that is, the probabilistic entropy flux) that they are expected to explain (Figure 14.1).

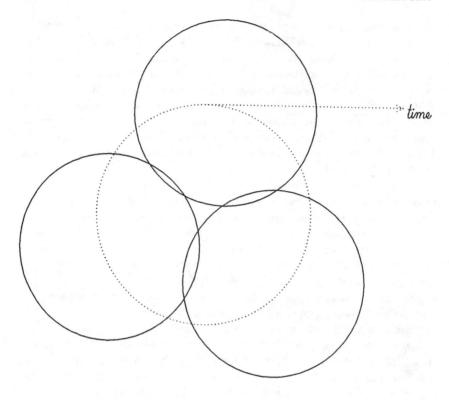

time

Figure 14.1 The hypercycle model.

Technological developments as agents of change

Let us apply this model of competing but potentially interacting specifications to technology studies. As is well known, Schumpeter (1939) distinguished between innovations as changes in the shape of the production function reflecting the possibility to generate more output from less input, and changes along the production function as factor substitutions. Thus, two different dynamics were postulated: adjustment with reference to an equilibrium (or steady state), and the generation of innovation upsetting the movement towards equilibrium. Note that these two mechanisms stand orthogonally in terms of shifts along or perpendicular to the production function.

The regulatory (for example, price) mechanisms has captured the attention of (neo)classical economics, but innovation has been considered as exogenous in this tradition. The identification of technological developments with the mechanism of change perpendicular to the production function provided evolutionary economics with a perspective for reducing the complexity in studying the dynamics of the system. Indeed, this perspective raises evolutionary questions, since the postulation of transitions among equilibrium states makes one wonder about trajectories or pathways in these transitions, their potential irreversibility, and the feedback between the emerging state and subsequent transitions.

Nelson and Winter (1977: 49) proposed that the feedbacks between technological trajectories and selection environments be ignored provisionally in favour of first developing conformable sub-theories about both mechanisms. The dynamics of innovation were then specified in terms of Markov chain models. A later comprehensive study (Nelson and Winter 1982) provided theoretical specifications for technological developments both in relation and in opposition to neoclassical economics. Their stated aim was to endogenize the innovation mechanism into economic modelling, but the interaction terms were not yet specified.

Economic historians, however, have emphasized the *interactive* nature of the relations among technologies and markets (see, for example, Rosenberg 1976). Sociologists have stressed the interdependence of variation and selection in social development processes (Bijker *et al.* 1987). Others have emphasized the *path-dependent* nature of technological developments and the consequent emergence of so-called 'lock-ins' (Sahal 1981; David 1985; Arthur 1988b). The idea that technological developments involve an 'internal momentum' (Winner 1977) suggests, first, that developments relate to their own previous state(s). Each development has both a self-referential axis − since it extends from a previous stage − and an extent to which it interacts with relevant environments. If a 'lock-in' among two axes occurs, a coevolution ('mutual shaping') can take off (cf. Nelson, this volume). The (super)system internalizes the two contexts as degrees of freedom. This procedure can be recursively reiterated.

The interactive and recursive terms introduce higher-order dynamics into the models. For example, a trajectory of transitions between equilibrium states can be considered as the result of interactions between the dynamics of innovation and the market mechanism. The resulting pattern, however, can recursively enter into another relation to its selection environment, and then generate a technological regime. While the Markov chain models develop towards a single steady state along a 'natural trajectory', more than one trajectory can be developed if the transition matrix for the system is allowed to vary in relation to changing selection environments. For example, by using parallel and distributed computing Allen (1988a) showed that in the curve of fish ('capital') against fishing ('labour') various densities − with their respective histories − could be originated in the simulation.

In the complex system, Nelson and Winter's 'search and selection processes' can with hindsight be considered as the organization at the interface between the two dynamics of technological innovation and market equilibria. Technological options ('search processes') and market opportunities ('selection processes') have to be combined socially into 'heuristics' that are attributed to firms or aggregates of firms into industries. The functions of the social system have to be carried by local actors, but, with reference to the complex system, these (aggregates of) actors should be considered as a distributed context that provides the evolving system with additional complexity, that is to say, with social organization as a third degree of freedom. The dynamics along a third dimension can be used for selections upon first-order selections (on variations in a first dimension) using a second-order cybernetics. As noted, the operation of two selective mechanisms upon each other ('coevolution') allows for the possibility of a subsequent feedforward, including a provisional stabilization.

Dosi (1982: 154) once used the metaphor of a 'cylinder' in a multi-dimensional space for describing a technological trajectory and its trade-offs. While a trajectory can still be considered as a dynamic trade-off between variation ('technological innovation') and selection (for example, 'the market mechanism'), the direction or stabilization of a trajectory requires an additional context (for example, a distribution of firms). Since firms are distributed, trajectories can only be localized provisionally and probabilistically. But if this (uncertain) localization offers specific advantages to enterpreneurs (cf. Atkinson and Stiglitz 1969; Sahal 1981), the local advantages can feed back to the dynamics of the system as a specific 'selection environment', and lead to 'increasing dynamic returns' over time. Thus, the additional feedback can lock the trajectory into a regime (Allen, this volume).

In other words, the coevolution of a specific combination of a selection environment with a probabilistically stabilized technological trajectory can lead to a globalized technological regime, or − in the case of an opposite sign − to the subsequent disintegration ('death') of the configuration (cf. Abernathy and Clark 1985). While the trajectory tends to be locally stabilized, a regime tends to be globalized in a four-dimensional hyperspace. The regime is by definition in transition; the hypercycle of a regime remains 'absent' if one studies observable events and relations in discursive models that use spatial metaphors (Giddens 1984).

Dosi's (1982) metaphor of a 'cylinder' appealed to a spatial representation, since the focus was on the 'stabilized' trajectory. The four-dimensional technological regime (or 'technological paradigm', as Dosi prefers to call it) is uncertain with respect to the three-dimensional 'cylinder' that it will consider as the representation of its past. In other words, the higher-order system contains a degree of freedom that enables it to make additional selections on lower-order stabilizations. The globalized system is both more responsive and more resilient (since better buffered) than each of its composing dynamics.

For example, if we consider the car system as a typical regime in our time, this system is responsive to policy measures like taxing leaded petrol. However, such policy measures do not lead to a shift towards public transportation, since the system is able to cope with this disturbance in terms of innovation as one of its constitutive cybernetics. The normative implication is that, on the one hand, policies may be able deliberately to influence technological *trajectories* in terms of, among other things, the relative use of various production factors. On the other hand, similar policies can have a range of effects in the case of technological *regimes* because of the additional degree of freedom in the self-organizing system. Although the latter system is able to exhibit more responsiveness to policy measures (for example, in terms of firm behaviour), one expects it to be resilient in restoring its own order.

In summary, the self-organizing regime is based on specific resonances among its constitutive cybernetics. Noise is continuously filtered out by the resonances among the lower-order systems. The self-organizing system returns to attracting states, and is therefore also self-cleaning as long as its hypercycle can be performed. The complex regime remains subject to the price mechanism, technological learning and social organization as its constitutive cybernetics; but it performs its own 'life' cycle, and thereby transforms the economy.

In an evolutionary model, one expects the various dynamics to be nearly decomposable: the subsystems interact in the observable events, but they tend to be reproduced as functional differentiations so that the system can organize as much complexity as possible. The emerging regime guides the order in the functioning of its subsystems by selecting *ex post*, while remaining a latent and *ex ante* condition for the instantiations at the next moment. As long as the lower-level systems run their cycles, the higher-order system is able to perform a hypercycle that sets the stage for dynamic developments at the lower levels. Since the sub-cybernetics tend towards functional differentiation (and therefore, near-decomposability in the frequency domain), the various composing cybernetics have to be rearranged periodically with functional reference to the further development of the hypercycle. When the higher-order system tends towards crisis the lower-level systems become less controlled and therefore more active. Thus, the model can guide the search for clusters of innovations in the frequency domain (cf. Rosenberg and Frischtak 1984).

Surplus value at the theoretical level

We have distinguished three functional dynamics for the emergence of a technological regime, namely the market system, technological innovation, and social organization in terms of firms and industries. The discourse of economics has introduced the market as a selecting device. As noted, substantive specification reduces complexity on the computational side by setting a filter on the wealth of possible models; by raising the question of the economic interpretability of the results, and by focusing on economic data.

Recent attention to technological innovation in evolutionary economics has brought the dynamic aspect of innovative change into the picture. If understood as two dynamics of a supersystem, the interaction terms are expected to generate 'business cycles', and thus to change the larger (social) system. This brings the sociology of technology into perspective. Thus, at least these three semantics are relevant, since they reflect interacting (but tendentially perpendicular) developments in the system.

Additionally, one would expect theories about all relevant interactions (cf. Simon 1973). But more importantly, one would expect a fourth orthogonal reflection of the system to be a subject of theorizing. This discourse addresses the problem of studying the hypercycle as an additional sub-dynamics. It abstracts from substances in the other dynamics, and reflects on fluxes instead of variables. Only reference to substance is left; the models tend to be formalized. The contribution, however, is to show that the actual regime or attractor is one among a range of attractors, and thus the model can sensitize the analyst to other possible dynamics.

One would expect the various discourses to interact, and to be functionally sorted again following interaction. The results may thus improve the understanding of technological developments in each of them, while not leading to a single comprehensive representation of the complexity of the processes under study. Each of the representations can specify sub-cybernetics in terms of expectations, but the specification of their interaction in the simulation model provides us with an additional angle to control for the quality of the expectation. Note that one can no longer predict, since the interactive effects are expected to be different from the expectation. But the interactive discourse is able to control for the quality of the expectation *ex post*, and it guides the specification of hypotheses on the basis of the results of simulations.

The new paradigm is based, among other things, upon the powerful tools of advanced computing for studying relations among specifications in nonlinear models. The possible occurrence of irreversible thresholds in stochastic processes, the occurrence of bifurcations and strange attractors, can be explored by using nested feedback loops for the recursive reduction of uncertainty. This discourse is mathematical; it uses a formalized language in which models can be formulated without a necessary relation to a specific instantiation in a system under study. Therefore, it allows one to generalize from the specifications to the state space, and in principle to suggest states other than those which are intuitively accessible. Thus, the system is able to bootstrap from specification to generalization. Note the analogy with the relation between stabilization and globalization.

The specification of the structural mechanisms that reduce the complexity can only be achieved by empirical research at the subsystems level. Grandiose and comprehensive schemes do not help us further, since each context in itself adds an infinite range of possibilities for the further development of the model. Integration can only mean elaboration of the theoretically useful differentiations in a reflexive discourse. For example, on the basis of previous knowledge about the aircraft industry a researcher might have reason to expect certain innovation patterns in the helicopter industry (cf. Saviotti 1988). Only by carefully testing the expectations based on the former industry in the latter case can one stepwise improve the understanding, and consequently the models. The choice of case studies, however, should anticipate the need for hypothetical generalization and formalization. Cases should be based, among other things, on considerations of sample choice in relation to populations. Remember that populations have first to be theoretically constructed, since one can no longer assume that they are given 'naturally'. The discourses can inform one another with respect to theoretical expectations, but they develop self-referentially. Additionally, the various bodies of knowledge interact reflexively as 'situated' perspectives by contributing to the further specification of models (cf. Haraway 1988).

Some normative implications

Considerations about the expected relations between technological trajectories and technological regimes provide us with a lead for the specification of normative implications. As noted, technological trajectories can be imagined in terms of three-dimensional pictures, while technological regimes organize themselves in the four dimensions of a hyperspace. Policies, however, cannot deliberately 'steer' complex dynamic systems, but only generate feedback on their 'instantiations'. The technological regime can be expected to react in a counter-intuitive way, and the intentional factors in the policy measures are self-referentially fed back into the political system as disappointments and occasions for learning (Luhmann 1990). Thus, the self-organization paradigm tends to emphasize the functions of subsystems; the degree of interaction remains an empirical question.

The more the developing regime is on the edge of crisis, the more receptive it will be to signals from its environments. Therefore, one might expect policies to be most effective when they support the 'creative destruction' of hypercyclic regimes. Schumpeter's well-known 'creative destruction' disturbs the system, and thereby generates room for innovation along new trajectories. As noted, the more the system disintegrates, the more active the sub-cybernetics can be. However, one should be aware that the resulting processes are self-organizing, and reflexively responsive. Thus, new policies have to be invented from time to time.

In concreto, this conclusion means that policies should support emerging trajectories. While the regime (for example, the car system) can be expected to restore its own order, taxing leaded petrol may be helpful for developing catalysts or cleaner engines.

Among the various sub-cybernetics distinguished above, the one most accessible to the political process is the dynamics of social organization (Etzkowitz, this volume). As noted, intervention at the level of each sub-cybernetics can be functional, since the regime is always challenged by disturbances in its sub-cybernetics. From this perspective, the debate over socialist intervention and liberal *laissez-faire* has grown obsolete: today's regimes contain both the dynamics of markets and those of social organization. Nowadays, the crucial question is whether interventions will prove to be functional in disturbing the ongoing process without laming it.

The political process has to organize the legitimation for intervention, but the intervention has to be assessed in terms of its effects in the relevant technological systems. Whenever two systems interact during the intervention, they can be expected to be functionally sorted thereafter. Note that this perspective provides us with a counter-intuitive set of evaluative standards for political action: not the effectiveness, but the (largely unintended) effects have to be assessed by a reflexive policy-maker. The more reflexive policy-maker will wish to register the unexpected effects, and to update his or her expectations. But since political expectations are normatively embedded, technological developments continuously generate tensions at the cultural level. These tensions can be considered as challenges to the future of technology studies.

Note

1. I use quotation marks for words like 'entropy', 'life' and 'death' in order to signal that the referent is not necessarily biological or physical. In nonlinear dynamics, one should use a probabilistic equivalent of entropy that is yet content-free (cf. Smolensky 1986).

Bibliography

Abernathy, W. J. and Clark, K. B. (1985) 'Innovation: Mapping the Winds of Creative Destruction', *Research Policy*, vol. 14, pp. 3–22.

Abernathy, W. J. and Utterback, J. (1978) 'Patterns of Industrial Innovation', *Technology Review*, vol. 50, pp. 41–7.

Acs, Z. J. and Audretsch, D. B. (1990) *Innovation and Small Firms*, Cambridge, MA: MIT Press.

Alchian, A. A. (1950) 'Uncertainty, Evolution, and Economic Theory', *Journal of Political Economy*, vol. 58, pp. 211–22.

Allen, P. M. (1976a) 'Evolution, Population Dynamics, and Stability', *Proceedings of the National Academy of Sciences of the USA*, vol. 73, pp. 665–8.

Allen, P. M. (1976b) 'Darwinian Evolution and a Predator–Prey Ecology', *Bulletin of Mathematical Biology*, vol. 37, pp. 389–405.

Allen, P. M. (1978) 'Dynamiques de centres urbains', *Sciences et Techniques*, no. 50, pp. 15–18.

Allen, P. M. (1982) 'The Genesis of Structure in Social Systems: The Paradigm of Self-Organization', in *Theory and Explanation in Archaeology*, New York: Academic Press, pp. 347–74.

Allen, P. M. (1984) 'Self-Organization and Evolution in Urban Systems', in Crosby, R. (ed.), *Cities and Regions as Non-linear Decision Systems*, AAAS Selected Symposia, no. 77, Boulder, CO: Westview Press, pp. 29–62.

Allen, P. M. (1985) 'Towards a New Science of Complex Systems', in *The Science and Praxis of Complexity*, Tokyo: United Nations University Press.

Allen, P. M. (ed.) (1986) 'Management and Modelling of Dynamic Systems', *European Journal of Operational Research*, vol. 25, no. 1.

Allen, P. M. (1988a) 'Evolution, Innovation and Economics', in Dosi et al. (1988: 95–119).

Allen, P. M. (1988b) 'Evolution: Why the Whole Is Greater Than the Sum of Its Parts', in Wolff, W., Soeder, C. J. and Drepper, F. R. (eds), *Ecodynamics*, Berlin: Springer-Verlag, pp. 2–31.

Allen, P. M. (1990) 'Why the Future Is Not What It Was', *Futures*, July/August, pp. 555–70.

Allen, P. M. (1991) 'Fisheries: Models of Learning and Uncertainty', in Cury, Ph. (ed.), *Pêcheries ouest africaines, variabilité, instabilité et changement*, Paris: ORSTOM.

Allen, P. M. and Ebeling, W. (1984) 'Evolution and the Stochastic Description of Simple Ecosystems', *Biosystems*, vol. 16, pp. 113–26.

Allen, P. M. and Lesser, M. (1991) 'Evolutionary Human Systems: Learning, Ignorance and Subjectivity', in Saviotti and Metcalfe (1991: 160–71).

Allen, P. M. and McGlade, J. M. (1986) 'Dynamics of Discovery and Exploitation: the Scotian Shelf Fisheries', *Canadian Journal of Fisheries and Aquatic Science*, vol. 43, no. 6.

Allen, P. M. and McGlade, J. M. (1987a) 'The Modelling of Human Systems: A Fisheries Example', *European Journal of Operational Research*, June 1987, vol. 30, pp. 147–67.

Allen, P. M. and McGlade, J. M. (1987b) 'Evolutionary Drive: The Effect of Microscopic Diversity, Error Making and Noise', *Foundations of Physics*, vol. 17, no. 7, pp. 723–38.

Allen, P. M. and McGlade, J. M. (1987c) *Managing Complexity: a Fisheries Example*, Report to the United Nations University, Tokyo.

Allen, P. M. and McGlade, J. M. (1989) 'Optimality, Adequacy and the Evolution of Complexity', in Christiansen, P. L. and Parmentier, R. D. (eds), *Structure, Coherence and Chaos in Dynamical Systems*, Manchester: Manchester University Press.

Allen, P. M. and Sanglier, M. (1978) 'Dynamic Models of Urban Growth', *Journal of Social and Biological Structures*, vol. 1, pp. 265–80.

Allen, P. M. and Sanglier, M. (1979) 'A Dynamic Model of Growth in a Central Place System', *Geographical Analysis*, vol. 11, no. 3. pp. 258–72.

Allen, P. M. and Sanglier, M. (1981) 'Urban Evolution, Self-Organization and Decision Making', *Environment and Planning A*, vol. 13, pp. 167–83.

Allen, P. M., Engelen, G. and Sanglier, M. (1983) 'Self-Organizing Models in Human Systems', in *Synergetics – From Microscopic to Macroscopic Order, Synergetics Series*, Berlin: Springer-Verlag, pp. 150–73.

Amable, B. (1992) 'Competition among Techniques in the Presence of Increasing Returns to Scale', *Journal of Evolutionary Economics*, vol. 2, pp. 147–58.

Amsterdamska, O. (1990) 'Surely You Are Joking, Monsieur Latour!', *Science, Technology and Human Values*, vol. 15, pp. 495–504.

Andersen, E. S. (1992) *Artificial Economic Evolution and Schumpeter*, Aalborg: Institute for Production, University of Aalborg.

Anderson, P. W., Arrow, K. J. and Pines, D. (eds) (1988) *The Economy as a Complex Evolving System*, Reading, MA: Addison-Wesley

Arrow K. and Debreu, G. (1954) 'Existence of an Equilibrium for a Competitive Economy', *Econometrica*, vol. 22, pp. 265–90.

Arnol'd, V. I. (1965) 'Small Denominators. I. Mappings of the Circumference onto Itself', *American Mathematical Society Translations*, vol. 46, pp. 184–213.

Arthur, W. B. (1988a) 'Self-Reinforcing Mechanisms in Economics', in Anderson *et al.* (1988: 9–32).

Arthur, W. B. (1988b) 'Competing Technologies: An Overview', in Dosi *et al.* (1988: 590–607).

Arthur, W. B. (1989) 'Competing Technologies, Increasing Returns, and Lock-In by Historical Events', *Economic Journal*, vol. 99, pp. 116–31.

Arthur, W. B. (1990) 'Positive Feedbacks in the Economy', *Scientific American*, vol. 262, February, pp. 80–5.

Atkinson, A. and Stiglitz, J. (1969) 'A New View of Technological Change', *The Economic Journal*, vol. 79, pp. 573–8.

Ayres, R. U. (1991) 'Evolutionary Economics and Environmental Imperatives', *Structural Change and Economic Dynamics*, vol. 2, no. 2, p. 255.

Baier, G. and Klein, M. (eds) (1991) *A Chaotic Hierarchy*, London: World Scientific Publishers.

Bailey, K. D. (1990) 'Why H does not Measure Information', *Quality and Quantity*, vol. 24, pp. 159–71.

Bainbridge, W. (1976) *The Spaceflight Revolution*, New York: Wiley.

Bak, P. and Chen, K. (1991) 'Self-Organized Criticality', *Scientific American*, vol. 264(1), pp. 46–53.

Barras, R. (1986) 'Towards a Theory of Innovation in Services', *Research Policy*, vol. 15, pp. 161–73.

Baum, E. B. (1988) 'Neural Nets for Economists', in Anderson *et al.* (1988: 33–48).

Batten, D. (1981) 'On the Dynamics of Industrial Evolution', *Regional Science and Urban Economics*, vol. 12, pp. 449–62.

Bennett, R. J. and Chorley, R. J. (1978) *Environmental Systems*, London: Methuen.

Bhargava, S. C. (1989) 'Generalized Lotka–Volterra Equations and the Mechanism of Technological Substitution', *Technological Forecasting and Social Change*, vol. 35, pp. 319–26.

Bhargava, S. C., Kumar, A. and Mukherjee, A. (1993) 'Stochastic Cellular Automata Model of Innovation Diffusion', *Technological Forecasting and Social Change*, vol. 44, pp. 87–97.

Bieshaar, H. and Kleinknecht, A. (1984) 'Kondratieff Long Waves in Aggregate Output? An Econometric Test', *Konjunkturpolitik*, vol. 30, pp. 279–303.

Bijker, W. (1993) 'Do Not Despair; There Is Life after Constructivism', *Science, Technology, and Human Values*, vol. 18, pp. 113–38.

Bijker, W., Hughes, T. P. and Pinch, T. (eds) (1987) *The Social Construction of Technological Systems*, Cambridge, MA: MIT Press.

Blank, S. C. (1991) '"Chaos" in Futures Markets? A Nonlinear Dynamical Analysis', *Journal of Futures Markets*, vol. 11, pp. 711–28.

Bloor, D. (1976) *Knowledge and Social Imagery*, London: Routledge & Kegan Paul.

Blume, M. and Stanbaugh, R. (1983) 'Biases in Computed Returns: An Application to the Size Effect', *Journal of Financial Economics*, vol. 12, pp. 33–56.

Bodewitz, H., De Vries, G. and Weeder, P. (1988) 'Towards a Cognitive Model for Technology-oriented R&D Processes', *Research Policy*, vol. 17, pp. 213–24.

Boldrin, M. (1988) 'Oscillations and Chaos in Dynamic Economic Models', in Anderson *et al.* (1988: 49–75).

Boulding, K. E., (1978) *Ecodynamics: A New Theory of Social Evolution*, Beverly Hills, CA: Sage.

Brock, W. A. (1988) 'Nonlinearity and Complex Dynamics in Economics and Finance', in Anderson *et al.* (1988: 77–98).

Brock, W. A., Hsieh, D. A. and LeBaron, B. (1990) *Nonlinear Dynamics, Chaos, and Instability: Statistical Theory and Economic Evidence*, Cambridge, MA: MIT Press.

Bruckner, E. (1980) 'Zur Frage der Anwendung des Eigen'schen Evolutionsmodells in der Ökonomie', manuscript (unpublished), Berlin.

Bruckner, E., Ebeling, W. and Scharnhorst, A. (1989) 'Stochastic Dynamics of Instabilities in Evolutionary Systems', *System Dynamics Review*, vol. 5, p. 176.

Bruckner, E., Ebeling, W., Jiménez Montaño, M. A. and Scharnhorst, A. (1993) 'Technological Innovations – a Self-organisation Approach', *WZB Papers* FS II 93-302, Berlin.

Brunner, H.-P. (1991a) 'Small Scale Industry and Technology in India: The Case of the Computer Industry', *Small Business Economics*, vol. 3, no. 2, pp. 121–9.

Brunner, H.-P. (1991b) 'Building Technological Capacity: A Case Study of the Computer Industry in India, 1975-87', *World Development*, vol. 19, no. 12, pp. 1737–51.

Callon, M. (1980) 'Struggles and Negotiations to Define What is Problematic and What Not', in Knorr, K. D., Krohn, K. and Whitley, R. (eds), *The Social Process of Scientific Investigation*, Sociology of the Sciences Yearbook IV, Dordrecht: Reidel, pp. 197–219.

Callon, M. (1986a) 'The Sociology of an Actor-network: the Case of the Electric Vehicle', in Callon *et al.* (1986).

Callon, M. (1986b) 'Some Elements of a Sociology of Translation: Domestication of the Scallops and the Fishermen of St. Brieuc Bay', in Law, J. (ed.), *Power, Action, and Belief*, London: Routledge & Kegan Paul.

Callon, M. (1987) 'Society in the Making: the Study of Technology as a Tool for Sociological Analysis', in Bijker *et al.* (1987).

Callon, M. (1992) 'The Dynamics of Techno-economic Networks', in Coombs, R., Saviotti, P. and Walsh, V. (eds), *Technological Change and Company Strategies*, London: Harcourt Brace Jovanovich, pp. 72–102.

Callon, M. and Latour, B. (1981) 'Unscrewing the Big Leviathan: How Actors Macrostructure Reality and How Sociologists Help Them to Do So', in Knorr-Cetina and Cicourel (1981: 277–303).

Callon, M., Law, J. and Rip, A. (eds) (1986) *Mapping the Dynamics of Science and Technology*, Houndsmill/London: Macmillan Press.

Camagni, R., Diappi, L. and Leonardi, G. (1986) 'Urban Growth and Decline in a Hierarchical System', *Regional Science and Urban Economics*, vol. 15, pp. 145–60.

Campbell, D. (1974) 'Evolutionary Epistemology', in Schilpp, P. (ed.), *The Philosophy of Karl Popper*, Library of Living Philosophers, La Salle, Ill.: Open Court.

Chandler, A. (1990) *Scale and Scope: The Dynamics of Industrial Capitalism*, Cambridge, MA: Harvard University Press.

Chen, P. (1988) 'Empirical and Theoretical Evidence of Economic Chaos', *System Dynamics Review*, vol. 4, no. 1–2, pp. 81–108.

Clark, K. B. (1985) 'The Interaction of Design Hierarchies and Market Concepts in Technological Evolution', *Research Policy*, vol. 14, pp. 235–51.

Clark, N. and Juma, C. (1987) *Long-run Economics – An Evolutionary Approach to Economic Change*, London: Pinter Publishers.

Clark, W. C. and Munn, R. E. (1986) *Sustainable Development for the Biosphere*, Cambridge: Cambridge University Press.

Clarke, R. and Davies, S. W. (1982) 'Market Structure and Price-Cost Margins', *Economica*, vol. 9 (August) pp. 277–87.

Cohen, L. and Noll, R. (1991) *The Technology Pork Barrel*, Washington, DC: Brookings.

Colding-Jørgensen, M. (1983) 'A Model of the Firing Pattern of a Paced Nerve Cell', *Journal of Theoretical Biology*, vol. 101, pp. 541–68.

Collins, H. M. (1985) *Changing Order*, London/Beverley Hills, CA: Sage Publications.

Cowan, R. (1990) 'Nuclear Power Reactors: a Study in Technological Lock-in', *Journal of Economic History*, vol. 5, no. 3, pp. 541–67.

Cowan, R. and Cowan, W. (1993) 'Strategic Complementarities and Spatial Equilibria: On the Nature and Degree of Technological Standardization', University of Western Ontario, Economics Department, mimeo.

Cyert, R. M. and March, J. G. (1963) *A Behavioral Theory of the Firm*, Englewood Cliffs, NJ: Prentice Hall.

Darwin, C., (1859) *On the Origin of Species by Means of Natural Selection of the Preservation of Favoured Races in the Struggle for Life*, London: John Murray.

David, P. A. (1985) 'Clio and the Economics of QWERTY', *American Economic Review*, vol. 75, no. 2, pp. 332–7.

David, P. A. (1988) 'Path-Dependence: Putting the Past into the Future of Economics', *Institute for Mathematical Studies in the Social Sciences Technical Report 533*, Stanford University.

David, P. A. (1991) 'Computer and Dynamo: The Modern Productivity Paradox in a Not-too-distant Mirror', in *Technology and Productivity*, Paris: OECD.

David, P. A. (1992a) 'Heroes, Herds, and Hysteresis in Technological History: Thomas Edison and the Battle of the Systems Reconsidered', *Industrial and Corporate Change*.

David, P. A. (1992b) 'Path-Dependence and Predictability in Dynamic Systems with Local Network Externalities: a Paradigm for Historical Economics', in Foray, D. and Freeman, C. (eds), *Technology and the Wealth of Nations*, London: Pinter Publishers.

David, P. A. and Foray, D. (1992) *Percolation Structures, Markov Random Fields and the Economics of EDI Standards Diffusion*, CEPR Publication no. 326, Stanford University.

David, P. A. and Greenstein, S. (1990) 'The Economics of Compatibility Standards: An Introduction to Recent Research', *Economics of Innovation and New Technology*, vol. 1, no. 1–2, pp. 1–32.

Day, R. (1983) 'The Emergence of Chaos from Classical Economic Growth', *Quarterly Journal of Economics*, vol. 98, pp. 201–13.

Debondt, W. and Thaler, R. (1987) 'Further Evidence on Investor Overreaction and Stock Market Seasonality', *Journal of Finance*, vol. 42, pp. 557–81.

Dopfer, K. (1991) 'The Complexity of Economic Phenomena: Reply to Tinbergen and Beyond', *Journal of Economic Issues*, vol. 25, no. 1, pp. 39–76.

Dorfman, N. (1982) *Massachusetts High Technology Boom in Perspective*, Cambridge, MA: MIT Centre for Policy Alternatives.

Dorfman, N. (1983) 'Route 128: The Development of Regional High-Technology Centres', *Research Policy*, vol. 12, pp. 299–316.

Dosi, G. (1982) 'Technological Paradigms and Technological Trajectories: A Suggested Interpretation of the Determinants and Directions of Technical Change', *Research Policy*, vol. 11, pp. 142–67.

Dosi, G. (1984) *Technical Change and Industrial Transformation*, Basingstoke/London: Macmillan Press.

Dosi, G. (1988) 'Sources, Procedures, and Microeconomic Effects of Innovation, *Journal of Economic Literature*, vol. 26, pp. 1120–71.

Dosi, G., Freeman, C., Nelson, R., Silverberg, G. and Soete, L. (eds) (1988) *Technical Change and Economic Theory*, London/New York: Pinter Publishers.

Dougherty, K. and Etzkowitz, H. (1993) 'The Hidden Industrial Policy: Science and Technology Policy at the State Level', Session on Economic Sociology, *American Sociological Association*, August.

Dyke, C. (1992) 'From Entropy to Economy: A Thorny Path', in Freese, L. (ed.), *Advances in Human Ecology*, Vol. 1, Greenwich, CT: JAI Press, pp. 149–76.

Dyke, C. (1993) 'Addition Accretion Accumulation Acceleration: Technology and Nonlinearity', manuscript for the Workshop 'New Developments in Technology Studies: Evolutionary Economics and Chaos Theory', Amsterdam, May.

Ebeling, W. and Feistel, R. (1982) *Physik der Selbstorganisation und Evolution*, Berlin: Akadamie-Verlag.

Ebeling, W., Feistel, R. and Engel, A. (1989) *Physik der Evolutionsprozesse*, Berlin: Akademie-Verlag.

Ebeling, W., Sonntag, I. and Schimansky-Geier, L. (1981) 'On the Evolution of Biological Macromolecules. II. Catalytic Networks', *Studia Biophysica*, vol. 84, p. 87.

Eckalbar, J. A. (1992) (Book Review of 'From Catastrophe to Chaos: A General Theory of Economic Discontinuities' by J. Barkley *et al.*), *Journal of Economic Literature*, vol. 30, pp. 2150–1.

Eigen, M. and Schuster, P. (1977–8) 'The Hypercycle', *Naturwissenschaften*, vol. 64, p. 541; vol. 65, p. 341.

Eigen, M. and Schuster, P. (1979) *The Hypercycle*, Berlin: Springer-Verlag.

Eldredge, N. (1985) *Unfinished Synthesis: Biological Hierarchies and Modern Evolutionary Thought*, New York/Oxford: Oxford University Press.

Etzkowitz, H. (1983) 'Entrepreneurial Scientists and Entrepreneurial Universities in American Academic Science', *Minerva*, vol. 21, pp. 198–233.

Etzkowitz, H. (1990) 'The Capitalization of Knowledge', *Theory and Society*, vol. 19, pp. 107–21.

Etzkowitz, H. (1992a) 'Individual Investigators and Their Research Groups', *Minerva*, vol. 30, no. 1, pp. 28–50.

Etzkowitz, H. (1992b) 'Redesigning Solomon's House: The University and the Internationalization of Science and Business,' in Sorlin, S. *et al.* (eds), *Sociology of Science Yearbook*, Amsterdam: Kluwer.

Etzkowitz, H. (1992c) 'The German–American Collaboration on Glass Research: The First Joint Meeting Between the NSF Industry–University Center for Glass Research at Alfred University and the Huttentechnische Vereinigung Der Deutschen Glasindustrie', *Report to the International Division, National Science Foundation*, 10 October.

Etzkowitz, H. (1992d) 'Capitalising Science in Post-socialist Eastern Europe', *Science, Knowledge and Technology*, vol. 6, no. 3.

Etzkowitz, H. (1993) 'Enterprises from Science: The Origins of Science-based Regional Economic Development and the Venture Capital Firm', *Minerva*, vol. 31, no. 3, pp. 326–60

Etzkowitz, H. (1994) 'Technology Centres and Industrial Policy: The Emergence of the Interventionist State', *Science and Public Policy*, May.

Etzkowitz, H. and Peters, L. (1991) 'Profit from Knowledge: Organizational Innovations and Normative Change in American Universities', *Minerva*, vol. 29, no. 2, pp. 133–66.

Fama, E. F. (1970) 'Efficient Capital Markets: A Review of Theory and Empirical Work', *Journal of Finance*, vol. 25, pp. 383–423.

Feigenbaum, M. (1978) 'Quantitative Universality for a Class of Nonlinear Transformations', *Journal of Statistical Physics*, vol. 19, pp. 25–52.

Feigenbaum, M. (1979) 'The Universal Properties of Nonlinear Transformations', *Journal of Statistical Physics*, vol. 21, pp. 669–709.

Feistel, R. and Ebeling, W. (1976) 'Dynamische Modelle zum Selektionsverhalten offener Systeme', *Wissenschaftliche Zeitschrift der Wilhelm-Pieck-Universität Rostock*, vol. 25, p. 507.

Fisher, J, C. and Pry, R. H. (1971) 'A Simple Substitution Model of Technological Change', *Technological Forecasting and Social Change*, vol. 3, pp. 75–88.

Forrester, J.W. (1977) 'Growth Cycles', *De Economist*, vol. 125, pp. 525–43.

Freeman, C. (1988) 'Japan: a New National System of Innovation', in Dosi *et al.* (1988).

Freeman, C. (1991) 'The Nature of Innovation and the Evolution of the Productive System', in *Technology and Productivity*, Paris: OECD.

Freese, L. (1988) 'Evolution and Sociogenesis' Parts I and II, in Lawler, E. J. and Markovsky, B. (eds), *Advances in Group Processes*, Vol. 5, Greenwich, CT: JAI Press, pp. 53–118.

Gabisch, G. and Lorenz, H.-W. (1987) *Business Cycle Theory*, Berlin: Springer-Verlag.

Galbraith, J. K. (1987) *A History of Economics*, London: Penguin.

Gandolfo, G. (1981) *Qualitative Analysis and Econometric Estimation of Continuous Time Dynamic Models*, Amsterdam: North-Holland.

Geiger, R. (1986) *To Advance Knowledge: The Growth of American Research Universities, 1900–1940*, New York: Oxford University Press.

Georgescu-Roegen, N. (1971) *The Entropy Law and the Economic Process*, Cambridge, MA: Harvard University Press.

Giddens, A. (1984) *The Constitution of Society*, Cambridge: Polity Press.

Glass, L., Schrier, A. and Belair, J. (1986) 'Chaotic Cardiac Rhythms', in Holden, A. V. (ed.), *Chaos*, Manchester: Manchester University Press.

Goodwin, R. M. (1967) 'A Growth Cycle', in Feinstein, C. H. (ed.), *Socialism, Capitalism and Economic Growth*, Cambridge: Cambridge University Press.

Goodwin, R. M., Kruger, M., and Vercelli, A. (1984) 'Nonlinear Models of Fluctuating Growth', Lecture Notes in Economics and Mathematical Systems, vol. 228, Berlin: Springer-Verlag.

Gort, M. and Klepper, S. (1982) 'Time Paths in the Diffusion of Product Innovations', *The Economic Journal*, vol 93, pp. 630–53.

Grabowski, H. G. and Vernon, J. M. (1987) 'Pioneers, Imitators, and Generics – A Simulation Model of Schumpeterian Competition', *Quarterly Journal of Economics*, vol. 52, pp. 492–525.

Grandmont, J. and Malgrange, P. (1986) 'Nonlinear Economic Dynamics: Introduction', *Journal of Economic Theory*, vol. 40, pp. 383–423.

Granovetter, M. (1985) 'Economic Action and Social Structure: The Problem of Embeddedness', *American Journal of Sociology*, vol. 91, pp. 481–510.

Grobstein, C. (1973) 'Hierarchical Order and Neogenesis' in Pattee, H. (ed.), *Hierarchy Theory: The Challenge of Complex Systems*, New York: George Braziller, Inc.

Groueff, S. (1967) *The Manhattan Project*, Boston: Little, Brown.

Grübler, A., Nakićenović, A. and Schäfer, A. (1992) 'Dynamics of Transport and Energy Systems', paper presented to the summer university course 'Communication Networks', Southern Stockholm.

Guilbaud, G. T. (1955) 'En marge de Schumpeter: quelques espérances mathématiques', *Economie Appliquée*, vol. 6, no. 1, pp. 243–70.

Gustave, L. B. (1895) *Psychologie des foules*. Reprinted as *The Crowd*, New York: Macmillan, 1922.

Gustin, B. (1975) 'The Emergence of the German Chemical Profession', Ph.D. dissertation, Department of Sociology, University of Chicago.

Haken, H. (1977) *Synergetics*, in *The Synergetics Series*, Heidelberg: Springer-Verlag.

Haken, H. (1983) *Advanced Synergetics*, Berlin: Springer-Verlag.

Hamilton, A. G. (1982) *Numbers, Sets, and Axioms: the Apparatus of Mathematics*, New York: Cambridge University Press.

Hamilton, W. B. (1966) 'The Research Triangle of North Carolina: A Study in Leadership for the Common Weal', *The South Atlantic Quarterly*, vol. 65, no. 2, p. 259.

Hammersley, J. M. and Welsh, D. J. (1980) 'Percolation Theory and its Ramifications', *Contemp. Phys.*, vol. 21, no. 6, pp. 549–603.

Hannan, M. T. and Freeman, J. (1989) *Organizational Ecology*, Cambridge, MA: Harvard University Press.

Haraway, D. (1988) 'Situated Knowledges: The Science Question in Feminism and the Privilege of Partial Perspective', *Feminist Studies*, vol. 14, pp. 575–99.

Harris, T. E. (1978) 'Additive Set-Valued Markov Processes and Percolation Methods', *Annals of Probability*, vol. 6, pp. 355–78.

Haxholdt, C., Kampmann, C. E., Mosekilde, E., and Sterman J. D. (1993) 'Entrainment in a Disaggregated Economic Long Wave Model', *Proceedings of the International System Dynamics Conference*, Mexico.

Henderson, R. (1991) 'Underinvestment and Incompetence as Responses to Radical Innovation: Evidence from the Photolithographic Alignment Equipment Industry', MIT, mimeo, October.

Henderson, R. and Clark, K. (1990) 'Architectural Innovation: The Reconfiguration of Existing Product Technologies and the Failure of Established Firms', *Administrative Science Quarterly*, vol. 35, pp. 9–30.

Hesse, M. (1980) *Reconstructions and Revolutions in the Philosophy of Science*, London: Harvester Press.

Hilpert, U. (1992) *Archipelago Europe*, Jena: Frederic Schiller University.

Hinton, G., McClelland, J. L., and Rumelhart, D. E. (1986) 'Distributed Representations', in Rumelhart *et al.* (1986, Vol. I: 77–109).

Hounshell, D. (1980) 'Edison and the Pure Science Ideal in America', *Science*, 8 February, pp. 612–17.

Hsieh, D. A. (1991) 'Chaos and Nonlinear Dynamics: Application to Financial Markets', *The Journal of Finance*, vol. 66, pp. 1639–877.

Hughes, T. (1987) *Networks of Power: Electrification in Western Society 1880–1930*, Baltimore, MD: Johns Hopkins University Press.

Janis, I. (1972) *Victims of GroupThink*, Boston: Houghton Mifflin.

Jantsch, E. (1980) *The Self-Organizing Universe*, Oxford: Pergamon Press.

Jencks, C. and Riesman, D. (1968) *The Academic Revolution*, Garden City, NY: Doubleday.

Jensen, M. H., Bak, P. and Bohr, T. (1983) 'Complete Devil's Staircase, Fractal

Dimension, and Universality of Mode-Locking Structure in the Circle Map', *Physical Review Letters*, vol. 50, pp. 1637–9.

Jensen, M. H., Bak, P. and Bohr, T. (1984) 'Transition to Chaos by Interaction of Resonances in Dissipative Systems. I. Circle Maps', *Physical Review A*, vol. 30, pp. 1960–9.

Jiménez Montaño, M. A. and Ebeling, W. (1980) 'A Stochastic Evolutionary Model of Technological Change', *Collective Phenomena*, vol. 3, pp. 107–14.

Johansson, B. and Nijkamp, P., (1987) 'Analysis of Episodes in Urban Event Histories', in Van den Berg, L., Burns, L. S. and Klaassen, L. H. (eds), *Spatial Cycles*, Aldershot: Gower, pp. 43–66.

Jordan, D. S. (1906) 'To What Extent Should the University Investigator be Relieved from Teaching', *AAU Journal*, vol. 30, pp. 34–42.

Kampis, G. and Csanyi, V. (1991) 'Coevolution and the Units of Evolution', in Smith, J. M. and Vida, G. (eds), *Organizational Constraints on the Dynamics of Evolution*, Manchester: Manchester University Press, pp. 385–98.

Kampmann, C. E. (1984) 'Disaggregating a Simple Model of the Economic Long Wave', *Working Paper no. D-3641*, Sloan School of Management, MIT, Cambridge, MA.

Kaneko, K. (1991) 'Climbing Up the Dynamical Hierarchy', in Baier, G. and Klein, M. (eds), *A Chaotic Hierarchy*, London: World Scientific Publishers, pp. 235–50.

Karmeshu, Bhargava, S. C., and Jain, V. P. (1985) 'A Rationale for Law of Technological Substitution', *Regional Science and Urban Economics*, vol. 15, pp. 137–41.

Katz, M. and Shapiro, C. (1985) 'Network Externalities, Competition, and Compatibility', *American Economic Review*, vol. 75, pp. 424–40.

Kesley, D. (1988) 'The Economics of Chaos or the Chaos of Economics', *Oxford Economic Papers* 40.

Kindermann, R. and Snell, J. L. (1980) 'Markov Random Fields and their Applications', *Contemporary Mathematics*, vol. 1, American Mathematical Society.

Klepper, S. (1992) 'Entry, Exit, Growth, and Innovation over the Product Life Cycle', Carnegie Mellon University, Discussion Paper.

Klepper, S. and Graddy, E. (1990) 'The Evolution of New Industries and the Determinants of Market Structure', *The Rand Journal of Economics*, vol. 21, pp. 27–44.

Knorr-Cetina, K. (1981) 'The Micro-sociological Challenge of Macro-sociology: Toward a Reconstruction of Theory and Methodology', in Knorr-Cetina and Cicourel (1981: 1–48).

Knorr-Cetina, K. and Cicourel, A. V. (eds) (1981) *Advances in Social Theory and Methodology: Toward an Integration of Micro- and Macro-sociologies*, Boston: Routledge & Kegan Paul.

Kondratieff, N. D. (1935) 'The Long Wave in Economic Life', *Review of Economic Statistics*, vol. 17, pp. 105–15.

Kuhn, T. S. (1962) *The Structure of Scientific Revolutions*, Chicago: University of Chicago Press.

Kwasnicka, H., Galar, R. and Kwasnicki, W. (1983) 'Technological Substitution Forecasting with a Model Based on Biological Analogy', *Technological Forecasting and Social Change*, vol. 23, pp. 41–53.

Langton, C. G. (1989) 'Artificial Life', in Langton, C. G. (ed.), *Artificial Life*, Redwood City, CA: Addison Wesley, pp. 1–47.

Larrain, M. (1991) 'Empirical Tests of Chaotic Behaviour in a Nonlinear Interest Rate Model', *Financial Analysts Journal*, vol. 47, Sept–Oct, pp. 51–62.

Latour, B. (1988) *The Pasteurization of France*, Cambridge, MA: Harvard University Press. First published in French in 1984 as Les Microbes: guerre et paix suivi de irréeductions, Paris: Editions Métailié.

Latour, B. (1987) *Science in Action*, Milton Keynes: Open University Press.

Lazonick, W. (1990) *Competitive Advantage on the Shop Floor*, Cambridge: Harvard University Press.

Leibniz, G. W., Letter to Christiaan Huygens, 8 January, 1692, in Huygens, C., *Oeuvres Complètes*, The Hague: Nijhoff, 1888–1950, Vol. X, p. 227.

Lenz, R. C. (1962) 'Technological Forecasting', Technical Report ASD-TR-62-414 (USAF Aeronautical Systems Division).

Leslie, S. (1993) *The Cold War and American Science: The Military-Industrial-Academic Complex at MIT and Stanford*, New York: Columbia University Press

Leydesdorff, L. (1992) 'Knowledge Representations, Bayesian Inferences and Empirical Science Studies', *Social Science Information*, vol. 31, no. 2, pp. 213–37.

Leydesdorff, L. (1993a) '"Structure"/"Action" Contingencies and the Model of Parallel Distributed Processing', *Journal for the Theory of Social Behaviour*, vol. 23, pp. 47–77.

Leydesdorff, L. (1993b) 'The Evolution of Communication Systems', paper presented at the Fourth International Conference of Bibliometrics, Scientometrics and Informetrics, Berlin, September.

Li, T.-Y. and Yorke, J. A. (1975) 'Period Three Implies Chaos', *American Mathematical Monthly*, vol. 82, pp. 985–92.

Long, C. D. (1940) *Building Cycles and the Theory of Investment*, Princeton, NJ: Princeton University Press.

Lorenz, H. W. (1989) 'Non-linear Dynamical Economics and Chaotic Motion', *Lecture Notes in Economics and Mathematical Systems*, vol. 228, Berlin: Springer-Verlag.

Lotka, A., (1920) 'Analytical Notes on Certain Rhythmic Relation in Organic Systems', *Proceedings of the National Academy of Sciences of the USA*, vol. 6, pp. 410–15.

Lotka, A. J. (1925) *Elements of Physical Biology*, Baltimore, MD: Wilkins and Wilkins.

Luhmann, N. (1984) *Soziale Systeme*, Frankfurt am Main: Suhrkamp.

Luhmann, N. (1989) *Ecological Communication*, Chicago: University of Chicago Press.

Luhmann, N. (1990) *Die Wissenschaft der Gesellschaft*, Frankfurt am Main: Suhrkamp.

Lundvall, B. A. (ed.) (1992) *National Systems of Innovation*, London: Pinter Publishers.

Mansfield, E. (1983) 'Long Waves in Technological Innovation', *American Economic Review*, vol. 73, pp. 141–5.

Marchetti, C. (1983) 'On the Role of Science in the Post Industrial Society: The Logos – The Empire Builders', *Technological Forecasting and Social Change*, vol. 24, pp. 197–206.

Marchetti, C. and Nakićenović, N. (1979) 'The Dynamics of Energy Systems and the Logistics Substitution Model', Research Report PR-79-13, Laxenburg, Austria: IIASA.

Marshall, A. (1920) *Principles of Economics*, London: Macmillan.

Maturana, H. R. (1970) *Biology of Cognition*, Report Biological Computer Laboratory 9.0, Urbana: University of Illinois.

Maturana, H. R. (1978) 'Biology of Language: The Epistemology of Reality', in Miller, G. A. and Lenneberg, E. (eds), *Psychology and Biology of Language and Thought. Essays in Honor of Eric Lenneberg*, New York: Academic Press, pp. 27–63.

Maturana, H. R. and Varela, F. (1975) *Autopoietic Systems*, Report Biological Computer Laboratory 9.4, Urbana: University of Illinois.

May, R. M. (1973) *Stability and Complexity in Model Ecosystems*, Princeton, NJ: Princeton University Press.

May, R. (1975) 'Simple Mathematical Models with Very Complicated Dynamics', *Nature*, vol. 261, pp. 459–67.

Medio, A. and Gallo, G. (1989) 'DMC – Dynamic Systems Analysis', Venice, mimeo.

Mensch, G. (1979) *Stalemate in Technology*, Cambridge, MA: Ballinger.

Merton, R. K. ([1942]1973) *Sociology of Science. Theoretical and Empirical Investigations*, Chicago: University of Chicago Press.

Metcalfe, J. S. (1986) 'Technological Innovation and the Competitive Process', in Hall, P. (ed.), *Technology, Innovation and Economic Policy*, New Delhi: Heritage.

Metcalfe, J. S. (1989) 'Evolution and Economic Change', in Silberston, A. (ed.), *Technology and Economic Progress*, London and New York: Macmillan.

Metcalfe, J. S. and Gibbons, M. (1986) 'Technological Variety and the Process of Competition', *Economie Appliqué*, vol. 39, pp. 493–520.

Meyer, B. (1990) 'Zur Messung des dynamischen Wettbewerbs: Eine empirische Analyse des evolutionstheoretischen Modells von Iwai', in Gahlen, B. (ed.), *Marktwirtschaft und gesamtwirtschaftliche Entwicklung*, Berlin: Springer Verlag.

Montroll, E. W. (1972) 'A Manner of Characterising the Development of Countries', *Proceedings of the National Academy of Sciences of the USA*, vol. 69, pp. 3019–23.

Morrison, F. (1991) *The Art of Modeling Dynamic Systems*, New York: John Wiley & Sons.

Mosekilde, E., Aracil, J. and Allen, P. M. (1988) 'Instabilities and Chaos in Non-linear Dynamical Systems', *System Dynamics Review*, vol. 4, p. 14.

Mosekilde, E., Feldberg, R., Knudsen, C. and Hindsholm, M. (1990) 'Mode-Locking and Spatiotemporal Chaos in Periodically Driven Gunn Diodes', *Physical Review B*, vol. 41, pp. 2298–306.

Mosekilde, E., Larsen, E. R., Sterman, J. D. and Thomsen, J. S. (1992) 'Nonlinear Mode-interaction in the Macroeconomy', *Annals of Operations Research*, vol. 37, pp. 185–215.

Mueller, D. and Tilton, J. (1969) 'Research and Development as Barriers to Entry', *Canadian Journal of Economics*, vol. 2, pp. 570–79.

Murphy, J. J. (1986) *Technical Analysis of the Futures Market*, New York: New York Institute of Finance.

Muth, J. F. (1961) 'Rational Expectations and the Theory of Price Movements', *Econometrica*, vol. 29, pp. 315–35.

Namenwirth, Z. (1973) 'The Wheels of Time and the Interdependence of Value Change', *Journal of Interdisciplinary History*, vol. 3, pp. 649–83.

Nelson, R. R. (1962) 'The Link Between Science and Invention: The Case of the

Transistor', in National Bureau of Economic Research, *The Rate and Direction of Inventive Activity: Economic and Social Factors*, Princeton: Princeton University Press, pp. 549–83.

Nelson, R. R. (1981) 'Research on Productivity Growth and Productivity Differences: Dead Ends and New Departures', *Journal of Economic Literature*, vol. 19, no. 3, pp. 1029–64.

Nelson, R. R. (1988) 'Institutions Supporting Technical Change in the United States', in Dosi *et al.* (1988).

Nelson, R. R. and Rosenberg, N. (1993) 'Technical Innovation and National Systems', in Nelson, R. R. (ed.), *National Innovation Systems: A Comparative Study*, New York: Oxford University Press.

Nelson, R. R. and Soete, L. G. (1988) 'Policy Conclusions', in Dosi *et al.* (1988: 631–5).

Nelson, R. R. and Winter, S. G. (1977) 'In Search of Useful Theory of Innovation', *Research Policy*, vol. 6, pp. 36–76.

Nelson, R. R. and Winter, S. G. (1982) *An Evolutionary Theory of Economic Change*, Cambridge, MA: Belknap Press of Harvard University Press.

Nicolis, G. and Prigogine, I. (1977) *Self-organization in Non-equilibrium Systems*, New York: Wiley Interscience.

Nicolis, J. S. (1986) *Dynamics of Hierarchical Systems: An Evolutionary Approach*, New York: Springer-Verlag.

Nijkamp, P. and Reggiani, A. (1992a) 'Spatial Competition and Ecologically Based Socio-economic Models', *Socio-spatial Dynamics*, vol. 3, no. 2, pp. 89–109.

Nijkamp, P. and Reggiani, A. (1992b) *Interaction, Evolution and Chaos in Space*, Berlin: Springer-Verlag.

Nijkamp, P. and Reggiani, A. (1993a) 'Space-time Dynamics, Spatial Competition and the Theory of Chaos', in Lakshmanan, T. R. and Nijkamp, P. (eds), *Structure and Change in the Space-economy*, Berlin: Springer-Verlag, pp. 25–47.

Nijkamp, P. and Reggiani, A. (eds) (1993b) *Nonlinear Evolution of Spatial Economic Systems*, Berlin: Springer-Verlag.

Nijkamp, P. and Reggiani, A. (1993c) 'Complex Behaviour in Spatial Networks', in Nijkamp and Reggiani (1993b).

North, D. (1990) *Institutions, Institutional Change, and Economic Performance*, Cambridge: Cambridge University Press.

Oleson, A. and Voss, J. (eds) (1979) *The Organization of Knowledge in Modern America, 1860–1920*, Baltimore, MD: Johns Hopkins University Press.

Opschoor, J. B. (1991) 'Economic Modeling and Sustainable Development', in Gilbert, A. J. and Braat, L. C. (eds), *Modelling for Population and Sustainable Development*, London: Routledge, pp. 191–210.

Osborne, M. F. M. (1964) 'Brownian Motion in the Stock Market', in Cootner, P. (ed.), *The Random Character of Stock Market Prices*, Cambridge, MA: MIT Press, pp. 262–96. (Originally published in 1959.)

Parker, L. (1992) *Academic–Industry Relations in Developing Countries*, Washington, DC: World Bank.

Pattee, H. H. (ed.) (1973) *Hierarchy Theory: The Challenge of Complex Systems*, NY: George Braziller, Inc.

Pavitt, K. (1984) 'Sectoral Patterns of Technical Change: Towards a Theory and a Taxonomy', *Research Policy*, vol. 13, pp. 343–73.

Penrose, R. (1989) *The Emperor's New Mind*, Oxford: Oxford University Press.

Perez, C. (1985) 'Microelectronics, Long Waves and World Structural Change: New Perspectives in Developing Countries', *World Development*, vol. 13, pp. 441–63.

Peters, E. (1989) 'Fractal Structure in the Capital Markets', *Financial Analysts Journal*, vol. 45, August, pp. 32–7.

Peters, E. (1991a) 'A Chaotic Attractor for the S & P 500', *Financial Analysts Journal*, vol. 47, March–April, pp. 55–81.

Peters, E. (1991b) 'R/S Analysis using Logarithmic Returns : a Technical Note', *Financial Analysts Journal*, vol. 47.

Pianka, E. R. (1978) *Evolutionary Ecology*, New York: Harper & Row.

Pinch, T. J. and Bijker, W. E. (1984) 'The Social Construction of Facts and Artefacts', *Social Studies of Science*, vol. 14, pp. 399–441.

Pondy, L. R. and Mitroff, I. I. (1979) 'Beyond Open System Models of Organization', in Staw, B. M. (ed.), *Research in Organizational Behavior*, Greenwich, CT: JAI Press, pp. 3–39.

Prigogine, I. (1976) 'Order through Fluctuation: Self-organization and Social System', in Jantsch, E. and Waddington, C. H. (eds), *Evolution and Consciousness*, Reading, MA: Addison-Wesley.

Prigogine, I. and Stengers, I. (1984) *Order out of Chaos*, New York: Bantam Books.

Prigogine, I., Allen, P. M. and Herman, R. (1977) 'The Evolution of Complexity and the Laws of Nature', in Laszlo, E. (ed.), *Goals for a Global Society*, Oxford: Pergamon Press, pp. 1–63.

Puffert, D. (1987) *Spatial Network Externalities – A Model with Application to the Historical Standardization of Railway Gauges*, Social Science History Workshop Paper, Department of Economics, Stanford University.

Radzicki, M. J. (1990) 'Institutional Dynamics, Deterministic Chaos, and Self-organizing Systems', *Journal of Economic Issues*, vol. 24, pp. 57–102.

Robson, M., Townsend, J., and Pavitt, K. (1988) 'Sectoral Patterns of Production and Use of Innovations in the UK: 1945–1983', *Research Policy*, vol. 17, pp. 1–14.

Rosenberg, N. (1976) *Perspectives on Technology*, Cambridge: Cambridge University Press.

Rosenberg, N. (1982) *Inside the Black Box: Technology and Economics*, Cambridge: Cambridge University Press.

Rosenberg, N. and Frischtak, C. R. (1983) 'Long Waves in Economic Growth: A Critical Appraisal', *American Economic Review*, vol. 73, pp. 146–51.

Rosenberg, N. and Frischtak, C. R. (1984) 'Technological Innovation and Long Waves', *Cambridge Journal of Economics*, vol. 8, pp. 7–24.

Rosser, J. B. (1991) *From Catastrophe to Chaos: A General Theory of Economic Discontinuities*, Dordrecht: Kluwer Academic Publishers.

Rozeff, M. S. and Kinney, W. R. (1976) 'Capital Market Seasonality: The Case of Stock Returns', *Journal of Financial Economics*, vol. 3, pp. 379–402.

Rumelhart, D. E., McClelland, J. L. and the PDP Research Group (1986) *Parallel Distributed Processing*, Cambridge, MA: MIT Press.

Sahal, D. (1981) *Patterns of Technological Innovation*, Reading, MA: Addison Wesley.

Sahal, D. (1985) 'Technological Guideposts and Innovation Avenues', *Research Policy*, vol. 14, pp. 61–82.

Samuelson, P. (1971) 'Generalized Predator – Prey Oscillations in Ecological Economic Equilibrium', *Proceedings of the National Academy of Sciences of the USA*, vol. 68, pp. 980–3.

Sanglier, M. and Allen, P. M. (1989) 'Evolutionary Models of Urban Systems: an Application to the Belgian Provinces', *Environment and Planning A*, vol. 21, pp. 477–98.

Saviotti, P. P. (1988) 'Information, Variety and Entropy in Technoeconomic Development', *Research Policy*, vol. 17, pp. 89–103.

Saviotti, P. P. (1991) 'The Role of Variety in Economic and Technological Development', in Saviotti and Metcalfe (1991: 172–208).

Saviotti, P. P. and Mani, G. S. (1993) 'A Model of Technological Evolution Based on Replicator Dynamics', paper presented at the workshop 'New Developments in Technology Studies: Evolutionary Economics and Chaos Theory', Amsterdam.

Saviotti, P. P. and Metcalfe, J. S. (1984) 'A Theoretical Approach to the Construction of Technological Output Indicators', *Research Policy*, vol. 13, pp. 141–51.

Saviotti, P. P. and Metcalfe, J. S. (eds) (1991) *Evolutionary Theories of Economic and Technological Change*, Chur and Philadelphia: Harwood Academic Publishers.

Savit, R. (1988) 'When Random is Not Random: An Introduction to Chaos in Market Prices', *Journal of Futures Markets*, vol. 8, pp. 271–89.

Savit, R. (1989) 'Nonlinearities and Chaotic Effects in Options Prices', *Journal of Futures Markets*, vol. 9, pp. 507–18.

Scheinkman, J. and LeBaron, B. (1989) 'Nonlinear Dynamics and Stock Returns', *Journal of Business*, vol. 62, pp. 311–37.

Schelling, T. (1971) 'Dynamic Models of Segregation', *Journal of Mathematical Sociology*, vol. 1, pp. 143–96.

Schumpeter, J. A. (1934) *The Theory of Economic Development*, Cambridge, MA: Harvard University Press.

Schumpeter, J. A. (1939) *Business Cycles: A Theoretical, Historical and Statistical Analysis of Capitalist Process*, New York: McGraw-Hill.

Schumpeter, J. A. ([1943]1976) *Capitalism, Socialism and Democracy*, London: Allen & Unwin.

Semmler, W. (ed.) (1986) *Competition, Instability, and Nonlinear Cycles*, Berlin: Springer-Verlag.

Servos, J. (1980) 'The Industrial Relations of Science: Chemical Engineering at MIT, 1900–1939', *ISIS*, vol. 71, pp. 531–49.

Shepsle, K. and Weingast, B. (1981) 'Structure Induced Equilibrium and Legislative Choice', *Public Choice*, Fall, pp. 503–20.

Silverberg, G. (1984) 'Embodied Technical Progress in a Dynamic Economic Model: The Self-organisation Paradigm', in Goodwin, R. M., Kruger, M. and Vercalli, A. (eds), *Nonlinear Models of Fluctuating Growth*, Berlin: Springer-Verlag.

Silverberg, G. (1988) 'Modelling Economic Dynamics and Technical Change: Mathematical Approaches to Self-organisation and Evolution', in Dosi *et al.* (1988: 531–59).

Silverberg, G. (1992) 'On the Complex Dynamics of Technical Change and Economic Evolution', *Journal of Scientific and Industrial Research*, vol. 51, pp. 151–6.

Silverberg G., Dosi, G. and Orsenigo, L. (1988) 'Innovation, Diversity and Diffusion: A Self-organization Model', *The Economic Journal*, vol. 98, pp. 1032–54.

Simon, H. A. ([1947]1965) *Administrative Behaviour: A Study of the Decision-making Process in Administrative Organization*, New York: Free Press.

Simon, H. A. (1969) *The Sciences of the Artificial*, Cambridge, MA: MIT Press.

Simon, H. A. (1973) 'The Organization of Complex Systems', in Pattee (1973: 1–27).

Smith, M. J. (1974) *Models in Ecology*, London: Cambridge University Press.

Smolensky, P. (1986) 'Information Processing in Dynamical Systems: Foundations of Harmony Theory', in Rumelhart *et al.* (1986, Vol. I: 194–281).

Soete, L. and Turner, R. (1987) 'Technological Diffusion and the Rate of Technical Change', *The Economic Journal*.

Sonis, M. (1991) 'Territorial Socio-ecological Approach in Innovation Diffusion Theory', *Systemi Urbani*, vol. 1–3, pp. 29–59.

Sonis, M. (1992) 'Innovation Diffusion, Schumpeterian Competition and Dynamic Choice: a New Synthesis', *Journal of Scientific and Industrial Research*, vol. 51, pp. 172–86.

Soros, G. (1988) *The Alchemy of Finance*, London: Weidenfeld and Nicolson.

Sparrow, C. (1980) 'Bifurcation and Chaotic Behaviour in Simple Feedback Systems', *Journal of Theoretical Biology*, vol. 83, pp. 93–105.

Sterman, J. D. (1985) 'A Behavioral Model of the Economic Long Wave', *Journal of Economic Behavior and Organization*, vol. 6, pp. 17–53.

Sterman, J. D. and Mosekilde, E. (1993) 'Business Cycles and Long Waves: A Behavioral Disequilibrium Perspective', *Working paper no. 3528-93-MSA*, Sloan School of Management, MIT, Cambridge, MA.

Stern, B. (1956) *Historical Sociology*, New York: Citadel Press

Stinchcombe, A. L. (1983) *Economic Sociology*, New York: Academic Press.

Stoneman, P. (1983) *The Analysis of Technical Change*, London: Oxford University Press.

Storr, R. J. (1953) *The Beginnings of Graduate Education in America*, Chicago: University of Chicago Press

Swenson, R. (1989) 'Emergent Attractors and the Law of Maximum Entropy Production: Foundations to a Theory of General Evolution', *Systems Research*, vol. 6, no. 3, pp. 187–97.

Technology Access Report (1992) 'MCC Launches Venture Capital Arm', October.

Teubal, M. (1979) 'On User Needs and Need Determination. Aspects of a Theory of Technological Innovation', in Baker, M. J. (ed.), *Industrial Innovation. Technology, Policy and Diffusion*, London: Macmillan Press, pp. 266–89.

Troitzsch, K.G. (1993) 'Evolution of Production Processes', in Haag, G. (ed.), *Economic Evolution and Demographic Change*, Berlin: Springer-Verlag.

Tushman, M. and Anderson, D. (1986) 'Technological Discontinuities and Organizational Environments', *Administrative Science Quarterly*, vol. 31, pp. 436–65.

Tushman, M. and Romanelli, E. (1985) *Organizational Evolution: a Metamorphosis Model of Convergence and Reorientation*, Greenwich, CT: JAI Press.

Tushman, M. and Rosenkopf, L. (1992) 'Organizational Determinants of Technological Change: Towards a Sociology of Technological Evolution', *Research in Organizational Behavior*, vol. 14.

Utterback, J. M. (1974) 'Innovation in Industry and the Diffusion of Technology', *Science*, vol. 183, pp. 620–6.

Utterback, J. M. and Abernathy, W. J. (1975) 'A Dynamic Model of Process and Product Innovations', *Omega 3*, pp. 639–56.

Utterback, J. and Suarez, F. F. (1993) 'Innovations, Competition, and Industry Structure', *Research Policy*, vol. 22, pp. 1–22.

Van den Belt, H. and Rip, A. (1987) 'The Nelson–Winter–Dosi model and synthetic dye chemistry', in Bijker *et al.* (1987: 135–58).

Van Duijn, J. (1983) *The Long Wave in Economic Life*, London: Allen & Unwin.

Veblen, T. (1915) *Imperial Germany and the Industrial Revolution*, New York: Macmillan.

Veysey, L. (1965) *The Emergence of the American University*, Chicago: University of Chicago.

Vincenti, W. (1990) *What Do Engineers Know and How Do They Know It?*, Baltimore, MD: Johns Hopkins University Press.

Volterra, V. (1931) *Leçons sur la théorie mathématique de la lutte pour la vie*, Paris: Gauthier-Villars.

Volterra, V. (1982) 'Variations and Fluctuations of Population Size in Coexisting Animal Species', in Pinto, F. O. and Conolly, B. W. (eds), *Applicable Mathematics of Nonphysical Phenomena*, New York: Ellis Horwood.

Wachtel, S. B. (1942) 'Certain Observations on Seasonal Movements in Stock Prices', *Journal of Business*, vol. 15, pp. 184–93.

Weber, B. H., Depew, D. L. and Smith, J. D. (eds) (1988) *Entropy, Information, and Evolution*, Cambridge, MA: MIT Press.

Weber, R. (1981) 'Society and Economy in the Western World System', *Social Forces*, vol. 59, pp. 1130–48.

Webster, A. and Etzkowitz, H. (1991) *Academic–Industry Relations: The Second Academic Revolution?*, London: Science Policy Support Group.

Weidlich, W. (1991) 'Physics and Social Science – the Approach of Synergetics', *Physics Reports*, vol. 204, p. 1.

Weiner, C. (1982) 'Science in the Marketplace: Historical Precedents and Problems', in *From Genetic Experimentation to Biotechnology: The Critical Transition*, New York: Wiley.

Weissburg, M., Roseman, L., and Chase, I. (1991) 'Chains of Opportunity: a Markov Model for the Acquisition of Reusable Resources', *Evolutionary Biology*, vol. 5, pp. 105–17.

White, D. R. and McCann, H. G. (1988) 'Cites and Fights: Material Entailment Analysis of the Eighteenth-century Chemical Revolution', in Wellman, B. and Berkowitz, S. D. (eds), *Social Structures: a Network Approach*, Cambridge: Cambridge University Press, pp. 359–400.

White, R. W. (1990) 'Transient Chaotic Behavior in a Hierarchical Economic System', *Environment and Planning A*, vol. 22, pp. 1309–21.

Wicken, J. S. (1992) 'The Natural Ecology of Human Ecology', in Freese, L. (ed.), *Advances in Human Ecology*, vol. 1, Greenwich, CT: JAI Press, pp. 101–18.

Wildes, K. and Lindgren, N. (1985) *A Century of Electrical Engineering and Computer Science at MIT, 1882–1982*, Cambridge, MA: MIT Press.

Williamson, O. (1985) *The Economic Institutions of Capitalism*, New York: Free Press.

Winner, L. (1977) *Autonomous Technology: Technics out of Control as a Theme in Political Thought*, Cambridge, MA: MIT Press.

Winter, S. (1984) 'Schumpeterian Competition in Alternative Technological Regimes', *Journal of Economic Behavior and Organization*, vol. 5, pp. 287–320.

Wolf, A. (1986) 'Quantifying Chaos with Lyaponov Exponents', in Holden, A. V. (ed.), *Chaos*, Manchester: Manchester University Press.

Wright, S. (1931) 'Evolution in a Mendelian Population', *Genetics*, vol. 16, pp. 97–189.

Young, G. L. (1992) 'Between the Atom and the Void: Hierarchy in Human Ecology', in Freese, L. (ed.), *Advances in Human Ecology*, vol. 1, Greenwich, CT: JAI Press, pp. 119–47.

Zuscovitch, E. (1986) The Economic Dynamics of Technologies Development, *Research Policy*, vol. 15, pp. 175–86.

Index